SYMBOLIZATION IN PSYCHOANALYSIS

Blucher

SYMBOLIZATION IN PSYCHOANALYSIS

The processes of subjectivation and the aesthetic dimension of psychoanalysis

Ruggero Levy

English technical revision
Marcella de Melo Silva

Symbolization in psychoanalysis: the processes of subjectivation and the aesthetic dimension of psychoanalysis

Publisher Edgard Blücher
Editor Eduardo Blücher
Editorial coordination Rafael Fulanetti
Production coordination Ana Cristina Garcia
Editorial production Lira Editorial
English technical revision Marcella de Melo Silva
Designer Lira Editorial
Proofreading Regiane da Silva Miyashiro
Cover Laércio Flenic
Cover image Istockphoto

Blucher

Rua Pedroso Alvarenga, 1245, 4º andar
04531-934 – São Paulo – SP – Brasil
Tel.: 55 11 3078-5366
contato@blucher.com.br
www.blucher.com.br

International Cataloging in Publication Data
Heytor Diniz Teixeira, CRB-8/10570

Levy, Ruggero
Symbolization in psychoanalysis : the processes of subjectivation and the aesthetic dimension of psychoanalysis/ Ruggero Levy. – São Paulo : Blucher, 2026.

304 p. : il.
Bibliography
ISBN 978-85-212-3092-2 (Printed)
ISBN 978-85-212-3090-8 (Electronic - Epub)
ISBN 978-85-212-2894-3 (Electronic - PDF)

Original title: *A simbolização na psicanálise: os processos de subjetivação e a dimensão estética da psicanálise*

1. Psychoanalysis. 2. Symbolization (Psychology). 3. Freud, Sigmund, 1856-1939. I. Title.

CDU 159.964.2

Index for the systematic catalog:
1. Psychoanalysis CDU 159.964.2

Acknowledgments

I would like to thank my parents and my sister for taking care of me and for the sense of justice and ethics they passed on to me;

To my wife, Andreia, and my children, Francisca, Ramiro, and Roberto, for their patience and tolerance of my hours of study and absence and for their constant and loving closeness;

To the Psychoanalytic Society of Porto Alegre, my second family – in the person of my analyst, my supervisors, teachers, and colleagues – who welcomed me and passed on psychoanalysis to me in accordance with the highest ethical and psychoanalytic principles.

Presentation, by Giuseppe Civitarese[1]

We can only welcome the arrival of Ruggero Levy's book with enthusiasm. The frontier of research in contemporary psychoanalysis revolves around the intersubjective and aesthetic dimensions of psychic birth. Aesthetics here does not refer directly to the world of artistic experience. Its meaning is mainly etymological. *Aisthesis* means sensation. At birth, the child is a bundle of sensations that already have a certain order due to anatomy and physiology, but this is not enough. The body is exposed to the environment and another agent, the maternal object, needs to be available to create a welcoming and ordering spatiality. The child is *infans*, it has no way of understanding the meaning of words, and yet, and this is the mystery of this process, it manages to form a mind. To create a mind requires another mind – in fact, many others, since each subject is, in fact, a group.

Thus, the paradox is that a link is generated in which the symbolic is both there and not there, depending on which point of view you choose to privilege. The narrative of the mother-baby relationship is central to Klein, Winnicott, and Bion, and yet psychoanalysis has always tended towards the pole of knowledge (of what is already of the order of the semantic meaning of the word) and not towards that of being and becoming (on the side of the signification that takes place on the semiotic plane). This orientation has been changing for some

1 PhD, training analyst of the Italian Psychoanalytic Society (SPI) and member of the American Psychoanalytic Association (APsA).

time and has changed even more recently in contemporary psychoanalysis. Emotion has regained a centrality as the place where meaning is generated and no longer as the place where psychic energy is discharged, as it basically is for Freud.

The basic psychology of psychoanalysis has also changed from the one-person psychology of Freud and Klein to the relational psychology of Winnicott (the child does not exist) and Bion (the analytic pair is a group). But it is difficult, I repeat, to take into account this sphere in which the process of subjectivation takes place (which, moreover, lasts a lifetime: one never stops being born) because it has to do with the construction of meaning at the level of corporeality and intercorporeality; in other words, with a dimension of being that escapes the domain of words. As Bion writes, you cannot sing potatoes (instead, just the word "potatoes"). An individual's affective and relational competence is more akin to pedaling a bicycle or playing the piano than to putting into practice a set of instructions that can be summarized in logical propositions.

Those who are going to help patients – who are inevitably deficient in these areas – to develop the ability to use their emotions to orient themselves in the world face the same difficulty. You cannot teach a child to ride a bike by telling them to find their balance and not to fall off. You have to invent something to talk to the body and the mind. Another essential aspect is that sense (semiotic) and meaning (semantic) are social by nature. To read the world, I need language and it is mine, but it is not mine either; I control only a small part of it, even if I contribute with others to expand it. That is why we say that the Self is the Other.

What do I mean by that? That today, if we want to deal, and we must, as the subtitle of the book says, with the processes of subjectivation and the aesthetic dimension of psychoanalysis, we must cure the serious disease of psychology which, for Binswanger, represents the division between subject and subject. In other words, a psychology of the subject in isolation is no longer adequate to support psychoanalytic research into these essential questions. What we need is a more precise theorization of what intersubjectivity means on an ontological and metapsychological level.[2] The implications are significant, both on a theoretical and technical level.

On a theoretical level: the unconscious ceases to be, as Freud says, the locus of evil or, as Klein says, essentially the locus of hatred and of the evil internal object becomes the function of the personality, but also inevitably and intrinsically transindividual, which allows experience to be given a personal meaning.

On a technical level: the reconceptualization of the unconscious and the dream, which we owe mainly to Bion, helps, especially in the developments of his thought that can be traced back to the theory of the analytical field, to consider not only the relational perspective of the *I/you,* in which a high rate of "suspicion" still circulates, but also the perspective of the we as a group of two.

To navigate these issues, Levy's book is a formidable "scout". What is remarkable about Levy is that he gives us a comprehensive view. While recognizing that this is a huge field and that he cannot deal with all the authors, Levy moves with extraordinary competence and agility between the various theories, from Freud to Green and the Botellas, from Bion to Meltzer, the Barangers, Rocha Barros and Ferro, from Winnicott to Ogden, and so on.

That said, Levy's theoretical choices are clear. He mentions them immediately when he refers to the mother-child model, as it is employed by Bion, if I am not mistaken, for the first time in the essay *A Theory of Thought.* The lexicon is therefore mainly Bionian and, in this book, Levy shows how fertile, in Brazil and around the world, are the seeds left by Bion in the lectures he gave in the last years of his life, testifying, like so many other scholars, to the importance of Bion's work in this country.

2 Cf. Civitarese, G. (2021). Intersubjectivity and the analytic field. *Journal of the American Psychoanalytic Association*, 69, 853-894.

The historical perspective is essential. It is important to recognize that it was Lacan more than anyone else who valued the *fort-da* game, which is one of Freud's most brilliant pages, as an activity of symbolization; but there is also Klein with *play as a dream*; and Bion with the *psychoanalytic game of* forgetting the past, desire and understanding in order to intuit, that is, visualize the emotions that move in the darkness of the analytical relationship.

Overall, the shift was from a focus on the symbol as content, for example, as Klein does when interpreting children's play, to the capacity to play or symbolize or dream, now seen more or less as synonyms; from the Freudian empire of representation to the centrality that emotion now has in Bion's psychoanalysis and that of the analytical field. As Levy points out when quoting Bion on the link between emotion and relationship, I put the former in my own words, emotion is the zero degree of symbolization (elsewhere I have called it a kind of primitive concept or abstraction).

One of the most effective ways of studying symbolization processes, and this is the one chosen by Levy, is to try to understand what happens when they fail. In reality, the analyst's area of expertise is the negative grid. There may be dreams that are not real dreams, which are therefore not the product of a successful symbolization activity. They do not usually elicit associations or emotional resonances. And the same can be said of many monotonous and repetitive analytical conversations: they are basically autistic. Unlike Meltzer, I would not see them as lying dreams. The word lie is misleading. On the one hand, lying implies being able to symbolize; on the other hand, from the point of view of unconscious meaning, lying is impossible, and in therapy, it is a non-problem. On the contrary, I would think that what we call a lie or falsehood is a deficit in symbolization, a deficiency in the ability to contain and thus give form to violent emotions or beta elements.

In the same way, the reason for –K is controversial, and with Bion even more so because he is faithful to Kleinian concepts but progressively empties them from within. In his essays, he interprets the patient's envy, still standing on the (partially) relational axis of *I/You*, but in the meantime, he creates new concepts that bend the theory towards the we (of the group). But then, if "envy" means the inability to contain and transform beta elements, the attack on the link should no longer be attributed to the patient alone or the analyst alone, but to both. –K becomes the name we can give to a certain quality that the link takes on at a given moment.

Similarly, with regard to the negative phenomena of symbolization, among so many expressions of the presence and the effects on the mind of real "black holes", one could see the trace of the search for existence as an attack on the process of symbolization; but also as a necessary moment of persecution[3] (as with the paranoid-schizoid position as opposed to the depressive one) before moving on to a new integration.

The question naturally arises as to how the analyst can intuit the existence of non-symbolic and anti-symbolic activities. Levy also shows us this in a series of long and beautiful clinical vignettes. The reader is thus really left to appreciate his great humanity (nothing new for those lucky enough to know him personally), theoretical preparation, and clinical expertise, as well as his use of the concepts brilliantly set out in the remaining sections of the book.

One of the most beautiful things in the book is the whole chapter on intimacy. If I had to summarize its essence, I would say that becoming a subject no longer involves the satisfaction of (impulse) desire, but rather, as Lacan effectively writes, the desire for the desire of the other and thus the experience of being loved.

The theme of intimacy is closely linked to that of symbolization. After all, in its origins, any symbolization is nothing more than a way of preserving intimacy with the object, even when it is temporarily

3 Cf. Civitarese, G. (2021). Bion's graph of "in search of existence". *The American Journal of Psychoanalysis, 81*, 273-280.

absent. If Ernst throws the reel away, it is not to make his mother disappear (the game is only apparently masochistic). Rather, it is to stage her magical reappearance, made possible by the thread, in the form of an internal representation.

Somewhere, Ogden wrote that Freud invented two new forms of human relationship that had not existed before: analysis and supervision. Certainly, one of the characteristics of these two new types of relationships is intimacy. But whereas in the past intimacy could be considered a non-specific or collateral factor of a given relationship of care, now, since the focus is not so much on knowing as on being, it has become the purpose of care.

Intimacy means that the patient and the analyst are no longer (too) afraid of each other, that they trust each other, that they gradually find themselves bound by something that can only be called a link of love. Of course, declined according to varying degrees of intensity and forms, depending on the case, as in life, if we use the concept of a love link it is to emphasize that deep down, on an unconscious level, there is an absolute symmetry in the therapeutic relationship. As Dante writes, "*Amor ch'a nullo amato amar perdona*"[4] can be read as stating that unrequited love is not love, but only illness or unhappiness.

What does this mean for the analysis? That the aesthetic conflict is not only between the child and the mother or the patient and the analyst but also between the mother and the child and the analyst and the patient. Could a patient ever overcome their distrust of the object if they did not feel that the love they were invested with was genuine? And could the analyst ever live up to Dante's definition of love, and thus feel recognized, if he did not feel the patient's gratitude was genuine? The same theme could be rephrased in terms of the concept of recognition, which is explained in the Phenomenology by Hegel as the path to self-consciousness; in short, to existence. In contemporary

4 *Inferno*, canto V, v. 103.

psychoanalysis, it is no longer possible to ignore the dialectic of difference but also of identity, which governs the process of subjectivation. For the same reason, any model of psychoanalysis that is still based on a psychology of the isolated subject is certainly obsolete, in my opinion.

Thus, the degree of intimacy achieved in the analysis by the patient and the analyst, without excluding conflict and turbulence and in strict (not "rigoristic") respect for the setting, is certainly the measure of the degree of success of the analysis. To analyze is to move the patient's inner world from a totalitarian regime to a democratic one. This can only be achieved by weaving many more emotional links, moments of unison in which something true for the analyst and the patient becomes part of the very substance of their subjectivity. To know how the process is going, the analyst must be conscious and therefore "asymmetrically" able to intuit the signs that reveal to him the nature of the analytic field at any moment, be it regressive or progressive.

Levy is right to recall the etymology of the word intimacy and to point out that it expresses the idea of something that penetrates the interior, "the superlative of the interior, or rather, as interior as possible… 'becoming the other'… 'being the other'". In this way, he refers to exactly what I have just referred to, mentioning the concept of recognition. For Hegel, it is by no means just conscious recognition, which is one way in which the concept has been trivialized in psychoanalysis by some. No, it means the unconscious and inherently dialectical process by which the subject somehow accepts being denied or destroyed by the other but also being created or established as a subject and vice versa.

The circle closes: it is the dialectic of the love relationship itself. After all, what Hegel, without using that word, and Husserl call "intersubjectivity", and Merleau-Ponty "the flesh of the world", is nothing more than the same subject that, in psychoanalysis, Freud investigates and baptizes as the unconscious. That is why on a page of

Transformations, Bion proposes replacing the finite and infinite with the conscious and unconscious; this is why thinking and working with Bion and the post-Bionians (I repeat, declared and important references for Levy) means using initial postulates regarding the unconscious and the dream that are no longer those of the classical tradition at all.

You can see how exciting the journey that Levy promises the reader in these pages is, and how – needless to say – he presents himself in the guise of Virgil. Nevertheless, he merely reproduces Freud's gesture: "*Acheronta movebo...*"; in other words: "I'm going to take you to hell, but don't worry, I'll be your guide!" Part of "hell" are the fears that accompany any growth in intimacy. Freud is very clear about this: "We are never so defenseless against suffering as when we love."[5] Emotions and affects are what matter in an analysis because the value people attach to their lives depends on emotions and affects. That is why we deal with this and not, for example, with complicated abstract reasoning.

The simple fact is that, as in the case of a concept, the formation of a symbol always implies a certain degree of destruction, aimed at the excess of difference that would make it difficult to individualize the common and consensual space. If a symbol has value, it has value for everyone, but in itself it also means losing a certain part of reality. Said like this, it may seem like nothing (the concept of a tree represents all trees and none in particular), but if we think that the prototype of this renunciation, as for little Ernst, is nothing less than the object of love, and that symbolizing, therefore, means engaging in a work of mourning: we see both the risks of the undertaking and the terrible ghosts that are always stirring in the air. We would not understand why, otherwise, it happens so often, not only for our patients but for each and every one of us at some point in our lives, that we are unable to do it and enter that terrain of negativity that Levy describes so well.

---

5 Freud, S. (1969). O mal-estar na civilização. In *Edição standard brasileira das obras psicológicas completas de Sigmund Freud* (Vol. XXI). Imago.

Contents

Preface

This book is the result of my interest in symbolization processes, which began many years ago. In the early 1980s, I worked with autistic children for almost ten years in a therapeutic community at the Pinel Clinic in Porto Alegre (RS). At that time, I was already interested in understanding how the first symbolizations were created; how and why they were not created; and why some of them were unable to develop their mental life and remained in a dementalized and predominantly dismantled state, to use Meltzer's concept.

During that period, I produced some work on these processes of subjectivation and non-subjectivation, especially one called "Echolalia and Childhood Autism,"[1] in which I studied the function of the word in the autistic child's echolalia, whether it had a symbolic function or not, and how the autistic child's mental space was constituted. That was when my interest in symbolization began.

Later, in 1995, my work for admission as an associate member of the Psychoanalytic Society of Porto Alegre (SPPA) also revolved around the theme of symbolization. Not coincidentally, I studied and reported the case of a patient with pseudomaturity and "don juanism", in which *acting outs* were very important and mental space was extremely restricted. His preconscious was extremely shallow and thin, with little capacity for symbolization. Throughout the

1 Levy, R. et al. (1980). Ecolalia e autismo infantil: comunicação preliminar a propósito de um caso clínico. *Revista de Psiquiatria do Rio Grande do Sul*, 2(3), 225-233.

analysis, it was possible to follow the expansion of his capacity for symbolization, the symbolic chain, and the chain of representations. Subsequently, my work to become a full member of the SPPA also revolved around symbolization and was called "From symbol to symbolization: a review of theoretical evolution and its repercussions on psychoanalytic technique".

Finally, in the last ten years, I have become interested, along with other psychoanalytic authors – inserting myself into this current of research – in this topic that is so prevalent in contemporary psychoanalysis: the issue of non-symbolization. In other words, what problems and failures in the process of symbolization are and how they occur; how the so-called *voids* in the symbolic web occur. As a result of my work and interest in the psychoanalysis of adolescence, I also began to study how the process of resubjectivation occurs at this moment of reconstruction of the subject's subjectivity.

In the first part of the book, in Chapters 1 to 5, a history of the conceptualization of symbolic processes will be presented, starting with Freud, of course, and evolving mainly along the path of the English school. Some contributions from the French school of psychoanalysis will be mentioned as well, especially from André Green and René Roussillon.

In the second part of the book, more contemporary aspects will be developed, especially with regard to flaws in the symbolic web, non-symbolizations and their repercussions on the psychoanalytic clinic, and the technical modifications that have been necessary to deal with the clinic with these patients. And also, more generally, the construction of analytic intimacy in this model of psychoanalysis.

In the third part of the book, the participation of symbolization processes in the resubjectivation of the adolescent subject will be studied, with adolescence understood as a major symbolization process.

This book is intended for psychoanalysts, psychoanalytically oriented psychotherapists, students of psychoanalysis and psychotherapy, who are interested in the study of symbolization processes, their pathologies, as well as the technique of psychoanalytic work with patients with disturbances in the construction of symbolic systems, that is, in their subjectivity.

Introduction

instead of defining man as an "animal rationale," we should define him as an "animal symbolicum".
Cassirer (1944/1997, p. 50)

Freud, with his discovery of the unconscious, shocked the culture of his time by revealing that human behavior was determined by a part of the mind that the subject himself did not know. What he did was denounce the existence of mental elements absent from immediate human perception, which could only be accessed through their derivatives, or their symbolic representatives, if we prefer. Since then, the understanding of symbolic processes has played a central role in the study of the functioning of the human mind.

The great divide between man and other animal species, according to Cassirer (1944/1997), is the existence of an intermediary symbolic system between the stimulus receptor system and the effector/motor system. Thought, as a symbolic system, mediates the immediate reaction, as Freud already said in "Formulations on the two principles of mental functioning" (1911/1969).

> *man lives in a symbolic universe. Language, myth, art, and religion are parts of this universe. They are the varied threads which weave the symbolic net, the tangled web of human experience. . . No longer can man confront reality immediately; he cannot see it, as it were, face to face,*

> except by the interposition of this artificial medium. *(Cassirer, 1944/1997, p. 48, my emphasis)*

Psychoanalysis, insofar as it sets out to understand and modify the human mind, has man's symbolic system as its "raw material". Psychoanalysis sets out to understand and act on what is most human in us, our symbolic system. This is the process of human subjectivation: moving from the perceptual, sensory and affective level of psychic functioning – present in all animals – to the symbolic level of the construction of the psyche. Subjectivation would mean moving from the body to the mind, from the corporeal to the mental, from the concrete to the symbolic, which is characteristic of the human being. Therein lies the human essence.

In this book, I intend to study not so much human symbolism, understood more generally, but symbolization from a psychoanalytic point of view, the creation of symbols in the human mind, in other words, the process of subjectivation. I will study the concept of symbolization, outline its meaning and evolution throughout the theoretical development of psychoanalysis, and highlight some consequences for psychoanalytic technique. Psychoanalysis, the science of the subjective, which seeks to study the subjective experience of reality by the human subject, has described the construction of this subjectivity from innumerable angles, in innumerable ways, all the way to more complex conceptualizations. However, I believe that all of them contribute to the theme and that is why they will be studied in this book.

The theme of symbolization runs through an endless series of questions that extend throughout psychoanalytic theory and technique: how are the first inscriptions in the psychic apparatus created and what are they? What about the creation of the psychic apparatus itself? What are mental contents? What about dreams? What about the transformations of the psychic apparatus? What about the ability

to think? What about "listening" to the latent through the manifest? Does one symbolize the other? There are countless others that could be listed, so in order not to lose objectivity and be exhaustive, I will focus on discussing some aspects that have interested me for many years.

In fact, they have interested me since the time when, at the beginning of my career as a child psychiatrist, I worked with autistic children. Children who did not speak, did not look at their interlocutor, did not play or take part in games. They spent hours, days, months in the therapeutic community, left to their own bodily sensations. How to help them speak? More than that, how do we inscribe them in the human world? How to help them move away from purely sensory, drive-based behavior towards human behavior?

On that occasion, I wrote a few articles to express the anguish generated by that experience, but also to share the challenge and even the wonder that came from it. Some children – very few, admittedly – managed to get in touch with other human beings and with themselves; others, unfortunately, did not, and had a sad evolution; sad because it was poor and deficient from the point of view of the acquisitions necessary for human development.

There I gained a profound understanding of the importance and centrality of the development of the symbolic function and its most obvious corollary, verbal language, for a being to become human. And today, many years later, this is still a subject of interest to me, I think because I am trying to help human beings who – on a different scale, it is true – also have difficulty thinking, communicating and relating.

There seems to be a common thread – which I have tried to follow in my research and which I try to expose in this book – along which the discoveries of psychoanalysis around the theme of symbolization extend. This thread runs from Freud, of course, through Ferenczi and Jones, to Melanie Klein, and from there to Winnicott, Bion, Meltzer and, more contemporarily, to Green, Ferro, Roussillon, Civitarese, and others. As we shall see, it is like a great jigsaw puzzle whose pieces we slowly find, putting them in place, giving us a sense of well-being and discovery, even though they were there waiting for us.

Of course, among these great thinkers of psychoanalysis, countless authors also made essential contributions because they clarified or synthesized what had been thought. These include Susan Isaacs, Hanna Segal, Harold Blum, and many others. I do not intend – and even if I did, I would not be able – to exhaust all the authors who have studied the subject, or even everything that each of these authors has written about it. Lacan, for example, has made great contributions to the subject, but to include him would take me months of study, or perhaps years. I will only mention those that I have been able to review and that have enabled me to achieve the objectives I set myself.

References

Cassirer, E. (1997). *Ensaio sobre o homem: introdução a uma filosofia da cultura humana.* Martins Fontes. (Originally published in 1944)

Freud, S. (1969). Formulações sobre os dois princípios do funcionamento mental. In *Edição standard brasileira das obras psicológicas completas de Sigmund Freud* (Vol. XII). Imago. (Originally published in 1911)

Part I
Conceptualization of symbolic processes in psychoanalysis

1. The symbol: general aspects

Initially, it is necessary to make some conceptual definitions, since the subject of symbolism and symbolization transcends psychoanalysis and these terms often refer to different concepts. Even within psychoanalysis itself, there are differences in the use of this terminology. As we shall see, after the Kleinian contributions, the concept has acquired a much wider scope, sometimes at the cost of some imprecision.

Several authors (Jones, 1916/1925; Green, 1975/1994; Laplanche & Pontalis, 1982/1997) trace the term "*symbol*" back to the Greek definition of *symbolon*, which consisted of an object cut into two pieces carried by two people belonging to the same sect who were separated and, therefore, a sign of recognition when the bearers met again and were able to reunite the pieces. In other words, the *symbolon* denoted the *link* between those two subjects.

Another interesting origin of the term symbol is given by Jones (1916/1925). He states that in Greek, "to symbolize" meant to *re-unite*, to *merge* and that the root of the term in Sanskrit (*gal*) designated the meeting of several rivers, an estuary. This is extremely interesting because it is precisely what we find in various symbolizations: the meeting, the confluence of various meanings that flow into a particular symbol.

In *The Language of Psychoanalysis*, by Laplanche and Pontalis (1982/1997), we see that it is possible to use the concept of symbolism in psychoanalysis in its broad form or its strict form and that Freud generally used it in the strict form. So says the dictionary:

> *a)* In a broad sense, *a mode of direct and figurative representation of an idea, a conflict, an unconscious desire; in this sense* we can consider any substitutive formation to be symbolic in psychoanalysis. *b)* In a strict sense, *a mode of representation that is distinguished by the constancy of the relationship between symbol and unconscious symbolized; this constancy is found not only in the same individual and from one individual to another, but in the most diverse domains (myth, religion, folklore, language, etc.) and in the most distant cultural areas between them. (p. 41, my emphasis)*

So we already have some definitions of what we call a symbol. In the non-psychoanalytic dictionary definition, the concept of symbol is limited to saying that it replaces something abstract or absent (Aurélio Digital, 2010). In the psychoanalytic definition of symbol, "absent" must include the notion of the unconscious: whether it is an unconscious idea or a repressed desire, which will be symbolized by something; or an unconscious elaboration of the absence of some object that can be replaced by a symbol.

However, as we will see throughout this chapter, even when it comes to the psychoanalytic concept of symbol, there is a great deal of variation in its conceptualization and, perhaps even greater regarding its creation; in other words, in the process of symbolization. For example, Freud and Jones understood the symbol in its restricted, supra-individual, collective sense, with constant meaning, while for Meltzer it is highly individual, personal, idiosyncratic.

Laplanche (1980/1988) criticizes Freud's position, by saying that, based on the discussion about the meaning of circumcision, it is a pre-psychoanalytical conception of symbolization. He says that this theory of symbolization considers the symbol and what it symbolizes to be two terms in a two-way correspondence, that is, a theory of the symbol as a simple designation of a specific object, disregarding what is known about the multiple chains and the complex weave between symbol and symbolized. He cites Jones himself to show how the links between symbol and symbolized are not two-way but rather constitute a network of associative chains: similarity of totality, part to part, links by metonymy (the part symbolizes the whole), links by the contrary. This wealth of associative chains was shown by Freud himself in relation to dreams, in which each element can refer to a multitude of associative chains, although Freud did not use the concept of symbol for these representations. We will see more about this later.

Thus, taking circumcision as an object of study, Laplanche shows that it becomes a complex symbol enclosing within itself relations of analogy (since castration and circumcision are two analogous acts since they cause an amputation); of metonymy since the part (foreskin) is taken for the whole (penis); but also of opposition, because the extirpation of the foreskin is understood as eliminating the "feminine" from the penis. Circumcision, then, is a symbolization of the double meaning of the threat of castration and, at the same time, a "masculinization," through the extermination of what would be "feminine".

Every symbolization introduces a new order, because when one symbolizes, one does not just introduce a new symbol, but a whole new symbolic set. To symbolize is to provide a new interpretation, which does not end with ambiguity or the possibility of new interpretations. The new symbol will have several meanings (Laplanche, 1980/1988). Step by step, we will try to understand each of these conceptualizations.

Perhaps the common element between the various conceptualizations of symbol and symbolization in psychoanalysis is that the production and use of the psychoanalytic symbol are unconscious, as is what is symbolized. Blum (1978) proposes a spectrum of symbolization that begins with conscious abstract and conceptual thought, passes through the allegorical expressions of preconscious metaphors, and reaches unconscious symbolism. His proposal combines the usual non-analytical notions of symbolism and psychoanalytical symbolism in a single framework. He raises the possibility that the same mechanism or process that leads to psychoanalytic symbols is related to the symbolic process that results in human language. He warns, however, that the differences are so great between the two types of symbolic processes that he does not think it is useful to place the two symbolic forms on a *continuum*, although they must have originated from a common, undifferentiated, protosymbolic matrix. He thinks that imagining a single symbolic function takes the emphasis off unconscious formations and the characteristics of psychoanalytic symbolism. As we will see below, this way of understanding the symbolic chain is close to the Bionian proposal evidenced in Bion's Grid (1965/2004), which organizes thoughts into levels ranging from the concrete (beta elements) to the most abstract levels (algebraic calculation).

Another distinction that might be worth making is between symbol, sign, and metaphor. The symbol not only represents an absent element but also brings with it an exchange of meanings. Meltzer (1984) goes on to say that this exchanged meaning enriches the two elements present in symbolization, the symbol and the symbolized. So, for example, if for one patient the "leper boy" symbolized his feeling of smallness and incontinent skin, we can see that not only the idea of leprosy enriches the idea of incontinent skin (insofar as it transfers to it a meaning of a disease, perhaps progressive, repulsive) but the idea of incontinent skin enriches the idea of leprosy insofar as it transfers to it the notion of the anguish of losing bodily limits.

As far as the sign is concerned, it is understood almost as an agreed sign to indicate something. A distinction can be made between the use of signs and symbols as follows: signs are elements that indicate or lead to a certain reaction when they have been associated, by concomitance, with certain stimuli (Langer, 1941/1989). They are the beginning of intelligence and the first manifestation of the mind.

Animals develop a language of signs, learned by trial and error, which tells them the most appropriate reactions for their biological functions. Therefore, even the animal mind works through a primitive semantics in which some phenomena are signs of others.

Humans can use signs differently: they can use them to indicate things, like animals, and they can also turn a sign into a symbol. For an animal, a certain word is a sign of the presence of something or of an immediate action; for a human being, it can be a way of talking about something absent, thus representing that object. Except that the signs used in this way are symbols (Langer, 1941/1989). For example, a traffic sign, which is primarily a sign, can, for someone, become a symbol of a certain highly emotionally significant experience: it can represent an accident, a romantic situation, carrying with it a highly personal and idiosyncratic emotional meaning.

For Cassirer (1944/1997), symbol and sign belong to two different universes of discourse: "a sign is part of the physical world of being; a symbol is part of the human world of meaning. Signs are 'operators' and symbols are 'designators'" (p. 58). A sign has a fixed and singular meaning, linked to the thing to which it refers, while "a genuine human symbol is not characterized by its uniformity, but by its versatility" (p. 65).

Making this distinction has not only an academic purpose, but a relevant clinical utility that will be explored in more depth at the end of this work. It is important, for example, to make a distinction between symbolic formation and creative thinking, on the one hand, and a "computerized" use of signs and a simplified use of experiences and ideas received from the past, on the other. "The creation of idiosyncratic symbols, as opposed to the manipulation of conventional signs, constitutes a watershed between personality growth and adaptation" (Meltzer, 1988/1995, p. 35). Or, if we prefer, between a creative life and an operative life. We will return to this essential aspect of mental functioning and psychopathology later.

To finish off this chapter, it may be worth mentioning other forms of indirect representation, such as analogy, metonymy, and metaphor. In analogy, relationships of similarity are established between the two terms being compared. In metaphor, a comparison is made and one of the two terms compared is removed. So instead of saying the fox is clever, John is clever, therefore John is a fox, you say straight out: John is a fox. A metaphor is used in order to economize on the description of attributes and adjectives of a given expression, to highlight a particular attribute and to immediately cause an affective impact on the interlocutor. According to Jones (1916/1925), insofar as it appeals to a more concrete, visual element, it uses a more primitive element and is therefore closer to the affects. Finally, metonymy uses a part to represent the whole. A sculpture, for example, can be said to be a bronze. These relationships of analogy, metaphor, and metonymy are then carried out consciously or preconsciously. However, I think that even in the process of unconscious symbolization, the type of relationship between the two terms varies, and can be symbolized by analogy, metonymy or metaphor.

References

Aurélio Digital (2010). Símbolo. In *Dicionário Aurélio da Língua Portuguesa* (5. ed.). Developed by Snowman Labs.

Bion, W. R. (2004). *Transformações: do aprendizado ao crescimento* (2. ed.). Imago. (Originally published in 1965)

Blum, H. P. (1978). Symbolic process and symbol formation. *International Journal of Psychoanalysis*, 59, 455-471.

Cassirer, E. (1997). *Ensaio sobre o homem: introdução a uma filosofia da cultura humana.* Martins Fontes. (Originally published in 1944)

Green, A. (1994). El analista, la simbolizacion, y la ausencia en el encuadre analitico. In *De locuras privadas.* Amorrortu. (Originally published in 1975)

Jones, E. (1925). La théorie du symbolisme. In *Traité theorique et pratique de psychanalyse*. Payot. (Originally published in 1916)

Langer, S. (1989). *Filosofia em nova chave*. Perspectiva. (Originally published in 1941)

Laplanche, J. (1988). *Problemáticas II: castração, simbolizações*. Martins Fontes. (Originally published in 1980)

Laplanche, J., & Pontalis, J.-B. (1997). *Vocabulário de psicanálise* (D. Lagache, Dir.). Martins Fontes. (Originally published in 1982)

Meltzer, D. (1984). *Vida onírica: una revisión de la teoría y de la técnica psicoanalítica*. Tecnipublicaciones.

Meltzer, D. (1995). *A apreensão do belo*. Imago. (Originally published in 1988)

2. Symbolization: some points of contact between philosophy and psychoanalysis

This chapter is not intended to provide an extensive review of philosophy's contributions to the concept of symbolization. However, it is interesting to make a small incursion by reviewing at least two authors, Cassirer and Susanne Langer, for the richness of their contributions and the influence they have had on psychoanalytic thinking, especially that of Bion and Meltzer. Of course, a more consistent review of the contributions of philosophy should include at least Kant, since he was Freud's interlocutor many times and for the influence of his thought on Bion; it should also include Heidegger, for the points of contact between his ideas and Winnicottian thought (Loparić, 1997). I will leave that for another paper, or for another colleague who is better qualified than me in this area.

Cassirer (1944/1997), in his book *An Essay on Man*, calls for unity in the search for something that explains the "real general character of human culture" (p. 43). To this end, he highlights the constant concern of philosophers to discover the nature of man and states that knowledge of oneself is the goal of philosophical inquiry.

Socrates inaugurated the anthropological vision of philosophy, seeking to define the nature of man. He tries to do this by describing man's virtues (goodness, courage, justice etc.), because he believes that man's nature cannot be detected like that of physical things. What is really interesting is Cassirer's statement that "man's character can only be understood in his immediate relations with other human beings" (p. 16). Man's truth ceases to be understood as something that can be grasped by the individual thinker and becomes tangible in confrontation, dialog, dialogical, or dialectical thinking. "It can only be obtained through the cooperation of subjects in mutual questioning and response" (p. 17). These ideas are noteworthy for their harmony with the appreciation of the intersubjective construction of meaning in psychoanalysis to discover the nature of the unconscious, ours and our patients'.

In the 19th century, Darwin, with his book on the evolution of species, established biology as the hegemonic science for understanding man's insertion into nature (Cassirer, 1944/1997). The theory of the evolution of species places man in a continuous line of evolution of life, but the question regarding *human culture* remains to be resolved: how do we understand it? "Is the cultural world, like the organic world, made up of accidental changes?" (p. 38). From this, various philosophical systems developed in the 19th and 20th centuries (Nietzsche, Freud, Marx) to understand what sets our thought and will in motion, producing culture as a result. A central thought (metaphysical, theological, mathematical, biological) is lost and we fall into a complete diversity of thoughts, each area approaching the problem from its own point of view.

The point of view that Cassirer will develop – and which, because of its nature, is quoted so extensively in this chapter – is that the symbol is the key to understanding the nature of man. He will say that in man, in addition to the receptor and effector systems found in all animals, there is the *symbolic system,* which indicates a qualitative change in the evolution of the human species. This acquisition has transformed the whole of human life.

We will see how close this is to the ideas defended by Freud in "Formulations on the Two Principles of Mental Functioning" (1911/1969). "There is an unmistakable difference between organic reactions and human reactions" (p. 48). Human reaction is mediated, "slowed down by a long, slow and complicated thought process" (p. 48). The last two sentences belong to Cassirer (1944/1997) but could be confused with Freud's in the aforementioned work, such as the statement that "language primarily does not express thoughts or ideas, but feelings and affections" (p. 49), which could be confused with Bion's statements that will be discussed later.

Language, myth, religion, and art are ways man has found to organize his feelings, desires, and thoughts. By analyzing these languages, we can build a theory about man. What distinguishes man from the other inhabitants of the planet is not his physical or metaphysical nature, but rather his work, what he produces: his language, his myths, his religion, art, science, and history. These productions are united by a common thread, which is the production of symbols.

It is also quite striking how much this view of man coincides with the most up-to-date contributions of historians and anthropologists, such as Yuval Harari (2020) in his book *Sapiens*. Based on various pieces of evidence, Harari develops the thesis that *Homo sapiens* prevailed over several species of hominids that lived together at the same time because thanks to its symbolic capacity, it was able to construct myths that were shared by growing groups of individuals and were therefore more powerful than other groups that did not have this capacity. And also because they were able to start drawing up more sophisticated hunting plans.

Drawing a dividing line between animal and human thought, the animal does not compare two things, nor does it confuse them; it does not think *about* it, but only *it* (Cassirer, 1944/1997). In other words, the animal does not place itself at a distance, discriminating the *self* from the object of thought in order to judge or compare it: it simply thinks the object in the sensory, concrete realm. In the development of the human individual, there is also an evolution from a concrete, sensory, pragmatic attitude to a symbolic attitude, and here we have a consensus between philosophy and psychoanalysis. Confirming this, we all have patients who, having difficulty entering the symbolic world, will live in automatism, and we will see that, in their way of behaving, they live in a world of signs, simply operating, as if the facts had no symbolic meaning for them. And they will tell us: "I just did it, I don't know if it means this or that, but if you're saying...".

The discovery of the symbolic universe represents a mental revolution because it opens up new horizons, introducing the subject to a world that transcends the world of concrete things, limited to things themselves. It introduces the subject into a world without limits, which is that of creative thought, of human creativity, of human culture. "Once in possession of this magic key (the word), the continuation of man's progress is guaranteed" (Cassirer, 1944/1997, p. 63).

One of the problems that psychoanalysis has come to deal with is precisely this: in individuals in whom there has been damage to the development of the symbolic function, or an attack on it as a form of escaping from internal reality (Bion, 1957/1988), we have a mind that cannot grow and develop. The apprehension of the internal and external world – in order to be thought about, not just felt – is mediated by the symbol. If its production is impaired, there will be a difficulty or inability to think about oneself and the world.

Finally, Cassirer defines that the *abstract space*, that is characteristic of man, has nothing to do with the space of the senses. It is a symbolic space, constructed through the apprehension of abstract relationships between things. Geometry is a typical example of this space. The concept of truth changes, because in it we are not dealing with the truth of things, but with the truth of propositions and judgments.

Since psychoanalysis deals essentially with abstract, symbolic space, its phenomena definitely do not belong to the domain of facts, of the world of the senses. Therefore, positivism, which essentially deals with real facts, cannot deal with the object of psychoanalysis. A new epistemology will be needed that can deal with truth not as a correlation to facts, but as a symbolic consensus (Rezende, 1997), as will be studied in more depth in the chapter on the construction of the possible truth in psychoanalysis.

Even if there is individual differentiation among higher animals (something that does not seem to exist in lower animals), with greater capacities in a given individual of a species, these capacities will not be passed on to the species due to a biological incapacity and will disappear with the death of that individual. Man's capacities, even if subject to the same biological law, can survive the individual to the extent that he expresses and records his works symbolically (Cassirer, 1944/1997). "Taken as a whole, human culture can be described as a process of man's progressive self-liberation. In the various cultural forms, man discovers and experiences a new power – the power to build a world of his own, an ideal world" (p. 371). This is also true for the individual: the ability to produce symbols that give meaning to their experiences frees the subject and gives him a sense of power, as it enables him to build a world of his own – the dream world, in Meltzer's (1984) sense.

Marilsa Taffarel (1997) makes an interesting study of the correlation between the concept of subjectivity in psychoanalysis and Cassirer's contributions, especially those in his first book, *The Philosophy of Symbolic Forms*. Taffarel believes that Cassirer's contributions are more in tune with those of Kleinian authors.

As we will see later, there is a very strong correlation between Cassirer's ideas and Kleinian conceptions of symbolization, since, especially since Segal (1957/1982), Kleinian theory defines two clear types of symbolization: the symbolic equation and the symbol itself.

It is Segal who clearly differentiates between them. It is only in the depressive position that the symbol itself can originate, the result of various separations; the *self* understands that the symbol only represents the object, it is not the object, and it endures this depressive pain. As in Cassirer, an evolution is conceived that goes from the concrete to the abstract, which will be extensively developed in the Bionian contributions.

Susanne Langer's (1941/1989) contributions in her book *Philosophy in a New Key*, highlighting the importance of symbolization in understanding man, are just as relevant as Cassirer's. She says that modern psychology (psychoanalysis) and modern logic have developed beyond their expectations due to their discovery of the power of symbolization. She says that modern psychology (psychoanalysis) and modern logic have developed beyond their expectations due to their discovery of the power of symbolization. She makes a epistemological consideration that is of great interest to psychoanalysts, stating that if we follow the scientific methods of the natural sciences, we get closer to histology, physiology, genetics, and biochemistry; however, if we want to study the human mind, by using these methods, we get further and further away from what we should be getting closer to. The scientific scheme of physicists that so seduces "psychologists" is useless for the study of mental phenomena.

The new concern with symbolization, both on the part of epistemology and psychoanalysis, even though they deal with different concepts of symbol, helps to shed light on the question of the functioning of the human mind, of the "*human response to the world*" (Langer, 1941/1989, p. 35).

The discovery of the importance of the symbolic function in man has shaken up the concept of intelligence: it is not a prodigious memory, or a superior mental speed, or an extremely sensitive perception (often found in animals) that makes man more intelligent, but rather it is his ability to operate with symbols, to speak, to record, to create culture, that designates his superiority over other animals. "Thus, our interest in the mind has increasingly shifted from the acquisition of experience, the domain of sense, to the *uses* of sensory data, the realm of conception and expression" (p. 38).

"The importance of the use of symbols, if admitted, soon becomes central to the study of intelligence, because the essential act of thinking is symbolization" (Ritchie quoted by Langer, 1941/1989, p. 38). The key to understanding mental life, which is characteristically human, not animal, is symbolization. This is centrally important, as it links the ability to create and operate with symbols with the individual's intellect, explaining why we have the impression of low intelligence in patients who have difficulties with their symbolic abilities.

What is most striking about Langer's contributions is their almost immediate connection with Bion's ideas. She believes that man has *a basic need, which is the need for symbolization, essentially human.* Symbolization can be crude, primitive, but it must exist.

> *The function of making symbols is one of the primary activities of the human being, just like eating, looking and walking. It is the fundamental process of the mind and it works all the time. Sometimes we are aware of it, sometimes we are merely faced with its results, and we understand that certain experiences have passed through our brain and have been digested there. . . For if the material of thought is symbolism, then the thinking organism must always be providing symbolic versions of its experiences in order for thinking to continue. In reality, symbolization is not the essential act of thought; it is essential to thought, it precedes it. Symbolization is the essential act of the mind and the mind takes in more than what is commonly called thought. (Langer, 1941/1989, p. 51)*

Langer (1941/1989) understands the brain far beyond its physiological function; she understands it as an organ that is always in activity, like the heart, lungs, and kidneys, "following its own law, actively translating its experiences into symbols" (p. 52), constantly carrying out a process of ideation. For her, the brain is a symbol-maker, an idea shared by Bion and Meltzer.

To conclude this topic, I would like to highlight her conception that "symbolization is pre-rationative, but not pre-rational. It is more general (and previous, I would say) than thinking, fantasize, or taking action. . . Each perception is sucked into the stream of symbols which constitutes the human mind" (p. 52).

References

Bion, W. (1988). Diferenciação entre a personalidade psicótica e não-psicótica. In *Estudos psicanalíticos revisados*. Imago. (Originally published in 1957)

Cassirer, E. (1997). *Ensaio sobre o homem: introdução a uma filosofia da cultura humana*. Martins Fontes. (Originally published in 1944)

Freud, S. (1969). Formulações sobre os dois princípios do funcionamento mental. In *Edição standard brasileira das obras psicológicas completas de Sigmund Freud* (Vol. XII). Imago. (Originally published in 1911)

Harari, Y. N. (2020). *Sapiens: uma breve história da humanidade*. Companhia das Letras.

Langer, S. (1989). *Filosofia em nova chave*. Perspectiva. (Originally published in 1941)

Loparić, Z. (1997). O Édipo de Freud a Bion. *Boletim Científico da SPRJ*, *18*(3), 375-381.

Meltzer, D. (1984). *Vida onírica: una revisión de la teoría y de la técnica psicoanalítica*. Tecnipublicaciones.

Rezende, A. M. (1997). *Investigação em psicanálise: uma procura da verdade.* Lecture given at the Ribeirão Preto Meeting, commemorating the centenary of Bion's birth.

Segal, H. (1982). Notas a respeito da formação de símbolos. In *A obra de Hanna Segal: uma abordagem kleiniana à prática clínica.* Imago. (Originally published in 1957)

Taffarel, M. (1997). A subjetividade básica na psicanálise e na "Filosofia das formas simbólicas". *Revista Brasileira de Psicanálise, 31*(2), 47-57.

3. Symbolization at the dawn of psychoanalysis

The question of symbolization and symbols in Freud's work, in general, is quite rich, complex and full of ambiguities, like many other aspects he studied. Any attempt to simplify it, to find a general concept, would impoverish the subject to such an extent that it would be regrettable. So, with the help of some authors, I will try to clarify how the subject was developed by him at the dawn of psychoanalysis.

Freud, with his keen clinical vein and unique scientific spirit, discovered and described the existence of two distinct mental processes, with different rules and laws, namely the primary and secondary processes. He described exhaustively and with great precision the contents of the primary process: the unconscious thoughts, their displacements and condensations, their associative and substitutive pathways. However, for fear of being confused with those he was fighting, he chose not to give the name symbolizations to these relations of substitution of repressed elements with other elements. He described condensations and displacements with brilliance and richness, but he did not specify that they occurred precisely because of the possibility of establishing symbolic relationships.

In the Freudian paradigm, there is a vectorial tendency, ranging from the drive to verbalization, which forms correspondence relationships based on a succession of retranscriptions between the different parts of the mind. A series of relationships is created in which one refers to the other. These relations are not only of opposition (censorship), "but of collaboration, since this is the way to move from one system to another, for example from a latent content to a manifest one" (Green, 1975/1994, p. 77). And although Freud did not call them that, Green believes that these are the *internal relations of symbolization,* which link the different elements of the same formation (dreams, unconscious fantasies, thoughts etc.) and ensure psychic continuity and discontinuity.

The symbol in Freud

Although Freud studied the various forms of *indirect representation* of the unconscious – as he used to refer to them – in dreams, symptoms, and parapraxes, he *did not refer to these indirect representations as symbols.* In most of his work, he reserved the term "symbol" to be used in a very restricted way, within the definition I referred to earlier using the description by Laplanche and Pontalis (1982/1997). In various works (1900/1969, 1901/1969, 1915b/1969, 1916/1969), Freud described symbols as supra-individual elements, belonging to culture, which the individual would use to mask the repressed elements of the unconscious.

It seems to me that one way of understanding Freud's ideas about symbols would be to study the area in which they would be most evident, namely his study of dreams. So, in his major work, *The Interpretation of Dreams* (1900/1969), although he described extremely rich processes of symbolic transformations in which repressed representations were replaced by others through displacement and condensation, once they met the conditions for representability, he would not call them symbolizations. He considered them to be mere substitution processes in which the unconscious used elements that were already ready to be used. He says this verbatim:

> *In fact, when we examine the matter more closely, we must recognize the fact that* the work of the dream does nothing original *in making these substitutions. In order to achieve its aims – in this case, to make possible a representation that has been blocked by censorship – it simply follows the pathways that it has already established in the unconscious; and it gives preference to the transformations of repressed material that can also become conscious in the form of chistes or allusions, and which are so full of the fantasies of neurotic patients. (p. 368, my emphasis)*

Freud adds later:

> *Everything leads to the same conclusion, namely that* there is no need to presume the operation of any symbolizing activity peculiar to the mind in dream work, *but rather that dreams make use of any symbolizations that are already present in unconscious thought, because they better fit the requirements of dream formation, by virtue of their representability, and also, in general, because they escape censorship. (p. 372, my emphasis)*

In this passage, Freud definitively clarifies his idea that there is no symbolizing activity peculiar to the mind during dreams. Meltzer (1984), in *Dream life*, tries to understand Freud's position and says that this is, in fact, an epistemological problem, since he could not conceive, given his historical context, of a creative activity during sleep. As if he could not imagine, given the margins of philosophical thought at the time, that the mind could be creative outside of wakefulness, even though he had discovered the creativity of the mind outside consciousness. I think the following passage illustrates what I am saying:

> *All the attributes that we value so much in our chains of thought and that characterize them as complex achievements of a higher order are found again in dream thoughts.* However, there is no need to assume that this thought activity is carried out during sleep, a possibility which would seriously confuse what has hitherto been our accepted picture of the psychic state of sleep *[he was referring to the regressive state of sleep]. On the contrary, it is quite possible that these thoughts originated the day before, went unnoticed by our consciousness from the beginning, and perhaps were already completed when sleep began. The most we can conclude from this is that it proves that the most complex realizations of thought are possible without the assistance of consciousness... (Freud, 1900/1969, p. 631, my emphasis)*

Even though he believed that the dream-formation processes he was studying were not symbolizations, Freud discovered and described highly creative dream activities, which he considered to be mere disguise and condensation. Studying the conditions of representability in dreams, he stated the following:

> *In some cases, this type of change of expression helps dream condensation even more directly, by finding a form of words that, due to its ambiguity, is capable of giving expression to more than one of the thoughts in the dream. In this way, the whole field of verbal mockery is put at the disposal of dream work. There is no reason to be surprised by the role played by words in the formation of dreams.* Words, being the nodal point of numerous representations, *can be considered as predestined to ambiguity; and neuroses (for example, in the structuring of obsessions and*

> *phobias), no less than dreams, make use at will of the advantages thus offered by words for the purposes of condensation and disguise. (p. 362, my emphasis)*

Here, Freud highlights how words, as signifiers, are loaded with countless meanings, creating a penumbra around them. This ambiguity of words allows them to carry various condensed thoughts. This is, in fact, a rich study of a type of symbolization – even if it has not been called that – which would be the transmutation of one type of language into another, studied by Meltzer (1984) in the chapter on the issue of dream interpretation in clinical practice.

Freud's main concern was the following: since symbols were considered to be universal, univocal elements with a constant meaning, they could be interpreted by the analyst directly, and not in the way that the good technique he created advocated, using the dreamer's associations to understand the specific meaning of the substitutions made in the dream. That is why he wanted to make a clear distinction between what he called the substitutive representations of dreams and symbols. And, consistent with this, he advocated that when symbols (in the restricted sense he considered) appeared in dreams, they could be translated directly, without the need for associations. This created a technical limitation, as he felt that not all psychoanalysts had this knowledge of symbols. He explicitly warned against this:

> *I would like to issue a categorical warning against overestimating the importance of symbols in dream interpretation, against restricting the work of translating dreams to a simple translation of symbols, and against abandoning the technique of using the dreamer's associations. The two techniques of dream interpretation should be complementary to each other; but, both in practice and in theory, the first place continues to be occupied by the*

> *process I described at the beginning, which gives decisive importance to the comments made by the dreamer, while the translation of symbols, as I have explained it, is also available to us as an auxiliary method. (p. 383)*

He returns to this concern in his 1916 *Introductory Lectures on Psychoanalysis*, especially in Lecture X, on "Symbolism in Dreams". This work is considered by Strachey to be the most important writing on symbolism in dreams. Freud begins by referring to "silent" dream elements in themselves, for which the patient has no associations and which he previously thought were a technical fault. He mentions some symbolic elements that would always appear representing the same thing in dreams and that, in order to elucidate these situations, he would interpret the "silent" dream elements (without associations) with his own resources. By making this kind of substitution, he was able to achieve the meaning of the dream. In this way, he obtained numerous uniform translations for certain dream elements, in the same way as popular dream interpretation books. He differentiates this technique of interpretation, through the translation of symbols, from the *associative technique.* Although it seems less reliable than interpretation by association, experience has shown it to be useful and valid as an auxiliary element.

In this lecture (Freud, 1916/1969), he makes an important definition: he calls the *constant* association between an oneiric element and its version in common use a *symbolic relationship.* It was the fourth type of relationship between the dream element and the "original" thing behind it. The three previous types of relationship were that of the part for the whole, that of allusion, and that of plastic representation. The symbolic relationship would therefore be a very specific type of dream representation. Freud says:

> *symbolism is perhaps the most remarkable chapter in dream theory. In the first place, as symbols are constant*

> *versions, they fulfill to a certain extent the ideal of the ancient, as well as the popular, interpretation of dreams, from which, with our technique, we have moved a long way away. In certain circumstances, they allow us to* interpret a dream without asking questions to the dreamer *who, in any case, would really have nothing to tell us about the symbol. If we are familiar with common dream symbols, and, moreover, with the personalities of the dreamer, the circumstances in which he lives, and the impressions that preceded the occurrence of the dream,* we will often be in a position to interpret a dream with certainty – to translate it by sight, so to speak. *(p. 181, my emphasis)*

I think this passage illustrates Freud's whole conception of dream symbolism (constant, non-original versions of the dreamer, let alone of a particular dream) and his concern to warn of the similarity with pre-psychoanalytic dream interpretation. He also warns that this type of symbolic, non-associative dream interpretation can give the impression of virtuosity, which the analyst must resist.

Freud, in his genius, recognized that, even if he believed that symbols had a universal and permanent meaning, there were situations, certain dreams, in which they should be understood in their *own sense and not symbolically*, that is, in a new sense other than the universal one; just as he accepted that in certain situations the dreamer did not use universal symbols to represent repressed desires, but any other element:

> *Often a symbol has to be interpreted in its proper sense, and not symbolically, while on other occasions the dreamer can draw from his particular memories the power to employ as sexual symbols all sorts of things which are not commonly employed as such. (Freud, 1900/1969, p. 375)*

In other words, in this passage, he broadened his concept of symbol and admitted that personal and idiosyncratic oneiric symbols could be created.

Laplanche (1980/1988) calls this set of fixed, universal symbols Freud's "symbolic" and says that it would be like an inherited language that transcends the individual and culture, a universal lexicon that appears in dreams, but also in culture in different ways. Freud was concerned about this because the interpretation of dreams by means of typical symbolism, as already mentioned, dispensed with free associations and the dreamer's biography, and could only be deciphered by knowing the meaning of the symbol. As this type of procedure was confused with the dream translations of almanacs, he was concerned that it would threaten the psychoanalytic method. Furthermore, concerned about some of Stekel's exaggerations, Freud did not want to fully accept the ambivalence of the symbol that he advocated. He did not let go of the analogical nature of the symbol and wanted to place some limits on its meaning: *you cannot make anything mean anything.*

So, for Freud, the symbol, in addition to its universal, collective character, implies that there is an internal power of representation. He would create a symbolic in which we will find biunivocal relationships between symbols and symbolized, sustained by "similarity", by a "natural" relationship between them. He thinks that "the imagination does not admit anything, and a solid, long object cannot be a feminine symbol, because its very shape imposes limits on the imagination" (Laplanche, 1980/1988, p. 246).

Jones, in his 1916 authoritative work "The Theory of Symbolism," gave consistency to this conception of symbolism and established a conceptual framework that would influence psychoanalytic conceptions for many decades, maintaining to this day the relevance of many of the statements contained therein. He begins by outlining the general characteristics of symbolism and then defines what true psychoanalytic symbolism is. He states: "The thesis will here be maintained

that true symbolism, in the strict sense, is to be distinguished from other forms of indirect representation" (Jones, 1916/1925, p. 209). So *true symbolism*, in the strict psychoanalytic sense, would be:

- *Representation of unconscious psychic elements:* this is what distinguishes it from other indirect representations of the mind; the process of symbolization takes place outside the mind, so the individual does not perceive the symbol he is using.
- *Invariable meaning:* despite defending this proposition, Jones thinks it should be toned down a little – there may be some variations, albeit small and very limited, according to the individual's social or cultural class. He implies that it is the individual who uses the symbol that already exists in the culture and does so unconsciously. It is formed in the culture by a succession of transformations over time and cultural and linguistic variations.
- *Non-dependence on individual factors*: Jones also mitigates this characteristic somewhat by saying that it is not completely independent of the individual, but *it is not dependent on the individual,* i.e. it is not conditioned solely by individual factors. The individual's freedom in creating the symbol is restricted. He goes on to say, quoting Freud, that "the individual cannot choose what idea shall be represented [...] he can choose what symbol out of the many possible ones shall be used to represent a given idea (Freud, 1900/1969). What he cannot do is to give another meaning to a given current symbol; he can choose symbols or even create a new one, but everyone who will use it will use it with the same meaning" (Jones, 1916/1925, p. 218).
- *It has a genetic meaning:* symbolism comes from the primitive mental functioning that tends to compare two ideas. Even in adults, he assumes that it is the "primitive infantile state of mind", which persists in the unconscious throughout life, that tends to make these comparisons that lie at the basis of all metaphor and symbolization. This primitive mental functioning found in

children, in savages, and during sleep, identifies different objects, merges different ideas, and registers similarities rather than differences. These are the most fundamental and primitive attributes of the mind.

- *It has linguistic connections:* the study of linguistics and semantics shows how, in their origins, certain words were linked to meanings that they carry with them.
- *Phylogenetic parallels:* the ubiquity of the same symbols in countless cultures, in different geographies, and historical moments is striking.

Jones goes on to say that the number of symbols is relatively high, perhaps in the thousands, but the ideas symbolized are few: the body, love, hatred, relationships with immediate relatives, birth, and death.

As for the genesis of symbolism, the author believes, as has been pointed out, that it comes from primitive mental functioning that tends to compare two ideas. However, Jones considers this factor of *mental insufficiency* to be the least important in the genesis of symbols and the most static. He believes that the factors linked to the pleasure/displeasure principle and the reality principle are more explanatory: the primitive mind ignores differences because this generates displeasure, while equating, feeling something as already known, generates pleasure. It is the function of identification (already described in 1913 by Ferenczi, which will see below) that forms *the basis of symbolism* and the adult, when their power to adapt is diminished, returns to their old, long-forgotten "childish games". He believes that every child ontogenetically recreates the steps of civilization, progressively deriving sexual energy for non-sexual purposes, through the sublimation described by Freud.

Another interesting concept by Jones, mentioned in this 1916 work, is the idea of symbolic equivalence, which I believe, along with Ferenczi's concept of *identification* (1913/1992), is the precursor to the concept of *symbolic equation* created by Segal in 1957. Jones says that B is the *symbolic equivalent* of A, if it can be identified with A and receive its meaning from it. It is not yet a symbol of A. It will only be when it can integrally replace A in a context in which A should appear. In his theory, the main condition necessary for B to symbolize A is that the latter suffers an *affective inhibition*. Affective inhibition can have various degrees, which will determine the type of symbolism in question: when inhibition is at its maximum, we will be facing the most typical form of symbolism: "I propose to reserve the name 'symbolism' only for this typical form par excellence" (1916/1925, p. 271).

The interesting thing is that, even though defining the psychoanalytic symbol in a restricted sense, Jones leaves open the possibility of thinking of symbolization as a more ubiquitous, individual, and omnipresent phenomenon in unconscious substitutive formations in general. He says that when the repression of some *affective tendency* occurs, it then results in a compromise formation in which both the repressed and the repressive tendencies are fused. The result of this fusion is manifested by the product of a substitution.

Jones (1916/1925) then defines psychoanalytic symbols as other compromise formations that involve conscious and unconscious elements and therefore play an important role in certain neurotic symptoms.

The curious thing about this idea is that, from the initial statement, I would have thought that Jones would finally define symbolism as occurring *in the* formation of every neurotic symptom. However, when he says that it is only in *a certain number of neurotic symptoms*, he takes up the idea that symbolism is something very specific, restricted, that only occurs in special situations. Perhaps, in fact, we are halfway between Freud's *symbolism* (Laplanche & Pontalis, 1982/1997) and a more extensive conception of symbolism. At the same time, nevertheless, Jones states in the same work that everything that is repressed is symbolized and that only the repressed needs to be symbolized, showing that in reality all neurotic symptoms are symbolized and not just some.

In summary, we could say that although the pioneers of psychoanalysis used the concept of symbol in a restricted sense, they did not fail to describe countless relations of mental representation that we consider symbolic relations today. Even though there was a certain "plastering" in their use of the concept, they sensed that the phenomenon of symbolization was more omnipresent than their restricted use of the concept.

As a conclusion to this section, we can already say that, without a doubt, and in agreement with the pioneers, the symbolization of repressed elements generates a type of symbolism; another conclusion, in the same sense, is that symbolization, in the psychoanalytic sense, occurs unconsciously. Another conception of symbolization that I will discuss later is that of Bion (1962a/1988, 1962b/1991), which happens in the formation of the mental, of that which belongs to the domain of the psychic, which can be thought about, which *allows* repression to exist, and which Freud called differently (association of mnemic registers, substitutive formations etc.). Another difference is that this type of symbolization described by Bion in his theory of the alpha function – the transformation of non-psychic elements into psychic ones – does not only occur in the genesis of the unconscious, but is part of daily dream life, expanding the unconscious infinitely (Rezende, 1994).

Freud: thoughts, symptoms, and symbolization

At the beginning of this chapter, I discussed the conceptualization of symbol, symbolism, and symbolization in the early theoretical developments of psychoanalysis. I now want to dedicate myself to discussing the first conceptualizations regarding the construction of the psychic apparatus, as well as the transformations that take place in it, whether to give rise to unconscious and conscious thoughts or to symptoms, since these are ultimately symbolic transformations. Since

I cannot review all of Freud's works in which these occur, I have chosen a few that I think are illustrative.

In Chapter VII of *The Interpretation of Dreams* (1900/1969), he sets out a model of the mental apparatus that he would maintain, except for a few modifications, for much of his work and which, as we shall see, would serve as the basis for the creation of very contemporary models on the origin of thinking, such as Bion's. The model is as follows: the perceptual system (*pcpt*) is bombarded by sensory perceptions in the frontal part and has no memory for them. Behind it is a second system, the mnemic (*mnem*), which *transforms* (there is a first transformation) the momentary excitations of the first system into permanent traces. And he points out that what is retained is more than just the content of the perception, indicating that some meaning has already been added to what has been retained. These perceptions are recorded in several mnemonic systems simultaneously, which maintain associations with each other. The associations are then made in the *mnem* system.

These memories are unconscious and act from there. We would thus have the origin of unconscious thinking, which would be the relationships, the links that are created between the various mnemic registers of sensory impressions. Character will be shaped by the mnemic traces of those impressions from early childhood, which have had the greatest effect on us and which never become conscious, considering all the reorganizations or re-inscriptions (Laplanche & Pontalis, 1982/1997) that can be made *a posteriori*.

Memories that become conscious through their association with verbal residues (Freud, 1911/1969) return without any sensory quality, or perhaps a minimal one. The model he creates is brilliant because these various mnemic registers of sensory experiences are articulated with more current points of view, such as those of Bion (1957/1988, 1962a/1988, 1962b/1991) and Stern (1988).

Bion, using a different frame of reference, but referring to similar events, I think, detailed that these first transformations of purely sensory elements into weaponizable mental records, already with emotional significance, would be the consequence of the action of the alpha function, which would result in the alpha elements. For his part, Stern mentions "clusters", which would be the recording in the mind of repetitive experiences with a specific affective quality. These are pre-verbal records with a predominant affective meaning. These records are the precipitates of the baby's first experiences.

In *The Ego and the Id* (1923/1969), Freud takes up the aforementioned model of the creation of thought and states that conscious thought originates from the relationships between mnemic registers and their connection to word presentations. He points out, however, that conscious thinking is possible without the link to word presentations, through a reversion to visual registers, which would be thinking in images. This, nonetheless, would be primitive thinking, closer to unconscious processes than thinking in words.

Another important contribution concerning thought in this work is found in the chapter in which he studies the role of the life and death drives in the new model of the mind that he introduces at this historical moment. He conceptualizes that desexualized libido displaced to the ego is *sublimated* energy and, considering the *binding* and *uniting* function of the life drive, he says that this energy helps maintain the ego's unity. He comments that if thinking, as an ego activity, is included among these sublimations, then thinking is also supplied by the life drive. This is of the utmost importance, as it shows how clear he was that the process of thinking occurs through the *link* between mental elements, creating a bridge to what will be described later by Bion (1957/1988): when the opposite predominates, the action of the death drive, there will be an attack on the *links* and an impossibility of thinking.

Freud enriches his model later on and it is perhaps worth pointing out that in one of his most important works on the genesis of thinking, "Formulations on the Two Principles of Mental Functioning" (1911/1969) – which will serve as another starting point for Bion (1962a/1988) in the creation of his theory of thinking – the word "symbol" does not appear. In this work, Freud masterfully describes the passage from the pleasure principle to the reality principle, or, if we prefer, from mental functioning aimed at the immediate relief of tension through motor discharge to that in which thinking is interposed, allowing greater tolerance to tension because it constitutes a special type of action. Cassirer (1944/1997), most likely influenced by Freud himself, will designate this type of interposition as a characteristic of the symbolic function that interposes itself between the sensory stimulus and the motor response.

Next, Freud (1911/1969) describes his idea of the evolution of thought, saying that it only becomes perceptible to consciousness after being linked to verbal residues. The evolution he traces, already described above, seems to be as follows: from sensory perceptions, multiple representations are created, mnemic records (which would be pre-symbolic, simple "notations" of reality); from there, relationships would be created between significant object presentations, giving rise to unconscious, primitive thinking; only then, from the link to verbal residues, would there be the possibility of conscious thinking.

In his work *The Unconscious* (1915a/1969), considered by Strachey to be Freud's most important metapsychological article, he makes important considerations about the psychic apparatus, its formation and its internal dynamics. He details how experiences are registered in the mind and how they are transformed from one register into another, or how they acquire symbolic qualities or symbolic retranscriptions. He studies what the *presentations of thing and word* are and their implications for the formation of the unconscious and the mind in general. Freud comments that:

> being linked to words, *the cathexes can be endowed with quality* even when they represent only relations between object presentations, *thus being unable to extract any quality from perceptions.* Such relations, which only become comprehensible through words, constitute one of the main parts of our thought processes. *As we can see, being linked to word presentations is not the same as becoming conscious, but merely makes it possible for this to happen; it is, therefore, something characteristic of the preconscious system (Pcs.), and only of this system. (Freud, 1915a/1969, my emphasis)*

Freud in *The Unconscious* has brilliant insights because he shows that the word goes far beyond giving a name to the sensory image, it grasps the quality of the *relationships* between object presentations. In more up-to-date language, I would say that Freud had realized that it was in the associations *between* object presentations that the emotional meaning of the experience was located and he believed that, in order to be made conscious, it needed to be transformed (symbolized, I would say), if it was not to remain in its raw state in the mind. He attributed this capacity to the word, which becomes even clearer in his classic work on aphasia (Freud, 1891/1969) when he says that *meaning* (symbolic, I would also say) is acquired by associating the presentation of a word with the corresponding presentation of a thing, and *asymbolic aphasia* results from the loss of the link between the presentations of a thing and a word. So, even though I have described the numerous relations, associations, retranscriptions, between the various contents of the psychic, he considered that symbolization only occurred when the presentations of things were linked to the presentations of words, although he did not explicitly call the process symbolization, as described above.

Even after describing his second topic, in 1923 and later (Freud, 1926/1969, 1938/1969), he maintains his general idea about the first sensory registers, their storage in memory, and their connection to the word in order to gain access to consciousness. He just places these processes in the new instances described, or more precisely, in the ego, now described in its unconscious and conscious activity.

I will now devote a few words to sublimation, considered a higher form of thought, and to symbolization. Although the term "sublimation" is conceptualized in different ways in different passages of his work, in his exquisite study on Leonardo Da Vinci, Freud (1910/1969) organizes his ideas on the subject in a fairly complete way. He states that sublimation is the capacity of the sexual drive to transform its immediate goals into others that are devoid of sexual character and can be highly valued.

Studying the capacity for research, scientific curiosity, he comments that it will be possible according to the "solution" given to infantile sexual curiosity and, ultimately, to sexual drives. In this sense, he says that the *impulse to research* can have three destinations. In the first case, it has the same fate as infantile sexuality: it succumbs to repression, curiosity is inhibited, and intellectual capacity is compromised for the rest of one's life; this is a neurotic inhibition. In the second case, intellectual development is "strong enough to resist the sexual repression that dominates it" (p. 74) and some time after the infantile sexual research has ceased, the child's intelligence, by its very force, resumes the association between research and sexuality, helps to avoid repression and resumes the old research activities in the form, now, of a *compulsive research curiosity*, eroticizing thought. It will be unfree thinking, sexualized, and exposed to the pleasure and anxiety typical of sexuality, characterizing compulsive neurotic thinking. The third destination is rarer and more perfect, according to Freud, because it escapes both inhibition and neurotic compulsion. Freud says that:

> *It is true that sexual repression also exists in him, but it does not manage to relegate any instinctive component of sexual desire to the unconscious. Instead, the libido escapes the fate of repression by being suppressed from the*

> *start into curiosity and by linking itself to the powerful instinct for research as a way of strengthening itself. (Freud, 1910/1969, p. 74)*

In this case, through sublimation, instead of returning to the unconscious, the drive can act more freely in the service of intellectual activity, with no connection to the original infantile sexual research. Repression also helps by removing any link to sexual themes. In other words, in this definition, sublimation is directly linked to the fate of infantile sexuality, its repression and/or sublimation, and presupposes a later stage of development.

In *The Ego and the Id* (1923/1969), Freud gives a more general conceptualization of sublimation. Studying the transformation of abandoned object-erotic cathexis into alterations of the ego through identification with the object, he comments that there is a transformation of object libido into narcissistic libido. He says that this transformation implies desexualization, constituting "a kind of sublimation" (p. 44), since, after the transformation and the desexualization, this energy is given another non-sexual destination, which is the strengthening of the ego itself and its functions. This more general way of understanding sublimation, linking it to the destinies of the libidinal drive of any abandoned object relationship, I think will be more linked to the way Ferenczi and Klein will refer to it, i.e. sublimation can occur from the beginning of libidinal development.

In any case, even if sublimation is understood as a desexualized energy placed at the service of the development of ego functions, in general, and thought, in particular, it is not conceptualized that symbolic transformations occur along this path; or rather, that sublimation occurs precisely because of the possibility of successive symbolic transformations in which the final product bears little relation to its origin. Segal (1991/1993) even recalls that Jones (1916/1925) differentiated symbolization from sublimation, narrowing the concept of symbolization even further.

Concerning the formation of symptoms, we will have some interesting contributions based on Freud's implicit concept of symbolization. By this I mean to emphasize once again that Freud did not state that he was studying symbolization, this is just some "digging" that I am doing. At the beginning of his scientific production, in his classic 1895 "Project for a Scientific Psychology", still not so rigorous in his restricted use of the concept of symbol, he refers extensively to the participation of symbolization in the understanding of what he calls "hysterical obsession". He says verbatim:

> *Before the analysis, A is an excessively intense idea, which forces its way into consciousness too often, and each time gives rise to weeping. The subject does not know why he weeps at A; he regards it as absurd, but cannot prevent it. After the analysis, it has been discovered that there is an idea B, which justifiably gives rise to weeping and which justifiably recurs frequently so long as a certain complicated psychical action has not been performed against it by the subject. The effect of B is not absurd; it is intelligible to the subject and can even be combated by him. B stands in a particular relation to A. For there has been an occurrence which consisted of B + A. A was an incidental circumstance; B was appropriate for producing the lasting effect. The reproduction of this event in memory has now taken a form of such a kind that it is as though A has stepped into B's place.* A has become a substitute, a symbol for B. *Hence the incongruity: A is accompanied by consequences which it does not seem worthy of, which do not fit in with it. (p. 459, my emphasis)*

Laplanche (1981/1992) tells us that this is Freud's description of the formation of a symbol. According to him, there is a relationship of contiguity between A and B, in the form of a metonymy, with A being a detail, or a part, which represents B. The latter, B, becomes repressed, and the affect that was attached to it is transferred to A. Freud (1895/1969) goes on to say that "the formation of symbols also occurs normally (outside of neurotic conditions). A soldier is capable of sacrificing himself for a multicolored rag attached to a flagpole, because it has become for him the symbol of his homeland, and no one considers this neurotic" (p. 459). The difference between symbolization in the neurotic and the non-neurotic person would be that in the former, what is symbolized is re-preserved, while in the normal person, it is not. Laplanche (1981/1992), using Freud's example of the gentleman who struggles to obtain a lady's glove, says that if the gentleman were to repress the idea that the glove represents the lady and lose sight of what he is fighting for, he would at most become a glove collector, with no chance of getting close to his beloved...

It is worth pointing out again that here Freud uses the term "symbol" in a broader sense than he did later, when he restricted it to symbols with a fixed and universal meaning. Another interesting aspect to which Laplanche (1981/1992) draws attention is that here Freud explicitly links the displacement (of affect from B to A, or from one representation to another) with symbolization.

One of Laplanche's conclusions (1980/1988, 1981/1992), which I find very interesting, is that at this point we arrive at Freud's concept of symbolization, even if it was not given this designation after 1895. There would be symbolization when an affect, *disconnected* from its original representation by the process of repression, was *linked* to a new representation. Symbolizing would mean "*linking*, retaining – and, of course, controlling – pure affect, in order to prevent it from appearing in an unspecified, unlinked form, that is, in the form of anguish" (Laplanche, 1981/1992, p. 88, my emphasis).

Laplanche (1980/1988), based on this conceptualization of the formation of symbols in the "Project..." and Freud's first theory of anxiety, i.e. that anxiety stems from the release of the affect that was linked to the repressed representation, draws interesting conclusions about what symbolization would be for Freud. Starting from the basic idea that to symbolize is to bring together, to unite, he asks: What does symbolization bring together? One answer is that it joins two representations. It replaces one representation with another, for example, the series of equivalences between the representations of feces, penises, and babies, or the study of the evolution of dangerous situations in *Inhibitions, Symptoms and Anxiety* (Freud, 1926/1969), in which he traces an evolutionary line of anxiety linked to separation from the mother/loss of the penis/loss of love from the superego.

Another answer is that symbolization brings together an affect and a representation. Freud discovered early on that affect is fluctuating, circulating between one representation and another. This is free energy. Bound energy is energy that is fixedly bound to a representation, with phobias being the classic example (the fear of Hans is bound to the representation of the horse). "Affect is transposed, displaced, from an unconscious representation to a conscious one, thus we have symbolization" (Laplanche, 1980/1988, p. 275).

These, then, are the functions of symbolization in the Freudian paradigm: the substitution of one representation for another (father for horse in the case of Little Hans) and the "linking" of the affect that was freed by the repression of the representation to which it was attached to another representation, in order to avoid anguish. In this sense, symbolization allows for a new psychic organization, insofar as it arises as an attempt to connect, to dominate a free and undifferentiated energy, generated after the autonomy acquired in relation to its original representation that was repressed. "It is affect that is the object of symbolization" (Laplanche, 1980/1988, p. 281). Affect always comes from the "undoing" of a previous symbolic network. "Anguish, which is the prototype of the unsymbolized in its raw state, would always be the unsymbolized in relation to a previous symbolization" (Laplanche, 1980/1988, p. 281). As we will see later, this point of view is in perfect harmony with later positions, for example, that of Bion (1962b/1991), who states that the impossibility of symbolic representation of emotional experiences implies a raw discharge of affects: either as anxiety, as Freud said, or as somatization, or as acting out, as Bion would say.

And what does the situation look like after Freud, in *Inhibitions...* (1926/1969), modifies his theory of anxiety? Laplanche (1980/1988) thinks that the theorizing of *Inhibitions...* – that it is anxiety that produces repression, and not the other way around – would be a step backwards regarding the first theory since it places too much value on the real, external danger of castration, and not on the threat that comes from the drive, from the affect freed from its representation.

Freud (1926/1969) begins by differentiating symptoms from inhibitions, describing the numerous possible inhibitions as an impairment of ego functions that have become eroticized. "It has been discovered as a general fact that the ego function of an organ is impaired if its erotogenicity – *its sexual significance* – is increased" (p. 110, my emphasis). Here, of course, he is saying that a non-sexual activity signifies, symbolizes, a sexual activity that is inhibited by what it symbolically signifies. It is almost inevitable that, in this work, he will use the word "symbol", which he had reserved for the other conceptualization. He then says so unequivocally:

> *As soon as writing, which causes a liquid to flow from a tube onto a piece of white paper, takes on the meaning of copulation, or as soon as* walking becomes a symbolic substitute *for trampling on the body of mother earth, both writing and walking are paralyzed because they represent the performance of a forbidden sexual act.* The ego renounces these functions, *which are within its sphere, in order not to have to adopt new measures of repression – in order to avoid coming into conflict with the id. (p. 110, my emphasis)*

From then on, at various points in the work, he will talk about this type of symbolic representation, in which a repressed drive or conflict is symbolically replaced by an ego activity and can therefore result in inhibition. The same is true when talking about symptoms: "A symptom is a sign and a substitute for an instinctual satisfaction that has remained dormant; it is a consequence of the process of repression" (p. 112).

In his theorizing on the origin of anxiety, he goes back to a concept he had created in "The neuropsychoses of defence" (Freud, 1894/1969) and later abandoned, saying: "Affective states have been incorporated into the mind as precipitates of primal traumatic experiences, and when a similar situation occurs they are revived as *mnemic symbols*" (Freud, 1926/1969, p. 114). In other words, the anxiety experienced in traumatic situations is recorded in the mind through affective symbols. Here he assumes that affective states are inscribed in the unconscious memory as symbols of certain primitive experiences and that in similar situations they are reactivated, released in the form of anxiety. He also refers these symbolic formations to primitive situations, as remnants of primeval times, but it can be assumed that in an individual these mnemic symbols are also created in traumatic experiences. So much so that he draws a parallel with hysterical attacks.

The important thing about this change in the theory of anxiety is that it is now conceived as being triggered not just by the economic explanation of the damming up, but by symbolic relations of meaning: because this (A) represents that (B), the ego emits a signal of anxiety. It seems to me that this theory of anxiety is more human, less physical-energetic and therefore less mechanistic than the previous one, because it takes more account of the symbolic aspects involved in triggering anxiety.

Giving the example of Little Hans, he shows how the horse replaced Hans's father: he wanted his father to fall and get hurt, so he feared being attacked by him. He explains that Hans had displaced his feelings for his father onto the horse. Hans did this because he had the symbolic capacity to symbolize the figure of his father in the horse, in other words, one representation has been exchanged for another. Underlying the mechanism of displacement is the symbolic capacity. Freud calls this symbolic representation a "substitute object". The symbol is a substitute object for something.

In all the clinical examples mentioned in *Inhibitions...* (Little Hans, the Wolf Man, the young American), their understanding of the dynamics of symptom formation denotes a more "symbolic" view of the neurotic symptom: symptoms are no longer understood from the previously preponderant economic perspective but in the light of their network of symbolic meanings. The young American, reading a story, identifies with the character to be eaten (the one made of spices) and identifies his father with the Arab chief who wanted to eat him.

The phrase "it was anxiety that produced repression and not, as I previously believed, repression that produced anxiety" (Freud, 1926/1969, p. 131) is brilliant not only for admitting self-criticism so transparently but for clarifying that it is the affects (anxiety), reactivated by the symbolic meaning of the situation, that give rise to defenses.

When he describes obsessive neurosis, he mentions a "motor symbolism", which is an act with an unconscious symbolic meaning whose purpose is the annulment of a previous act.

> *The view that in a phobia the ego is able to escape anxiety through avoidance or inhibitory symptoms fits very well with the theory that anxiety is just an affective signal and that no change in the economic situation has occurred. (p. 149)*

The interesting thing about this passage is that it definitively excludes any economic change in the generation of anxiety reducing it exclusively to an affective sign generated by a mnemic symbol.

In this way, it seems to me that Freud, although he conceptually maintained the restricted definition of symbolism that I have repeatedly referred to, implicitly operated, at many points in his work, with the idea that symbolization, which is personal, idiosyncratic, and highly variable from one individual to another, needed to be elucidated in order to understand the formation of symptoms and mental functioning in general.

References

Bion, W. R. (1988). Diferenciação entre a personalidade psicótica e não-psicótica. In *Estudos psicanalíticos revisados*. Imago. (Originally published in 1957)

Bion, W. R. (1988). Uma teoria sobre o processo de pensar. *Estudos psicanalíticos revisados*. Imago. (Originally published in 1962a)

Bion, W. R. (1991). *Aprendiendo de la experiencia*. Paidós. (Originally published in 1962b)

Cassirer, E. (1997). *Ensaio sobre o homem: introdução a uma filosofia da cultura humana*. Martins Fontes. (Originally published in 1944)

Ferenczi, S. (1922). Ontogênese dos símbolos. In *Obras Completas* (Vol. 2). Martins Fontes. (Originally published in 1913)

Freud, S. (1969). Sobre a concepção das afasias: um estudo crítico. In: *Edição standard brasileira das obras psicológicas completas de Sigmund Freud* (Vol. III). Imago. (Originally published in 1891)

Freud, S. (1969). As neuropsicoses de defesa. In *Edição standard brasileira das obras psicológicas completas de Sigmund Freud* (Vol. XII). Imago. (Originally published in 1894)

Freud, S. (1969). Projeto para uma psicologia científica. In *Edição standard brasileira das obras psicológicas completas de Sigmund Freud* (Vol. I). Imago. (Originally published in 1895)

Freud, S. (1969). A interpretação dos sonhos. In *Edição standard brasileira das obras psicológicas completas de Sigmund Freud* (Vol. IV). Imago. (Originally published in 1900)

Freud, S. (1969). Sobre os sonhos. In *Edição standard brasileira das obras psicológicas completas de Sigmund Freud* (Vol. V). Imago. (Originally published in 1901)

Freud, S. (1969). Leonardo Da Vinci e uma lembrança de sua infância. In *Edição standard brasileira das obras psicológicas completas de Sigmund Freud* (Vol. XI). Imago. (Originally published in 1910)

Freud, S. (1969). Formulações sobre os dois princípios do funcionamento mental. In *Edição standard brasileira das obras psicológicas completas de Sigmund Freud* (Vol. XII). Imago. (Originally published in 1911)

Freud, S. (1969). O inconsciente. In *Edição standard brasileira das obras psicológicas completas de Sigmund Freud* (Vol. XIV). Imago. (Originally published in 1915a)

Freud, S. (1969). Suplemento metapsicológico à teoria dos sonhos. In *Edição standard brasileira das obras psicológicas completas de Sigmund Freud* (Vol. XIV). Imago. (Originally published in 1915b)

Freud, S. (1969). Conferências introdutórias sobre psicanálise. In: *Edição standard brasileira das obras psicológicas completas de Sigmund Freud* (Vol. XV). Imago. (Originally published in 1916)

Freud, S. (1969). O Ego e o Id. In *Edição standard brasileira das obras psicológicas completas de Sigmund Freud* (Vol. XIX). Imago. (Originally published in 1923)

Freud, S. (1969). Inibições, sintomas e ansiedade. In *Edição standard brasileira das obras psicológicas completas de Sigmund Freud* (Vol. XX). Imago. (Originally published in 1926)

Freud, S. (1969). Esboço de psicanálise. In *Edição standard brasileira das obras psicológicas completas de Sigmund Freud* (Vol. XXIII). Imago. (Originally published in 1938)

Green, A. (1994). El analista, la simbolizacion, y la ausencia en el encuadre analítico. In: *De locuras privadas*. Amorrortu. (Originally published in 1975)

Jones, E. (1925). La théorie du symbolisme. In *Traité theorique et pratique de psychanalyse*. Payot. (Originally published in 1916)

Laplanche, J. (1988). *Problemáticas II: Castração, simbolizações*. Martins Fontes. (Originally published in 1980)

Laplanche, J. (1992). *Problemáticas IV: O inconsciente e o id*. Martins Fontes. (Originally published in 1981)

Laplanche, J., & Pontalis, J.-B. (1997). *Vocabulário de psicanálise* (Daniel Lagache, Dir.). Martins Fontes. (Originally published in 1982)

Meltzer, D. (1984). *Vida onírica: una revisión de la teoría y de la técnica psicoanalítica*. Tecnipublicaciones.

Rezende, A. M. (1994). *A metapsicanálise de Bion: Além dos modelos*. Papirus.

Segal, H. (1982). Notas a respeito da formação de símbolos. In *A obra de Hanna Segal: uma abordagem kleiniana à prática clínica*. Imago. (Originally published in 1957)

Segal, H. (1993). Simbolismo. In *Sonho, fantasia e arte*. Imago. (Originally published in 1991)

Stern, D. N. (1988). Affect in the context of the lived experience: some considerations. *International Journal of Psychoanalysis, 69*(pt. 2), 233-238.

4. Towards a broader concept of symbol

As I said earlier, it seems to me that, of the pioneers, Ferenczi was the one who ventured to broaden the concept of symbol and symbolization, becoming a "bridge" to Melanie Klein's conceptualizations.

The work "Stages in the development of the sense of reality" (Ferenczi, 1913a/1992), considered a classic in the theory of the development of symbolization, is a reference for Freud and Klein. He is also regarded as a pioneer in the study of the development of the ego's adaptive capacities. It also contains the embryos of what Winnicott would later describe, in a more detailed, rich way, about the illusion of omnipotence provided by parents to the young child and the passage from subjectivity to objectivity. He takes Freud's "Formulations on the Two Principles of Mental Functioning" (1911/1969) as his starting point and constant reference. It is remarkable that this work, Freudian in its conceptualization, later became the point of departure and permanent reference for Isaacs (1943/1978) and Bion (1962/1991).

Ferenczi (1913a/1992) says that Freud, when describing the transition from the pleasure principle to the reality principle, did not specify whether this occurs immediately or gradually and, in the latter case, how it would happen. He then describes the various stages that the subject goes through as they lose their omnipotence, from birth to adulthood:

- *Period of unconditional omnipotence:* this is the intrauterine period, when the child's desires and drive needs were met unconditionally, without frustration or the need for any action on the environment.

- *Period of magical hallucinatory omnipotence:* this is the period in which the newborn tries to re-establish the intrauterine experience, the good days when there was omnipotent gratification of all its desires. There is a hallucinatory reinvestment in the lost state of satisfaction. For the child, the only change that has occurred in this phase is that now, to obtain complete satisfaction of its desires, it needs to invest what it wants in a hallucinatory way; it does not need to act on the environment. The mere representation of its satisfaction is felt as an omnipotently powerful force. But even then, *frustration* sets in, for the environment is not always ready. The child begins to feel that it has to intervene in the environment in order to satisfy itself.
- *Period of omnipotence by the help of magical gestures:* the child begins to use a series of signals to change the environmental situation. At first, these are motor discharges as magical signals. Over time, the signals become more complex and specific. Then *frustration* sets in again, however, forcing the child's ego to realize more clearly that the *objective* world differs from its *subjective* world and to differentiate between its desire and the external world's resistance to them at times. This broadens the self/non-self differentiation.
- *Animistic period:* despite the greater differentiation between self and non-self, the child attributes the characteristics of his ego and drives to the world, "trying to find in each thing its own organs or functioning" (p. 47). It invests the world with its libido, taking an interest in objects that remind it of its autoerotic activities, or that lend themselves to being "identified". These are "profound relationships, persistent throughout life, between the human body and the world of objects, which we call symbolic relationships" (p. 47). With this symbolic improvement, the child will be able to mark the desires that concern its body as those that concern the external world, now recognized as such. The remarkable thing is

that the beginnings of symbolization are located here: from the differentiation of self/non-self and frustration.

- *Period of magical thoughts and words:* gestural symbolism is gradually replaced by verbal symbolism, sounds *identified* with desires and situations evolve into words "which allow a much more economical and precise version of desires. At the same time, *verbal symbolism makes conscious thought possible* since, by associating itself with unconscious thought processes, it gives them perceivable qualities. Conscious thought through verbal signs is therefore the highest achievement of the psychic apparatus, the only one that allows adaptation to reality, delaying reflex motor discharge and the release of pleasure" (p. 48, my emphasis). Even here, the child continues to believe in its magical power, now executed through words and thoughts.

Then there comes a moment in development when the pleasure principle gives way to the reality principle, and *feelings of omnipotence are replaced by the recognition of reality and its circumstances*. The illusion of omnipotence gives way to the recognition of limitations and that one depends on favorable "conditions" for the fulfillment of desire. This is outlined in latency, I believe.

In his work "The ontogenesis of symbols" (1913b/1992), Ferenczi makes several clarifications. Firstly, that not every comparison between two terms constitutes a symbol in the psychoanalytic sense; only when one of the two terms is repressed. There is a "sexualization of the universe" (p. 107). In the same way that the objects of the world are identified with the parts of the child's body, the child identifies the upper part of the body (mouth, teeth, eyes) with the lower part (anus, vagina, penis), but they only become symbolizations after cultural education causes the repression of the most important term of the analogy and the other, more insignificant in its origin, receives a supplement of affective importance: it becomes its symbol. Thus, the "identification" between two terms is the precursor to true symbolization.

In this work, Ferenczi differentiates between *representation* and psychoanalytic symbols. He says:

> *We can only consider symbols, in the psychoanalytic sense of the term, to be things (representations) that come to consciousness with an affective investment that logic can neither explain nor justify, and whose analysis allows us to establish that they owe this affective overload to an unconscious identification with another (the symbol) thing (representation), to which this affective supplement actually belongs. (p. 106)*

I believe that both the self/non-self differentiation and frustration, highlighted by Ferenczi as occurrences in the animistic period, will be considered by authors from all psychoanalytic currents as fundamental preconditions for the development of the symbolic capacity in its fullness. Furthermore, according to Petot (1991a), Ferenczi is the author of the idea – a revolution of the apex – that the objects of the external world are of no interest to the child: it does not perceive them, it does not think about them, until it can extend its libido to them.

He ends his article by describing art as the space in which man preserves the illusion of omnipotence and denies the limitations exposed by the sense of reality, which, as we shall see, will be further developed and conceptualized by Winnicott (1951/1975).

Klein: from Freud and Ferenczi to a new conception of symbolization

At the beginning of the chapter dedicated to the study of Freud, I stated that any attempt to simplify would lead to impoverishment, and the same can be said of Melanie Klein's contributions to the subject of symbolization. As will become clear next, we will find at least three different ways of conceptualizing symbolization and its vicissitudes in this important author.

The centrality of the libido

Petot (1991a, 1991b), in his exquisite and detailed study of Klein's work, defines what would be the proto-Kleinian period, in which Melanie's theoretical contributions do not yet have all the originality and independence acquired later. As far as symbolization is concerned, although there is already originality in the conceptualizations, there is a marked presence of the contributions of Freud, Jones, and Ferenczi.

In the proto-Kleinian period, then, symbolization is understood by Klein (1923a/1981, 1923b/1981) basically in the light of the vicissitudes of the libido, like the descriptions of her contemporaries. Adhering to Ferenczi's ideas (1913b/1992), she argues that there is initially an *identification* between parts of the body, especially the upper half and the lower half, based on superficial similarities (teeth/penis, mouth/vagina).

Identification – influenced by Jones' theory of symbolism (1916/1925) – and the entire psychogenesis of symbolism were based on the pleasure principle, i.e. the possibility of obtaining similar pleasure from two different parts of the body: "I will have the same pleasure with my mouth as I have with..." One can then replace the other. In this sense, the body image is not a construction based on the cognitive functions of the ego but depends on a movement of the libido, governed by the pleasure principle. Hence, from libidinal equivalences between parts of the body, the subject evolves, from libidinal investment to equivalences between subject and object, or body and objects of reality. By themselves, the objects of reality are of no interest, but only to the extent that they are libidinized.

The *identification* between different parts of the body and between the body and other objects is the precursor to symbolization in this theoretical model. In this period, there is a primitive confusion of the symbolized with the symbol (Petot, 1991a). It is from the repression of sexual activity that *identification* is transformed into a symbol.

Primary sublimations, based on *identification*, would occur through the attraction of libido to ego activities that generate non-sexual organ pleasure (motor skills and speech). The libidinal cathexis would give these activities a sexual character. *Secondary sublimations*, on the other hand, would not depend on an attraction to a previous organ pleasure, but would occur due to a tendency of the libido to seek new gratifications and would lead, over the course of development, to the formation of new symbols. They would occur due to a propagation of the libido to objects of reality and to more complex interests and activities of the ego, so that, for example, rising and falling, or raising and lowering one's voice are equated with the sexual act (Klein, 1923b/1981). As we can see, it is very similar to Ferenczi and Jones.

Petot (1991a) states that this is a dialectical process, in which the child sees the world from its body and gives new representations to its body from things in the world. For example, it can represent the inside of its body, which it has only felt through cenesthetic sensations, using objects from the world (the train with coal, for instance, can symbolize the intestine with faces). Likewise, the world will be seen as an extension of one's own body, as Ferenczi (1913b/1992) aptly illustrated with the boy who, on looking at the Danube, commented: "What a lot of spit!". "The outside world and the body symbolize each other" (Petot, 1991a, p. 62).

So, to clarify, the process develops because, as the libido is not satisfied with these substitutions and substitutive gratifications, it goes in search of new substitutes, new investments, in a continuous repetition of creating new symbols and new sublimations. A chain of sublimations is created, a veritable edifice, and the first of the secondary sublimations is play. For this upward process to take place without inhibitions, previous sublimation must not have been repressed. The degree to which play is rich or poor will be diagnostic of whether or not there are inhibitions in the process of libidinal investment (Petot, 1991a).

Melanie Klein (1923b/1981) said: "the constant impulse to carry out, by means of fixations, a libidinal cathexis of recent ego activities and interests genetically linked (i.e. by means of sexual symbolism) to each other, and to create new activities and interests, would be the driving force in the cultural evolution of humanity" (p. 146). In other words, she completely agrees with Freud (1910/1969) that sublimation occurs through a transformation of sexual goals into new activities, with new purposes. She only adds that this occurs because one symbolizes the other. This is relevant, since sublimation is no longer understood solely from an energetic, economic point of view, but from the perspective of symbolic processes. Even her idea of primary sublimations occurring very primitively is very close to Freud's concept presented in *The Ego and the Id* (1923/1969) – interestingly, released in the same year! – already discussed, in which he discusses the strengthening of ego activities by a desexualized energy and claims that it would be a *kind of sublimation*.

This *identification* will allow the *primary sublimations* to occur, based on the libidinal cathexis of parts of the body and activities and interests of the ego not originally invested in this way. These would be sublimations to the extent that the libido would be given a new purpose, namely, to invest in and reinforce non-sexual activities. Speech and bodily movement, for example, would be the first skills/activities invested in, becoming identified with sexual activities. Subsequently, over the course of development, *secondary sublimations* would occur, through the spreading of libido to objects of reality and to more complex interests and activities of the ego. The concept of sublimation is expanded and used much more freely, like symbolization.

Even though the libido loses its role as the driving force of the symbolization process for Klein and acquires a secondary role, we will see that aspects of this theorizing will continue to be used later (Isaacs, 1943/1978).

Sadism and symbolization

The second moment in Kleinian theorizing about symbolization is related to the introduction of the idea that sadism will play the primary role in the process of symbolization. With the primacy of aggression, the idea of the libidinal nature of sublimation is no longer maintained as a primary process, but secondary to aggressive investments. It will be secondary to the reparation of the object by the libido, after the damage caused has been verified in fantasy. The general outline of the genesis of symbolism is preserved, albeit at the cost of a radical change in perspective: the whole process is attributed to the death drive. The endogenous anxiety generated by the death drive triggers defense mechanisms – projection –, generating persecuting objects in which the subject will take an interest in order to defend himself against their threat. Petot (1991a) says that "the train has been connected to another locomotive, but the order of the wagons is the same" (p. 75). The new locomotive is sadism.

In her classic paper "The Importance of Symbol Formation in the Development of the Ego", Klein (1930/1981) assumes that in the oral phase there is an increase in sadism to the maximum degree (which will decline in the first stage of the anal phase) which leads the child to want to devour the mother's breast or the whole mother. This is the phase in which the Oedipus begins, and its onset coincides with the period of great sadism.

In this way, the child expects to find inside the mother's body: a) the father's penis; b) excrement; c) children; all of which are homologized as edible. The infantile sexual theory of this period consists of the belief that, during coitus, the penis, or the entire father, is incorporated by the mother. Thus, sadistic attacks on the mother's body are aimed at both mother and father. These attacks give rise to the persecutory anxiety of being vengefully attacked by both parents with the same fury.

Klein then explores the ego defenses used in this primitive moment. She says that, concerning sadism, the defense *is its expulsion* and, concerning the attacked object (which immediately becomes a source of danger), it *is its destruction.*

She once again uses Ferenczi (1913a/1992) and Jones (1916/1925) to support her theory of symbolization: Ferenczi's theory of identification as a precursor to symbolism, and Jones' idea that, through the pleasure principle, the child equates two different things by a similarity of pleasure and interest.

She comments that, in her 1923 work, she had discovered that symbolism was the foundation of all sublimation, since it is through the *symbolic equation* that things, activities, and interests become the subject of libidinal fantasies. She claims that she can now add that sadism also interferes in this process. Along with libidinal interest, it is anguish, a product of sadism, that sets the mechanism of identification in motion. Since it wants to destroy the organs (breast, penis, vagina) that represent the objects, it fears them.

> *Anxiety helps them to equate these organs with other things; because of this equation, they in turn become objects of anxiety. And so the child feels impelled to make new equations which form the basis of his interest in new objects, and of his symbolism . . . Symbolism, therefore, is not only the foundation of all fantasy and sublimation, but it is also* the basis *of the subject's entire relationship with the outside world and reality in general. (p. 297, my emphasis)*

As the object of sadism and the epistemophilic impulse is the inside of the mother's body, for Klein, at that moment, these sadistic fantasies constitute the first and basic relationship with the outside world and with reality. At first, the child lives in a fantastic reality in which it feels surrounded by sadistically charged objects like feces and organs, which cause it great anxiety. Gradually, its ego should be able to develop a more realistic relationship with reality and, for this to happen, a balance must be struck in its personality.

> *A sufficient amount of anxiety is the necessary basis for the abundant formation of symbols and fantasies; in order for anxiety to be elaborated, for this fundamental phase to have a favorable outcome and for the ego to develop successfully, it is essential that the ego has an adequate capacity to tolerate anxiety. (p. 298)*

However, if the ego cannot tolerate this anxiety, it will set up defenses that will inhibit the process of symbol formation. Inhibition will now be understood as a function of the anxiety resulting from sadism and an intolerance of it.

Klein illustrates her theory with the Dick case, in which, as a result of developing up in an environment devoid of love and of a complete, constitutional inability to tolerate anxiety and, therefore, the *formation of a premature defense* against intense sadism, the formation of symbols came to a halt. The ego stopped being interested in reality and stopped developing its fantasy life. Isolated and unrelated to reality, it could not carry out new sublimations. The equations needed to explore reality ceased because of the intolerable anxiety this caused. Klein realized that *what was causing the halt in the formation of symbols was Dick's fear of the punishment he would suffer (from his father's penis) when he penetrated his mother's body.* In addition, because of the intolerable anxiety it caused, he developed strong defenses against his own destructive impulses, which resulted in an impediment to development. He was incapable of aggression. The defenses against sadistic impulses resulted in the cessation of fantasies and the cessation of symbol formation.

In Dick's mind, there were no *affective or symbolic relationships* with objects. Regardless of the disagreements we may have with her conceptualization, this work is brilliant because, like Freud with Dora, Klein transforms, with Dick, the obstacle to treatment (which was the non-formation of symbols) into a development of technique of the utmost importance: the work of helping the patient to develop his capacity to make symbolic representations. Klein herself recognizes that she had to make a change to her usual technique and that she was only able to resume it once the patient had developed his symbolic capacity. Again, despite the restrictions that may be placed on her theorizing, in terms of her concern for developing the symbolic capacity of patients who need it, she was the forerunner of the most up-to-date psychoanalytic technique.

She initially gave meaning to toys that had no meaning for the patient: it was the train/Dick and the train/Dad, to which he added the station that she called mama. Encouraged by Klein's interventions, Dick became interested in objects that acquired new meanings and, as he "entered his mother's dark body", he felt anxious and developed a sense of dependence on Klein.

Klein assumes that, due to the premature development of the ego, Dick felt empathy with the suffering of objects, which would have initiated his aggressive impulses. As his latent anxiety diminished and he was able to manifest more of it, he let his sadism show more and more and, progressively, extended his interest to new objects and expanded his vocabulary. The extension of the interest to new objects allows anxiety to be mitigated, making it more tolerable for the ego. And once the anxiety became manifest, Klein was able to resolve it through interpretation.

The importance given to sadism in symbolization continues in her 1932 work, "Early stages of the Oedipus conflict and of super-ego formation". In it, Klein states that the fear of introjected persecuting objects causes the child to displace the origin of this fear and place it in the outside world.

> *By this process, its organs, its objects, its faeces, its internalized objects, as well as everything else, are* equated *with external objects; at the same time, it distributes its fear of an external object among a large number of objects,* equating them *with each other. (p. 200, my emphasis)*

She comments that this functioning, based on anguish and a series of *equations*, will be the basis of phobias.

Klein describes the transition from libidinal and aggressive interest in the only object, the breast, which represents the mother at the beginning, to the multiplication of this interest: libidinal and aggressive interest in the interior of the mother's body (also the object of epistemophilic impulses).

> *As its sadistic fantasies increase, the child imagines the inside of its mother's body, and this part of her body comes to represent the mother's whole person as an object,* symbolizing *both the outside world and reality. (p. 201, my emphasis)*

So, originally it was the breast that represented the outside world and now it is the inside of the mother's body, with its multiplicity of objects and thanks to libidinal and aggressive investment, that represents it. "Thus, sadistic fantasies about the mother's body constitute a fundamental relationship with the outside world and reality" (p. 201). She goes on to say that not only aggression but also libido plays a fundamental role, as it allows us to counterbalance the fear of internal and external enemies with the belief in protective, kind objects. It is through libidinal investment and the perception of the reality of objects that the terrifying objects of the primitive superego are softened. And it is also through this that reparation will be possible.

Reparative processes are based on genital drives which, for Klein, have been present since the primitive Oedipus: it is the decrease in sadism that allows for reparation, especially from the guilt arising from attacks on the beloved object. According to Petot (1991b), it was in this 1932 work that Klein (1932/1975) discovered reparation, even before she had better structured her conceptions of the depressive position.

The depressive position and the arrival at a more definitive conceptualization of symbolization

Klein (1934/1981), in "A contribution to the psychogenesis of manic-depressive states", defines that, as the ego matures, the internalized *imagos* – as she called the internal objects at the time – become closer to reality, the relationship with partial objects moves to the relationship with the total object and the child becomes concerned with its preservation. The decrease in the splitting allows the child to see that the "bad" object that is attacked is the same as the "good" object that is loved. She then points out that "only after the object has been loved as *a whole* can its loss be felt as a *whole*" (p. 358, my emphasis).

It is at this point in development that ambivalence and true guilt appear from the Kleinian point of view. Says Petot (1991b):

> *Since all love and all sublimation rest on reparation, they derive from the form of guilt that is prolonged in this mechanism. Depressive anxiety is only truly complete when feelings of guilt are fully experienced and* symbolic reparative behaviors are successful. *(p. 9, my emphasis)*

Petot (1991b) comments that the tragic accident that occurred in 1934 (the death of her son Hans in the Swiss mountains) while involving Klein in a significant process of mourning, was not responsible for this theoretical creation, but rather all her previous theoretical elaborations.

In the great works of synthesis of 1952, published in the book *Developments in Psychoanalysis* (1946/1978, 1952a/1978, 1952b/1978), Klein completes and consolidates the concept of the depressive and paranoid-schizoid positions, stating that in each of them, a type of object relationship is established that will determine the quality of the symbolization process. These contributions, with the subsequent clarifications and in-depth studies by Susan Isaacs (1943/1978) and Hanna Segal (1957/1982, 1991/1993), will be original and will have a strong presence in psychoanalytic theorizing about symbolization.

Klein (1946/1978, 1952a/1978, 1952b/1978) describes an expansion in children's interests, a strengthening and development of the ego, greater libidinal organization, and, as a consequence, a broadening of the scope of fantasies, with greater elaboration and differentiation of these, as well as a change in their nature. The processes of synthesis in object relations take precedence and ambivalence comes into being. The notion of the total object and the fear of losing it due to previous sadistic attacks are created.

The ego's processes of synthesis and integration allow for a greater apprehension of both psychic and external reality. The notion of the total object and the guilt over the potential damage to the beloved object makes reparative tendencies stronger. It creates "a superlative urgency to make reparation and to preserve or revive the loved and damaged object" (Klein, 1952a/1978, p. 233). As reparative tendencies come from the life instinct, they bring with them libidinal fantasies and desires. The reparative tendency will become part of sublimation and will be the major means by which depression is elaborated and kept under control.

The adequate development of the depressive position depends on how the previous development was carried out, i.e. whether an adequate incorporation of the good object as the integrating nucleus of the ego was established and, therefore, whether the processes of division of the ego were not excessive. In the depressive position, by repairing the loved and attacked object, it is re-established in the internal world, recovered and restored. Evidently, there is a reference here to a mental reconstruction of the object, in fantasy, which already presupposes a high degree of symbolization. But, according to Klein and Isaacs (1943/1978), unconscious fantasy and some kind of symbolization exist already in the paranoid-schizoid position, from the beginning of life.

We have also seen that, in her early theorizing, Klein assumed sublimation from the beginning of life and, even though she changed her mind about what set the process of symbolization and sublimation in motion, she continued to believe this. It is therefore necessary to understand, in the light of Klein's ideas, how thoughts and the mental apparatus develop from the beginning of life.

Perhaps the most complete study is that of Susan Isaacs, together with Segal's later contributions. In "The nature and function of phantasy", Isaacs (1943/1978) goes to great pains to specify and detail the mental functioning described by Klein and, at the same time, tries to articulate it with Freudian contributions. She will first conceptualize what she means by unconscious fantasies and then detail a whole evolutionary line of these.

Her first definition is that they are always inferred, that is, the psychoanalytic concept of fantasy implies that they are always unconscious. For her, "fantasies are the primary content of unconscious processes" (p. 96). She makes a connection with Freud when he argues that the id receives instinctual needs from somatic processes and gives them mental expression. Thus, "the mental expression of instinct is the unconscious phantasy... There is no impulse, no instinctual urge or response which is not experienced as unconscious 'phantasy'" (p. 96). She believes that "the first mental processes, the psychic representatives of bodily impulses and feelings, i.e. of libidinal and destructive instincts, are to be regarded as the earliest beginnings of phantasies" (p. 96). But in her conceptualization, she says that *not only impulses but also defenses and all feelings are experienced in fantasies* that give them mental life. It follows that fantasy is the way in which experiences take on a mental quality, they become contents of the mind itself, they cease to be somatic, they leave the terrain of sensoriality and move on to the mental.

Isaacs also describes the omnipotent and concrete characteristics of unconscious fantasies: primitively, in its early days, the child not only desires something but feels that it is doing what it desires. "It is only slowly that he learns to distinguish between the wish and the deed" (p. 99). Here, it becomes clear that the first fantasies are so concrete that they are confused with perceptions, as in the hallucinatory satisfaction of desire described by Freud in "Formulations on the Two Principles…" (1911/1969).

Isaacs adds that the first fantasies are a long way from words and logical thought. Only later can they be expressed in playing and, later still, in words. That is to say, meanings are in the mind long before verbal signifiers. But these will be the corollary of the whole symbolization process. Isaacs, nevertheless, makes clear her view that complex fantasies in terms of meaning can exist in visual and auditory form, that is, visual or auditory elements functioning as mental symbols of complex affective experiences. She adds that dreams illustrate how complex and dramatic experiences can be represented in visual terms alone. And through art, we know that "a wealth of implicit meaning can reside even in a shape, a colour, a line, a movement, a mass, a composition of form or colour, or of melody and harmony in music" (p. 103).

She even more precisely describes that the most rudimentary fantasies are very close to sensory experience and are *affective interpretations of bodily sensations*. I have highlighted this passage because its concept presupposes that, primitively, what occurs are not just mnemonic records of sensory experience; there is already an affective meaning in these records. This primary process dominates the mind at first, but soon, in the second month, "there is a very considerable degree of integration in perception and behaviour, with signs of memory and anticipation" (p. 112), in other words, the development of the secondary process of arranging experience begins.

Isaacs then traces an evolutionary axis of fantasies:

The most primitive are oral somatic sensations (taste, smell, oral touch), cenesthetic, and visceral sensations.

These sensations are concrete bodily experiences, felt in the body. These *internal sensations are not distinguished from external perceptions*. There is still no notion of continent skin, distinction between internal/external reality. The sensation of living in the world of things predominates. Perhaps, at this and the next evolutionary moment, we are in the domain of the paranoid-schizoid position and at the level of symbolic equivalences (Jones, 1916/1925) or symbolic equations (Segal, 1957/1982).

The visual element slowly increases. *The first images are very concrete*, becoming confused with perceptions.

Gradually, it *differentiates internal/external* and from there *real "images"* of objects are created with the distinction that the object is outside and the image is inside. This seems to be the domain of the depressive position and the symbolic itself.

These images affect the mind because they are inside it, just as their somatic precursors, which would now have been repressed, are in the unconscious. This unconscious, formed by these primitive fantasies, is felt to be shaped by the drives and objects to which they refer.

The establishment and strengthening of the visual element in the evolutionary trajectory of unconscious fantasy is seen as the turning point: from this point onwards, distinction between inner/outer and the more symbolic character of mental contents begin. Isaacs' description of how fantasies begin with the first sensory impressions, from the beginning of life, is very reminiscent of Bion's model, which we will see next. It places frustration with the evanescent character of the hallucinatory gratification of desire as a stimulus for adaptation and thinking about external reality.

Isaacs mentions that libido extends to objects, using the first theory of libidinal investment as studied in *The Centrality of Libido,* and mentions her adherence to Ferenczi's theory: "The external physical world is, in fact libidinized largely through the process of symbol-formation" (p. 125). In other words, in 1943 these aspects of the 1923 symbolization model remained valid. She says that the interest in reality occurs because it symbolizes the body, so its exploration is sublimation. However, from Klein's work in 1946 and 1952 onwards, it becomes clear that true symbolism occurs in the depressive position, directly linked to reparative processes.

Segal: an integration of Kleinian ideas

Segal (1957/1982, 1991/1993) will play a fundamental role in ordering the concept of symbol and symbolization in Kleinian contributions integrating the various elements mentioned so far. Her work "Notes on symbol formation" is a brilliant classic which, despite being written in 1957, remains extraordinarily up to date. Expressing one of the most contemporary ideas in psychoanalysis, she says that often, rather than being interested in the symbolic content in the patient's mind, the analyst should be interested in the process by which symbols are formed, in other words, symbolization, especially in those patients who show some inhibition in the formation or use of symbols.

Segal offers a quick appraisal of Jones' concepts (1916/1925), disagreeing with him on his restricted use of the concept of symbol. In her opinion, his differentiation between symbols and sublimations is too restrictive of the concept. For him, when there was a sublimation, that is, when the affect for the symbolized idea underwent a transformation in its quality, this did not consist of symbolization. Symbolization would only occur when the symbol unconsciously replaced the symbolized, without transforming the affect. Segal, based on Klein's discovery back in 1923 that the child's play – a sublimated activity – was a symbolic expression of its anxieties and desires, believes that the concept of symbol should also be extended to sublimations. She asks: *how could sublimation occur if not through the formation of symbols?* She thinks that broadening the concept of symbol brings it closer to the way it is used in other areas of knowledge.

On the other hand, she agrees with Jones (1916/1925) in his assertion that it is from the child's interest in its body and that of his parents that, through symbolization, other interests emerge. She makes it clear that these shifts in interests are possible thanks to symbolization.

She initially defines symbolization as an intrapsychic phenomenon and a relationship between three terms: the thing symbolized, the thing that symbolizes, and the person for whom one represents the other. And then she adds, anticipating Bion's more contemporary idea of understanding symbolization as an inter-subjective phenomenon, that "the problems of symbol formation must always be examined in the context of the ego's relation with its objects" (p. 81).

Finally, here we have the theoretical integration of the concept of symbolization with Klein's theory of object relations and the paranoid-schizoid and depressive positions, and it is no longer understood as a process of the individual alone, unipersonal. Symbol formation begins with the onset of object relations and transforms as the nature of the ego's relationship with its objects and with reality changes. To the extent that projective identification predominates in the paranoid-schizoid position, disturbances occur in the differentiation between the ego and the objects and, consequently, between the symbolized and its symbol. What she will conceptualize as *symbolic equations* are formed, giving rise to a representation that is taken concretely as if it were the original symbolized object itself. The subject treats these symbolic equations as he would treat the pursuing object itself, i.e. through annihilation, causing a permanent impoverishment insofar as the products of thought have to be eliminated.

As development takes place, there is a gradual transformation of primitive symbols until true symbolism is formed. This will only occur from the depressive position onwards, i.e. from the moment the projective processes and the splitting diminish and, therefore, there is a better differentiation between the internal and external worlds, ego and object, and true symbolic representations can be created. These are taken as productions of the ego and are therefore abstract, products of thought rather than concrete elements of the material world. Guilt, the fear of losing the loved and attacked object, results in a longing to restore, repair, and finally recreate the object in the internal world. It is interesting to note that true symbolization, in this theoretical context, is necessarily detached from the repression of one of the terms and is linked to the reduction of projective processes. In fact, it was inevitable that the new perspective introduced by Klein, emphasizing the importance of primitive processes in the constitution and structuring of the mind, would also affect the concept of symbolization.

The need to protect the now total object from its own aggressiveness and possessiveness leads to an inhibition of direct drive goals, both libidinal and aggressive. This need to redirect drives becomes a powerful stimulus for the formation of symbols: symbols of objects to which aggression can be displaced, for example, reducing guilt and fear of loss. This displacement aims to leave the original object safe. Symbols are created in the inner world and projected into the outer world, which then takes on new symbolic meanings.

Segal (1957/1982) admits that, even when the depressive position has been reached, there is the possibility of regression to more primitive modes of symbolization in situations where the ego regresses to a more primitive mode of functioning and object relations. Bion (1957/1988) expanded this concept: it is not just a question of chronological regressions but of different modes of representation in different parts of the personality. Later, in 1962, Bion gave a new character to the paranoid-schizoid and depressive positions, defining them in a synchronic context, in a constant oscillation between modes of mental functioning. Segal went on to describe another important function of the ego in the depressive position, which is to symbolize previous conflicts, including those of the paranoid-schizoid position, in order to attenuate anxiety and resolve these conflicts.

Framing the issue of symbolization within the problem of the absence/presence of the object, Segal defines that symbolic equations, due to their concreteness, serve to deny the absence of the object, as they create the illusion of its presence. The symbol itself, available for sublimation, is felt to *represent* the absent object. It is used to overcome the loss, not to deny it, as will be illustrated in the clinical material I will describe.

Filling a gap that, from my point of view, remained in Freud's descriptions of retranslations between different topics of the mind, Segal will define that both internal and external communication is carried out by means of symbols that do not necessarily have to be verbal, in a conceptualization that, in my opinion, differs from Freud's. Internal communication, between unconscious fantasies and their derivatives, is carried out by means of symbolic transformations, resulting in the fact that people who are more capable of carrying out these transformations will be *more in touch with themselves.* This is where the theoretical conceptions that will lead to changes in the theory of technique are located, in the sense of giving greater emphasis to the importance of increasing the capacity to carry out symbolic transformations as a way of broadening the subject's contact with himself.

Thus, we see that Segal's contribution highlights the various junctions, connections, made by the process of symbolization (past/present; unconscious/conscious; subject/object etc.) and, insofar as the symbol is that which connects, we could say that it is one of the most common manifestations of the life drive.

In 1991, in her work "Symbolism", Segal (1991/1993) revisits her 1957 concepts of symbolic equations and symbols proper, or true, because they *represent* the object and *are not felt to be the object.* It is interesting because she mentions a gradual evolution between symbolic equations and true symbolism, with intermediate stages in which an incipient symbol is easily realized.

Still concerned with the theme of the evolution of symbolic equations to symbol, she will state that concrete symbolization probably underlies pathological mourning. If we feel the dead person as a concrete body inside, or feces, then mourning is not possible. Mourning is only possible if we can feel that the dead person is symbolically introjected and that the internal object symbolizes the lost person. Only then can the internal reparation necessary to overcome grief be achieved. A dead person cannot be brought back to life any more than feces can become milk. I mention this last idea of her because it relates directly to the clinical case I will present next.

She also takes up the idea that, especially since the concept of projective identification, the issue of symbol formation has been clarified. When this predominates, the triple relationship of symbolized, symbol, and the person who symbolizes is lost. Boundaries are blurred, differentiation is lost, subject and object are confounded and the symbol, which is the creation of the ego, is confused with the symbolized. It is only with the advent of the depressive position, in which separation and loss are experienced, that fuller symbolic representation can occur.

The use of projective identification aims to deny inner psychic reality by getting rid of a part of oneself and taking and controlling an object. "Symbols *are necessary* to overcome the loss of the object and to protect the object from one's aggressiveness. A symbol is like a precipitate of mourning for the object" (Segal, 1991/1993, p. 54, my emphasis). The symbol only *represents* the object and can therefore be used freely to express the subject's aggression towards it.

In this same work, Segal helps to articulate the question of Oedipus and triangulation with symbolization. Including the Oedipus in the context of the depressive position, she states that the acceptance that the mother and father form a couple is fundamental for the development of symbolic capacity and that mourning for the mother is included in this context: the acceptance of the father as a total person, the mother's partner, and not as a partial object, the mother's possession, confused with her, as a combined object.

In an interesting contribution, which explains the importance of triangulation in symbol formation, she places the father as an interceptor of the chain of projective identifications in the mother. *He comes to be seen as necessary for the proper formation of symbols.* The depressive processes allow the child to recognize the father as a separate object and, at the same time, "discovering" him as such becomes a necessary factor in the subsequent elaboration of the depressive position. This process will allow for a growing capacity for abstraction which will be fundamental for the ability to verbalize.

From Ferro's point of view (Ferro & Gaburri, 1988), the Kleinian contributions will bring about a change in the way we understand the psychoanalytic symbol and symbolization:

> *The symbol is no longer something deformed to be unveiled with a pre-constituted value, but something displaced from the internal to the external and from one object to another that is introduced into the child's (or patient's) phantasmatic relationship with the objects themselves. The ability to symbolize, whether due to the analysis of*

> *children or psychotics, it will be seen as a capacity that can develop, suffer interruptions or even be lost. (p. 292)*

I agree with Ferro that, in Kleinian theory, there is progress in considering symbolization in the heat of the object relationship. From his point of view, however, with which I also agree, even though Segal defines symbolization as a three-term process (symbol, thing symbolized, and person symbolizing), in the classic Kleinian view, symbolization still understands the process only intra-psychically, observing the patient's inner world, his objects, his fantasies, to the relative exclusion of the *presence of the other person's mind* in the process. This will only change with the Bionian contributions.

References

Bion, W. R. (1988). Diferenciação entre a personalidade psicótica e não-psicótica. In *Estudos psicanalíticos revisados*. Imago. (Originally published in 1957)

Bion, W. R. (1991). *Aprendiendo de la experiencia*. Paidós. (Originally published in 1962)

Ferenczi, S. (1992). O desenvolvimento do sentido de realidade e seus estágios. In *Obras Completas* (Vol. 2). Martins Fontes. (Originally published in 1913a)

Ferenczi, S. (1992). Ontogênese dos símbolos. In *Obras Completas* (Vol. 2). Martins Fontes. (Originally published in 1913b)

Ferro, A., & Gaburri, E. (1988). Gli sviluppi kleiniani e Bion. In: A. A. Semi. *Trattato di psicanalisi*. Raffaello Cortina Editore.

Freud, S. (1969). Leonardo Da Vinci e uma lembrança de sua infância. In *Edição standard brasileira das obras psicológicas completas de Sigmund Freud* (Vol. XI). Imago. (Originally published in 1910)

Freud, S. (1969). Formulações sobre os dois princípios do funcionamento mental. In *Edição standard brasileira das obras psicológicas completas de Sigmund Freud* (Vol. XII). Imago. (Originally published in 1911)

Freud, S. (1969). O ego e o id. In *Edição standard brasileira das obras psicológicas completas de Sigmund Freud* (Vol. XIX). Imago. (Originally published in 1923)

Isaacs, S. (1978). A natureza e a função da fantasia. In M. Klein et al., *Os progressos da psicanálise*. Zahar. (Originally published in 1943)

Jones, E. (1925). La theorie du symbolisme. In *Traité theorique et pratique de psychanalyse*. Payot. (Originally published in 1916)

Klein, M. (1975). Primeiros estádios do conflito edípico e a formação do superego. In *Psicanálise da criança*. Mestre Jou. (Originally published in 1932)

Klein, M. (1978). Notas sobre alguns mecanismos esquizoides. In M. Klein et al., *Os progressos da psicanálise*. Zahar. (Originally published in 1946)

Klein, M. (1978). Algumas conclusões teóricas sobre a vida emocional dos bebês. In M. Klein et al., *Os progressos da psicanálise*. Zahar. (Originally published in 1952a)

Klein, M. (1978). Sobre a observação do comportamento dos bebês. In M. Klein et al., *Os progressos da psicanálise*. Zahar. (Originally published in 1952b)

Klein, M. (1981). O papel da escola no desenvolvimento libidinal da criança. In *Contribuições à psicanálise*. Mestre Jou. (Originally published in 1923a)

Klein, M. (1981). A análise infantil. In *Contribuições à psicanálise*. Mestre Jou. (Originally published in 1923b)

Klein, M. (1981). A importância da formação de símbolos no desenvolvimento do ego. In *Contribuições à psicanálise*. Mestre Jou. (Originally published in 1930)

Klein, M. (1981). Uma contribuição a psicogênese dos estados maníaco-depressivos. In *Contribuições à psicanálise*. Mestre Jou. (Originally published in 1934)

Petot, J-M. (1991a). *Melanie Klein* (Vol 1). Perspectiva.

Petot, J-M. (1991b). *Melanie Klein* (Vol 2). Perspectiva.

Segal, H. (1982). Notas a respeito da formação de símbolos. In *A obra de Hanna Segal: uma abordagem kleiniana à prática clínica*. Imago. (Originally published in 1957)

Segal, H. (1993). Simbolismo. In *Sonho, fantasia e arte*. Imago (Originally published in 1991)

Winnicott, D. W. (1975). Objetos transicionais e fenômenos transicionais. In *O brincar e a realidade*. Imago. (Originally published in 1951)

5. The contemporaries: Bion, Meltzer, Winnicott, and later contributions

Meltzer (1984) believes that Klein and Bion extended psychoanalytic metapsychology beyond the four initial metapsychological dimensions defined by Freud, namely: the dynamic, the genetic, the economic, and the topographical. Melanie, with her concepts of the internal world and the interior of the object, created a new metapsychological dimension, the *geographical dimension* of the mind, with all its implications: the notions of inside/outside the *self* and inside/outside the object. Bion, in addition to developing the study of the geography of mental spaces and the communication between them and expanding the concept of projective identification created by Klein, created the *epistemological dimension of* the mind by characterizing the central importance of knowledge, the creation of thoughts and thinking in the structuring of the mental apparatus. We will see that these extensions will also affect our object of study, symbolization.

Bion, thoughts, and thinking

Bion (1957/1988, 1959a/1988, 1959b/1994, 1959c/1994, 1962a/1988, 1962b/1991), based on Freud and Klein, made brilliant contributions to the theme of symbolization. Throughout his work, he defined that what drives the process of symbol formation is not the libido (L – *love*), nor the death drive (H – *hate),* but the desire to know (K – *knowledge),* as long as L and H are subordinate to K. Here, the desire to know is elevated to the status of a drive (Meltzer, 1988). He will define, as we will see next, that the ability to think is created not in the paranoid-schizoid position, nor in the depressive position, but in the permanent oscillation between them (Ps ⇔ D). He will also define that symbolic transformations depend not on the subject or the object, but on the link and the affect experienced between them, in other words, the relationship between container and contained.

Assuming you are all familiar with them, I will give you a quick summary of Bion's main ideas that are relevant to the topic I am discussing.

Freud's strong presence is noted when, in *Learning from experience,* Bion (1962b/1991) is interested in studying "the relationship that exists between the 'pleasure principle' and the 'reality principle' and the choice that a patient can make when faced with the possibility of modifying a frustration or evading it" (p. 22), in an explicit reference to "Formulations on the Two Principles of Mental Functioning" (1911/1969).

Klein's concepts of *splitting*, projective identification, depressive position, paranoid-schizoid position, and envy are, on the other hand, fundamental to his conceptualization (Bion, 1959c/1994). I emphasize this because I have sometimes heard a discussion – sterile, from my point of view – about whether or not Bion is Kleinian. Klein is as central to Bion as Freud is. I think that Bion went beyond Klein and in this sense, he is not a classic Kleinian; but if we remove Klein from Bion, there is no Bion! Bion's central concepts do not work without Klein's concepts. So let's finally get to his ideas.

Bion (1959c/1994), in "Dream-work-α", describes a series of mental functions that he claims are already well known to psychoanalysis. His description is the origin of what he later calls the alpha function. The characteristics of alpha are: 1) it is continuous day and night; 2) it operates on stimuli received from inside and outside the mind and on the ideational counterpart of external facts. He claims that alpha transforms raw sensory impressions so that they can be stored and recalled. The sensory impression is transformed into an ideogram, or "ideogrammaticized". For example, if the experience is one of pain, the psyche may receive an image of a tear-stained face or a scratched elbow... And, in an explicit link with "Formulations on the two principles..." (1911/1969), he says that if the *reality principle is dominant* (frustration tolerated), the ideograms created will be stored (by memory) and recalled (by attention) later and can also be synthesized with each other. If the *pleasure/pain principle is dominant*, the ideogram will be evacuated.

It is interesting that he called this function *the alpha dream work*, because it is a foreshadowing not only of what he will describe as the alpha function, but also of the capacity for *rêverie*. *Rêverie* comes from the French word *réver*, which means to dream. Bion uses this term not in the sense of the dream itself, but in the sense that "raw" emotional and sensory experiences need to be "dreamed", transformed, in order to leave the realm of the sensory and move into the realm of the mental.

He goes on to relate the alpha dream work to projective identification: a dream, for example, can have the purpose of simply evacuating a set of emotions in the analyst, rather than being destined for recording and psychic elaboration. He imagines that he might be asked: if an image has been created, has not there been alpha work and, therefore, visual symbolization? He replies that, in a way, yes. It does seem that some feelings have been ideogrammaticized, but not for the purpose of mental digestion, but rather to be placed in a receptacle that gives the feeling of being free of them.

"In that case, the visual image itself is used as a target for projective identification and then is used as a missile container for further projective identification" (p. 66). The dream, in this case, is felt as a "real object" and serves as a container for projective identification, it is not felt as a healthy phenomenon, it is felt as if it were a hallucination.

Later (Bion, 1962b/1991), ordering and expanding his ideas, he created the following model: the alpha function operates on sensory impressions and emotions, which he calls beta elements, transforming them into alpha elements.

> *The alpha elements are visual images, auditory and olfactory models, and are suitable for use in oneiric thoughts, in the unconscious thought of wandering, in dreams, contact barriers, memory. (p. 48)*

"The alpha elements resemble, and may in fact be identical to, the visual images with which we are familiar in dreams" (p. 26) and are considered by him to be mental forms capable of being thought about or stored, while the beta elements are equated with things in themselves, belonging to the field of the phenomena and not ideas, in other words, they cannot be thought about.

The alpha elements belong to the thinking domain and the beta elements to the sensory domain. The alpha function is necessary for conscious thought and for relegating a certain thought to the unconscious if we want to free our consciousness from it. If there are only beta elements, which cannot be unconscious, there can be no repression. The alpha function then allows the formation of the unconscious/conscious barrier (contact barrier): so, in wakefulness, the subject can remain "asleep" to perceptions and emotional experiences that are stored in the unconscious by it. The alpha function enables dreaming by forming alpha elements that give rise to oneiric thoughts. It also allows the sense of reality to develop, which, in the Bionian theoretical model, is as important for the mind as food, drink, air, and evacuation are for the body. The contact barrier, as we will see next, results from the adhesion between the alpha elements.

Therefore, to learn from experience, it will be necessary for the alpha function to operate on the emotional experience, whether in day or night life, transforming it into knowledge and memories that can be stored.

Regarding the genesis of thoughts, Bion (1962b/1991) believes that thoughts themselves occur in the absence of the expected object, that is, in a lack of fulfillment, or in the context of frustration. Bion puts it literally:

> *Thoughts then, or these primitive elements that are proto-thoughts, are bad, needed objects to be got rid of because they are bad. They can be got rid either by evasion or modification. The problem is solved by evacuation, if the personality is dominated by the impulse to evade frustration, and by thinking the objects if the personality is dominated by the impulse to modify the frustration. (p. 115)*

In other words, the next step, running away from frustration or changing it, will depend on your ability to tolerate frustration. If one can tolerate frustration, the non-breast, the bad object, the proto-thought, becomes a thought, giving rise to what Freud called the reality principle. If one cannot tolerate it, one will run away from it, and "what should be a thought becomes a bad object, indistinguishable from a thing-in-itself, and which lends itself only to evacuation" (p. 103). In the predominance of intolerance of frustration, permanent measures will be taken to flee from it, intensifying projective identification, confusing the distinction between *self* and external object, consequently preventing the perception of dualities, the formation of true symbols, and developing, instead of a thinking apparatus, a thought-evacuation apparatus.

It is important to highlight the appearance in Bion of the importance of frustration and the self/object differentiation in symbolization, already highlighted in Ferenczi (1913/1992), as has been pointed out. So, in the Bionian model, if a pre-conception followed by a non-realization leads to a thought proper, a pre-conception followed by a realization, i.e. the presence of the expected object, will result in a concept.

One of Bion's surprising and interesting formulations is that thoughts precede the ability to think them, which implies that the fact of having thoughts does not mean that the patient has the ability to think. It will depend on how and for what the thoughts are used: whether they are evacuated or articulated with each other; whether they are used simply for discharge or to modify the environment. In the first case, they are similar or identical to beta elements. In these cases, the mind functions like a musician who continuously discharges beta elements, which only lend themselves to evacuation, are felt as things, and can be sensorially perceived in the body as somatizations and in external reality as hallucinations. It is implicit that numerous clinical conditions in which evacuative processes predominate in the soma, in the passage to the act, or in the form of hallucinations, will be understood as having at their base problems in the capacity for symbolic transformation.

Alpha elements, on the other hand, can be thought of because they can integrate, establish links between themselves. Caper (1996/2002), in an interesting article on the alpha function, explains that, in the Bionian sense, the quality of having meaning is linked to the possibility of establishing connections. In other words, an idea is meaningful if it can be connected to another idea. Therefore, an idea is potentially thinkable if it belongs to a network of interconnected ideas.

In the work "Differentiation of the psychotic from the non-psychotic personalities" (1957/1988), Bion highlights his idea that the psychotic, or the psychotic part of the personality, due to an intolerance of the perception of a painful reality, attacks parts of the personality capable of perceiving reality. In particular, he describes an attack on the links that are established within the thought processes themselves. Referring explicitly to Freud (1911/1969), he says that primitive thought occurs through the possibility of establishing links between sensory impressions. It is these connections that give meaning to sensory impressions. Bion says:

> *All these links are now being attacked, until it finally becomes impracticable to join two objects in such a way that each one, despite keeping its respective intrinsic qualities, can nevertheless generate a new mental object by combining it with another. Consequently, the formation of symbols, the therapeutic effect of which depends on the ability to unite two objects so that their similarity is evident and the difference between them is blurred, now becomes difficult. (p. 51)*

He goes on to say that the patient attacks and expels from the mind that which binds. In this brilliant paragraph, several ideas become evident that are of interest to my objective: Bion conceives and calls "symbol formation" the primitive processes, already mentioned by Freud and cited by me previously, of association, of linking sensory impressions, and he anticipates, in 1957, what he will later call the *alpha work* (1959c/1994) and *alpha function* (1962b), that is, that sensory impressions, in order to acquire meaning and significance, need to establish connections and associations between themselves. Another fact that I would like to highlight and which I will develop next is that when Bion talks about an element that connects (that-which-binds), he is presupposing a three-way relationship: one element, another element, and that which connects them. Dana Birksted-Breen (1996) described the penis – not the phallus – as a mental structure, as that which creatively connects the father and the mother. We will look at this later.

The alpha elements, due to their capacity for articulation, give rise to a reticulum that Bion (1962b/1991) called the alpha screen. The alpha screen forms a contact barrier that, on one side, separates the conscious from the unconscious and, on the other, allows contact between the two. It is the alpha screen that creates the possibility of the unconscious existing insofar as it creates the mental elements capable of being organized and carrying the meaning of the emotional experiences that will form the unconscious. Caper (1996/2002) makes a direct correlation between the ability to form symbols described by Segal (1957/1982) and Bion's contact barrier. So, as I have already said, in Bion, it is the ability to form symbols that will enable repression.

The screen of beta elements, which cannot be articulated with each other, serves more to expel and aims to provoke reactions in the analyst. The use of words is more an action to free the psyche from an increase in stimuli than a language as such.

Bion (1962b/1991) also describes the possibility of *reversal of the alpha function*. There will be a destruction of the contact barrier so that "the alpha elements are stripped of all the characteristics that distinguish them from the beta elements and are then projected, thus forming the beta screen" (p. 46). In this way, bizarre elements are formed.

One of Bion's great differences from Klein is that, as well as creating a theoretical model of what goes on intrapsychically, he conceives of the mother/baby relationship in such a way that what goes on inside the infant's mind becomes inseparable from the link established with the mother and what goes on in her mind. At the beginning of life, the baby, faced with inevitable frustrations, will need to get rid of the beta elements and will project them into the mother. Bion (1962a/1988, 1962b/1991) then, taking a new theoretical step, considers that the mother will play an essential modulating role, "managing" the baby's personality so that it can develop its mind. In other words, this development will not only depend on the baby's constitutional characteristics (amount of death/life drive and frustration tolerance), but *also* on the mother's mental capacity to "metabolize" and transform the baby's initial projections.

Considering that the alpha function does not operate from the beginning of life, the baby will depend on the mother's alpha function and her capacity for *rêverie* to "alphabetize" (Ferro, 1995) its emotional experiences. The mother's *rêverie* is understood by Bion (1962a/1988) as the "receptor organ for the harvest of sensations" (p. 106) from the baby that have been projected into her. It is the *rêverie* that satisfies the infant's need for love and understanding. If the nurturing mother has no capacity for *rêverie* or if *rêverie* occurs, but without love for the baby *or its father* (!!), this fact will be communicated to the baby, even if it is incomprehensible to it. "Rêverie *is a factor in the* mother's alpha *function*" (p. 59). In other words, from Bion onwards, the mother is seen as performing structuring functions in the baby's mind. Just as she feeds it milk, she feeds it "thoughts" by putting her alpha function at the baby's service. This is much more than presenting the object of the baby's need or desire.

Bion (1962a/1988, 1962b/1991) then added a new way of operating *normal* projective identification, namely for communicative purposes: the baby awakens unpleasant sensations in the mother that it wants to get rid of; the mother accepts these sensations and "reacts therapeutically" (1962a/1988, p. 105), modifying the projection so that the baby feels, after reintrojecting what was projected, that it is receiving its personality back in a tolerable way. This would be a +content/contained relationship that would lead to the development of the thinking apparatus. If, on the other hand, the mother, reacting with anxiety and incomprehension, does not accept the projections, or accepts them but does not attenuate them and gives them back, increased by her own anxiety, the baby feels that it is in a relationship with an evil, despoiling, jealous object and feels invaded by a *nameless terror*. This emotional state will, in turn, lead to a further increase in projective identification, contributing to the development not of the thinking apparatus, but of an apparatus that serves more for evacuation. I will return later to the details of the container/contained relationship.

Bion (1962b/1991) made an original contribution by linking *frustration tolerance* with the ability to make realistic, normal projective identifications; if frustration tolerance is lower, projective identification has a less real counterpart in external reality, which Klein calls *excessive*. It leads to an *excess* of expulsion through greater intolerance of unwanted feelings and without taking into account the data of reality. In this case, the transformation of the experience will depend even more on the mother's capacity for *rêverie*. If the mother fails, there will be a new overload on the baby's limited capacity to tolerate frustration, increasing projective identification. In the opposite situation, an infant, in order to survive in the presence of a mother with no capacity for *rêverie*, will need to have an enormous tolerance for frustration. He then describes a spectrum of proportional relationships between maternal *rêverie* capacity and the infant's frustration tolerance.

Based on the idea that thoughts precede the ability to think them, Bion (1962b/1991) describes a second factor responsible for the development of the thinking apparatus, which is the Ps ⇔ D oscillation (Grinberg, Bianchedi & Sor, 1991), the first factor being the possibility of establishing a positive container/contained relationship. As we shall see, the Ps ⇔ D oscillation has numerous implications for the psychoanalytic technique. Drawing on the ideas of mathematician Poincaré, Bion describes how, based on successive emotional experiences, the alpha function forms alpha elements which, at first, lack coherence and organization. At a certain point, based on a selected fact, they can be organized into a coherent model and acquire meaning for the subject. The selected fact would be "the name of an emotional experience, the emotional experience of a sense of discovery of coherence" (Bion, 1962b/1991, p. 104). Thus, the selected fact precipitates the mental model to be created.

But in order for emotional experience to be used to create this model, its sensory data must have been transformed into alpha elements so that they can be united, articulated and organized. The model, in this description, would already be an abstraction of emotional experience and a concretization of later abstractions that could be made. The mind is described in a line of development that goes from concrete experience to increasing degrees of abstraction resulting from successive symbolic transformations. In his clinical practice, the psychoanalyst must have the negative capability to tolerate the moments of incoherence characteristic of Ps until a selected fact allows him to arrive at D and, only then, to create a model of what is happening in the session. Thinking depends on reaching an integration, a synthesis (D), after a period of incoherence and fragmentation (Ps). Ogden (1996) states that the reverse is also true: in order to arrive at a new thought, it is necessary to leave D, there needs to be a "de-structuring" of what is already known. Always staying in D would have more to do with omniscience than with true knowledge.

I think it is already possible, tentatively, to make some integrations and raise the following hypothesis: for Bion, the first symbolizations, which he calls "proper" thoughts (the non-breast), are unequivocally related to the absence of the object and the ability to *contain* the anxiety arising from this absence; the records made in the presence of the object, which he calls concepts, could perhaps be what Freud called mnemic records of sensory impressions. These records, I believe, would become symbolic records if, *a posteriori*, subjected to the alpha function, linked to the affect felt in the experience, they were articulated, transformed into alpha elements and began to evoke, to represent, the absent, loaded with the meaning of the affective experience in question.

Thinking and links

Bion (1962b/1991) is categorical in stating that an emotional experience cannot occur in isolation from a relationship. He assumes that three types of links can unite X and Y: X loves Y; X hates Y; X knows Y. He uses the three signs already known to refer to love, hate, and knowledge, and then defining L, H, and K. The K link is an emotional experience between X and Y and is a becoming, not something that is possessed. It is the search for the truth of what you are trying to know. The feeling inherent in this experience seems to be painful and, in order to proceed, it will depend on your tolerance for frustration.

The result of the K link is the production of a statement that represents the emotional experience lived, and the sense of truth is ensured by common sense, by a correlation of feelings. This representation is an abstraction of the experience. In our field, Rezende (1998), studying the scientific status of psychoanalysis and its truth criteria, classifies this methodology among other truth criteria used by psychoanalysis, such as truth by symbolic correlation.

It is implicit in Bion's theorizing that it seems to him that the Freudian model in "Formulations on the Two Principles..." clarified how consciousness and attention apprehend the sensory qualities of experience and that, for him, the question goes further, that is, it also aims to clarify how psychic qualities are apprehended in which sensory data do not contribute. Bion (1962b/1991) states that, for personalities incapable of true dreaming, in other words, of transforming beta into alpha, describing the conscience as an organ for apprehending psychic qualities is not satisfactory – it is not a false description, but an unsatisfactory one, because the consciousness can only apprehend psychic qualities if there is this transformation; otherwise it can only apprehend sensory qualities.

What is interesting to note is that, although Bion believes that what builds the mind is the possibility of creating statements about lived experiences or, if we prefer, symbolic representations of experiences, he places the emotion experienced in the link at the center of the process, inaugurating what will be called the aesthetic dimension or model of psychoanalysis, which will be discussed in subsequent chapters of this book.

Delving a little deeper into his concepts, Bion (1962b/ 1991) will affirm that the first manifestation of a K link is in the mother-baby relationship and that container and contained are impregnated and united by emotion: L and H are factors of K. In other words, reaching K will depend on the emotion that binds container and contained. If L predominates in the K link, a commensal relationship is established, as both mother and baby gain mental growth from this experience. This shared activity is introjected by the baby "in such a way that the container/contained apparatus is installed in the infant as part of the alpha function apparatus" (p. 123).

The development of the container occurs through the formation of a reticulum in which the gaps are like vacuoles to be filled by thoughts and the threads that make up the mesh are emotion. The growing container/contained set provides the basis for an apparatus for learning from experience. Thus, from thoughts and the development of thoughts, comes the apparatus for thinking them. Learning depends on this apparatus being both integrated and flexible. This creates a mental state in which the individual can retain his knowledge and experiences and at the same time be prepared to reconstruct past experiences in the light of a new one. Emotion plays a fundamental role in uniting the container and the contained to produce a commensal relationship and, therefore, K. According to Bion, however, not all emotions do. There are emotions that lead to –K, the link constituted by *not* understanding, in other words, *misunderstanding.*

He considers envy to be one of the factors that lead to –K when it is the emotion that unites the container and the contained. Considering envy as an expression of the death drive, that which disconnects, he understands that it does not lead to the creative production of something. Envy makes a commensal relationship impossible. In –K, the baby feels that the breast strips it of what is good and forces a worthless residue inside it. "The baby who started out afraid of dying ends up containing a nameless terror" (p. 128).

The negative container/contained relationship "presents itself as a superior object that asserts its superiority by showing flaws in everything" (p. 130). There is a hatred of any new development, as if it were a rival to be destroyed. The search for truth is met with destructive attacks. The contained are included in a container that strips them of value and deprives them of meaning. This envious divestment contrasts with the process of abstraction inherent in K's container/contained relationship. There is an inversion: –container/contained converts alpha elements into beta. In other words, the abstract is converted into things-in-themselves, unlike +container/contained.

The thinking apparatus then develops through the Ps ↔ D oscillation and the container/contained relationship. Container and contained are part of the alpha function. This integrated and flexible apparatus, as described earlier, which can accept and transform emotional experiences, expands infinitely, leading to constant mental growth.

As a preliminary conclusion, we could say that Bion places symbolization not only in the warmth of the object relationship, as Klein had already done, but in the dependence on this object performing functions of containment and transformation of the emotional experience. That is to say, the mental functioning of the object is taken into account. What is more, it places emotion as the driving force and starting point of the symbolization process. Subsequently, the individual, identified with the container function of the object, will gain the ability to "alphabetize" his emotional experiences and thus build his psychic apparatus. The assertion is that the activity of the permanent alpha function, on a prolonged basis, presupposes a permanent expansion of the alpha screen and of the mind itself.

The protomental, the unison and the negative

Although Bion made a point of leaving the concepts of alpha function and alpha elements open, covered by a shroud of uncertainty, other authors (Meltzer, 1984, 1988/1995; Segal, 1991a/1993, 1991b/1993; Green, 1975/1994; Ogden, 1996; Ferro, 1995, 1998; Gaburri & Ferro, 1988) make it clear that it is the process of symbolization that Bion is studying.

Perhaps Bion, with his acknowledged concern to encourage openness to new ideas, avoiding them being equated with familiar ideas, avoided using old names. If we can assimilate Bion's new ideas, preserve their originality and what they bring, I think we can use names that have already been used. As Ogden (1996) shows in his beautiful book *Subjects of analysis*, as long as we can preserve the originality and purity of the various psychoanalytic concepts, we must try to articulate them, put them in relation, bring them together to the maximum limit and then differentiate them. This allows us to explore the creative potential of psychoanalytic theory.

Meltzer (1984) equates the alpha elements with symbols and the alpha function with symbolization and says so verbatim:

> *In equating alpha elements and symbols, I follow Bion's suggestion that alpha elements are in themselves unobservable... the symbol is not a sign, it is a recourse for exchanging meaning, a form of linkage that expresses congruence, but which carries in itself an increment of meaning for both terms. (p. 81)*

Except that, in the Bionian theoretical context, symbols and symbolization will be understood as something extremely dynamic, constant, created in the context of an emotional relationship and subject to the most diverse vicissitudes. A psychopathology of symbolization will be described: the reversal of the alpha function, the appropriation by a perverse part of the personality, the expulsion from the mind of the possibility of making connections, all leading to disturbances in the constitution or functioning of the mental apparatus itself.

In his various contributions to the study of symbolization, in addition to clarifying Bion's contributions, Meltzer (1975/1979, 1984, 1988/1995; Meltzer et al., 1986/1990) also adds originality to various concepts. For instance, he will say that Bion, in defining the container/contained relationship as fundamental in the generation of symbols and thinking, complements Klein in the sense that she described introjection and projection, but was not concerned with describing how the concept of internal space arises in the mind.

Then, following Bion's description of the mother's need to function as a container and the baby's internalization of this function, Meltzer, in *Explorations in Autism* (1975/1979), described the passage from two-dimensionality to three-dimensionality. In this book, based on Esther Bick's ideas (1967/1991) about the skin, he shows how the possibility of using projective identification, symbolizing, and thinking depends on developing the notion that the self and the object have an internal space. In two-dimensional mental functioning, there is no possibility of symbolization, since there is no notion of inside/outside, so since everything is joined edge to edge, there is nothing to represent. There is no discriminated perception of objects.

In *Sexual states of mind*, Meltzer (1973/1979) described creativity as coming from the internalization of a pair of parents united in creative coitus. He poetically said that the subject does not create, he only discovers what the internal parents have created! Thirteen years later, in *Extended metapsychology* (Meltzer et al., 1986/1990), a book in which he dedicated himself to studying the clinical application of Bion's contributions, he referred to the *mysterious process of generating symbols* as the core of human creativity. The symbolic area will come to be understood as the essence of the mind, whose purpose is to create symbols to represent the meaning of emotional experiences so that they can be stored as memories, used for thinking and transformed into a variety of symbolic forms for communicating ideas and for artistic creation.

Increasingly, Meltzer (1988/1995) will stress the creative, aesthetic nature of symbolization, insofar as it creates a form that carries the meaning and emotion of the experience. I think this is illustrated in the following statement:

> *The mind is the metaphor-generating function that uses the big computer (brain) to write its poetry and paint its pictures of a sparkling world of meaning. And meaning is, in the first instance, the fundamental manifestation of the passions of the intimate relationship with the beauty of the world. (p. 35)*

The poetic way in which Meltzer tries to describe Bion's ideas and his aesthetic vision of the process is also illustrated in this comment:

> *Through a mysterious creative act of the mind, the data provided by the different senses are introduced into the container ("the dark chamber of virginal thought" – Keats) where the thirst for knowledge (link K) and the dynamics of concern for loved objects (Ps ↔ D, catalyzed by the selected fact) are capable of producing a dreamlike image where meaning is apprehended, to borrow an image from Bion, "like the light of a diamond". This mysterious process can be reversed "halfway" to produce a web of lies and false representations. (Meltzer et al., 1986/1990, p. 112)*

Concerned with discriminating between human relationships that take place in the heat of emotions and others that are devoid of them, he will differentiate between two areas of human experience. There is an area of human life and development that is dementalized and resembles the stimuli received by young animals, where what predominates is learning through training, mimicry, and conditioning. This would be the area marked by the presence of signs and conventions, rather than the symbols themselves. It is an essential area for survival. But it is hoped that another area will develop in the human being, in which intimate relationships are established that are charged with emotional experiences and that can be learned about through thinking, from which the imagination constructs an image of the world. Taking Bion's ideas as far as possible in this respect, he would say that emotion is the first manifestation of the "meaning" of an experience and symbolic meaning is its working-through. In other words, it is emotion that gives the quality of what is experienced and, as long as there is a possibility of containment, this is elaborated, recorded, and stored through symbolic representation.

Meltzer will finally define clearly the boundary between the *protomental* and the *mental*: it is delimited by the alpha function, responsible for the mysterious process of symbol formation (Meltzer et al., 1986/1990). He will also say that the protomental apparatus instigates action outwards (acting) or inwards (psychosomatic), while the mental apparatus restricts action and promotes thinking, drawing a parallel between the beta elements – which Bion had already called proto-thoughts and which belonged to the protomental – and the alpha elements, which constituted the mental. Thus, various phenomena linked to the relief of stimuli, to sensory experiences and their recording, would belong to the domain of the protomental.

Segal (1991b/1993), in her article "Mental space and elements of symbolism", makes a theoretically important integration between her own concepts and those of Bion. She highlights all the clinical relevance of Bion's theory of thinking, particularly the container function of the object and the identification with this function in order to develop a mental apparatus capable of symbolizing. She states that a good container/contained relationship presupposes a space in the container to contain the contained and that this is what will give rise to the mental space. Whenever the child or the patient feels that there is no mental space to accommodate his/her projections, these will come back worse.

She makes several attempts to articulate beta elements and symbolic equations. First, she says that "they are like a very primitive form of what I call 'symbolic equations'" (p. 64). She also adds that perhaps symbolic equations are made up of beta elements. But then she says – and this is the view to which she leans – that it might be better to consider that symbolic equations are halfway between beta and alpha. She concludes that they cannot be equated, for symbolic equations are not always minutely fragmented and are therefore more recognizable; their meaning is more easily recognized and they already have some symbolic meaning. If we follow her suggestion, we might arrive at the following line of evolution: *beta elements → beginning of the transformation into alpha → symbolic equations → alpha elements → symbol itself.*

As for the alpha elements, she will point out, in line with Bion, that they are the elements of oneiric thought, myth, and symbolism, and the alpha function, like Meltzer, she believes is closely related to the symbolic function. The unsaturated nature of the alpha elements makes them susceptible to countless articulations and open to infinite transformations. This means that there can be many symbols for one situation and one symbol can represent several situations. It occurred to me from this that one could imagine the alpha reticulum as a three-dimensional structure in which each point articulates with countless others, on several different planes. I believe this results in symbolic relativity (Rezende, 1988/1998). Each of these articulations gives a different emphasis, meaning, and significance. Each of these meanings will exist depending on the type of articulation that is made at each moment.

Returning to Segal (1991b/1993), she compares her idea of the passage from equation to symbol being linked to the passage PS → PD with Bion's conception of oscillation Ps ↔ D. I think they are different conceptions: the oscillation conceived by Bion is much more an oscillation of mental state than of well-defined positions in development; it is a more synchronic than diachronic concept.

Gaburri and Ferro (1988) say that Bion studied less the symbol, understood as mental content, and more symbolization as a creative mental function, the mind as a generator of symbols. In fact, the whole technique that Ferro advocated concerned the expansion of symbolic capacity (Ferro, 1995, 1998). In his 1988 work, he stated that current conceptualizations of the symbol are related to the way projective identification is conceived: if it serves communication and if thought formation occurs through the mind of the other, *symbolization becomes a twosome process and the symbol a relational success.* Less importance is given to the "veracity" of the symbolic meaning itself and less importance is given to the patient's relationship with his/her own objects and fantasies:

> *there is another mind, that of the analyst, with its own objects and fantasies, which, by transforming emotions and operating "in unison", favors the function of symbolizing. This is why the revelation of preconceived meanings can be accompanied by the formation of new meanings, new connections and new possibilities. (Gaburri & Ferro, 1998, p. 297)*

Symbolization will come to be seen as a creative conjunction: the symbolic area is that partition shared by two objects immersed in a reciprocal relationship and the creative configuration will be the crucial element in the formation of symbols (Gaburri & Ferro, 1998). This will have numerous implications for psychoanalytic technique, as we will see next.

If so far we have seen and studied ideas about the formation of symbols, which would be a representation of the "truth" of emotional experience, Meltzer (1984) follows up on Bion's ideas by trying to understand what he calls anti-symbols. He then describes his concept of *lying.*

> *The credibility of a lie does not depend on its quantitative relationship with the truth, but on its structural or functional congruence, just as with symbols. A lie is a disfigurement of the truth, in which* false symbols *are used. (p. 86, my emphasis)*

"The formation of symbols is at the service of representing the truth and the formation of anti-symbols is at the service of disfiguring it" (p. 88). Meltzer, in a personal conversation, went so far as to say that Bion bequeathed to future psychoanalytic thinkers the development of a negative form of the grid that would encompass the formation of lies, foreseeing that lies can be created at various levels of thought and serve different uses. He adds that we cannot consider that dreams always tell the *truth*. "The truth they tell is the treatment that emotional experiences receive in the depths of the mind; but truth is not always treasured here, for it is freighted with mental pain" (p. 101).

In the view of expanded metapsychology, the geographical dimension of the mind poses some difficulties in understanding dreams: *the mind is not one and the mental world is divided into multiple spaces*. Thus, in the metaphor of the *theater for the generating of meaning* used by Meltzer (1984), it is useful to follow the roles of the various aspects of the personality in dreams, as well as the geographical location of dream action. Meltzer will emphasize the importance of delimiting which part of the personality is in charge of "directing" the dream and whether this part is interested in producing a truth, however painful, or a lie as a way of relieving psychic pain.

In *Studies in extended metapsychology* (Meltzer *et al.*, 1986/1990), Meltzer continues with his idea of the need to create a negative grid to describe the genesis of lies or misrepresentations of the truth. He says that the "mysterious process [of symbol formation] can be reversed, 'halfway', to produce a web of lies and false representations" (p. 112). In his conception, it is as if the alpha function formed the symbol, which, because it generates a considerable amount of pain, would need to be covered with a cloak of lies. Here is a significant difference with Bion: Meltzer believes that the reversal of the alpha function does not destroy the newly created alpha elements but covers them with a "cloak of lies". If this is so, says Meltzer, "the true symbol is not destroyed, but covered over, leaving the hope that it can shine through this covering again and thus illuminate the mind from its penumbra" (p. 116). The theme of the negative with regard to symbolization will be dealt with in another chapter of this book: the creation of false symbols, the "de-representations", in Meltzer's words, or Bion's own bizarre objects (1957/1988, 1962a/1988, 1962b/1991).

With everything presented so far about Meltzer's ideas, we create a conception in which the external world acquires meaning from that which is generated in the internal world. Meltzer (1984) will say: "Oneiric life is the theater that generates meaning and the external world is devoid of meaning until it is created in the internal world and spreads outwards" (p. 104).

Mental space, transitional space, triangulation, and the integration of primitive experiences

As I mentioned earlier, Klein introduced a new metapsychological dimension by defining the geography of mental spaces. She described the inner world, the fantasies about the interior of the maternal body, and the interplay between them through projective and introjective processes. Bion described how the notion of inner space is created from the introjection of the container/contained relationship. Klein also traced the Oedipus complex, with all that it represents for the notion of triangulation, back to the beginnings of development. Winnicott (1951/1975, 1971/1975) made an enormous contribution by conceptualizing the existence of a space that lies between the interior of the subject and the interior of the object, namely the transitional space. All these concepts about the geography of mental spaces and triangulation will have fundamental implications for the contemporary notion of symbolization.

In relation to the *third object*, Segal (1991b/1993) will highlight Bion's notion that when there is a good container/contained relationship, this gives rise to a third object, so that the two objects share a *third to the advantage* of all three, and when the relationship is not good, it gives rise to a *third that is destructive* to all three.

The depressive position; the perception of the father as a third element; the importance of this in reducing the projective processes and projective identification, giving rise to the discriminated subject/object perception; and the container/contained relationship giving rise to the third are all factors that contribute to the formation of the mental space, subject/object discrimination and, therefore, symbolic formation. Britton (1989/1992) described that the *triangular space*, with its three vertices, implies the recognition of the three people in the oedipal relationship and their potential relationships. The third, who can observe the other two in a benevolent and interested way, not destructively, is crucial for the development of a mental space where it is possible to observe, see, understand, gain *insights*, and is the basis for epistemophilic curiosity. Segal (1991b/1993) argues that the triangular space is also a space for a new, unsaturated baby. It allows the birth of new thoughts: two can come together like parents in coitus, to produce a third, new thought.

Winnicott (1962/1979, 1971/1975) made countless contributions to the subject of symbolization, but I am going to focus on two in particular: transitional space and the constitution of alterity, or the objective object. One of his great contributions to the study of the "geography" of mental spaces and to symbolization was his concepts of transitional space and transitional object. In 1951, he produced his famous work "Transitional objects and transitional phenomena" (1951/1975), expanded in 1971 in *Playing and Reality* (1971/1975).

He describes an intermediate area of the human experience, which lies between the internal and external worlds: an intermediate area of *experimentation* in which both internal and external reality contribute. He is studying the sphere of *illusion*, which, in adult life, is inherent in art and religion. It is an intermediate area between the subjective and the objective.

Through primary creativity, the baby creates a subjective object, exactly where and when it appears in reality. The mother's ability to adapt to the baby's needs gives it the illusion that it has created the object. The mother must then also have the ability to gradually disillusion it through frustration in bearable doses. This gradual evolution allows the perception of the mother as an objective object to gradually emerge.

In fact, in 1962, Winnicott described more than this. He said that maternal *holding* fosters the integration of the baby's ego and the development of the feeling of being "me", "selfhood", in the words of Ogden (1996). Next comes the notion of not-self and, soon after, of existing by exchanging experiences with the not-self. The transitional object is situated precisely in this process as the first non-self possession, a material object, but one that is not the mother and is under the baby's control. All of this will be directly linked to the capacity for symbolization.

Winnicott (1971/1975) then describes a series of activities with one's own body or with objects of personal use, which are sucked or caressed and can become vitally important for sleeping, for example. These are transitional phenomena and constitute a defense against depressive anxiety. The object used becomes a transitional object.

Next, he studies the relationship between the transitional object and symbolism:

> *It is true that the piece of blanket (or whatever it is) is symbolical of some part-object, such as the breast. Nevertheless the point of it is not its symbolic value so*

> *much as its actuality. Its not being the breast (or the mother) is as important as the fact that it stands for the breast (or mother). (p. 395)*

In fact, it seems that although Winnicott recognizes a link between his concept of the transitional object and that of the symbol, he recommends maintaining the difference between what he wants to describe with the notion of the symbol. When the symbol is used, the baby already differentiates between fantasy and fact, internal and external objects, primary creativity, and objective perception. Winnicott advocates for the use of the term transitional object, because it seems to be halfway there, it opens up space for the process of becoming able to accept *difference and similarity*. It is halfway between subjective and objective objects; between omnipotence and the perception of reality; between indifferentiation and the differentiation of self/non-self. He believes it is at the *root of the ability to symbolize*.

Although there are characteristics specific to the transitional object (its materiality, for example), it is interesting to note that what Winnicott says about it also applies to the symbol in general: for the psyche, the fact that the symbol is not the thing itself is just as important as representing it. This dialectical relationship of simultaneously being and not being is the essence of symbolization. This is precisely the characteristic of symbolic relationships: ensuring continuity (one element refers to another) and discontinuity (one is not the other). This is what makes symbolization so fundamental to mental functioning.

It seems to me that another of Winnicott's great contributions, which will also have repercussions on the psychoanalytic technique, is to conceive that transitional objects and transitional phenomena, which mark the beginning of symbolic formation, in his view, are created in the space *between* the mother and the child. In comparing the ideas of Bion and Winnicott, Segal (1991b/1993) says that there are major differences between them because in Bion it is an active mental space that performs the transforming alpha function, "it is not a neutral space. This space is not between the mother and the child – *it is an internal mental space formed by the introjection of a breast capable of containing the baby's projective identifications and giving them meaning*" (p. 69).

Although I agree with Segal that there are major differences between the concepts of container space (Bion) and transitional space (Winnicott), I think that each of the two has its own richness and are therefore useful concepts for thinking about symbolization, for example. One of the uses of the Winnicottian concept – apart from understanding an extremely frequent evolutionary phenomenon and a whole area of human creativity – is to clarify that the true symbol is created in the presence/absence dynamic, it depends on the differentiation of self/non-self, subjective/real.

In *Beyond the Pleasure Principle*, although he did not describe the same type of phenomenon as Winnicott, Freud (1920/1969), with his brilliant intuition, describes the development of a symbolic play activity, the *fort-da*, which had the aim of working out the depressive anxiety of an 18-month-old boy when he was separated from his mother. It deals, without describing it explicitly, with the same presence/absence dynamic – implicit in the dynamic of the creation of the transitional object – and the driving force of this dynamic for symbolic formation: it is in order to work out the depressive anxiety that the reel is set to go back and forth…

The paper "Phallus, penis and mental space" by Dana Birksted-Breen (1996), in my opinion, should be included among the classics of psychoanalysis. She conducts an in-depth study of the problem of triangulation and its importance in the formation of mental space and symbolization. She differentiates between two mental structures: the *penis* as a link and the *phallus*. The penis would be a structure on a more genital level that admits lack, incompleteness, and the relationship between parents established through it, and therefore implies triangulation. The phallus, on the other hand, would be equated with an idealized object which, when possessed by the subject, would lead to a narcissistic feeling of self-sufficiency, completeness, and superiority.

The introjection of the penis as a link leads to the *expansion of mental space*, as it admits the link between two objects (male/female) in order to create a third (baby/new idea). The introduction of the phallus, on the other hand, leads to the *constriction* of mental space, as it consists of a fusion with the idealized object and therefore leads to omniscience. The co-connection I might make with Bion's ideas would be that the penis, conceived in this way, would be something equivalent to what Bion describes as the thing-that-binds. Even though they are different concepts, both presuppose that there needs to be a structure in the mind that connects them in order to create a third, and that this is central to symbolization.

The desire to *have or be the phallus* is an attempt to supply the structuring function of the penis as a link when it is lacking, which can be obtained temporarily in the phallic structure. This "solution", due to its *manic character* and its *concreteness*, is flawed, which leads to the need for permanent action.

The expansion of mental space is due to the admission – in the case of the penis as a link – of the third *position*, of the third party, and therefore of a new perspective, more distanced from the self. It allows thoughts to come together, to connect, which implies a reduction in the compulsion to act out.

> *Mental space and the ability to think are created by the structure that allows* separation and linking between internal objects, between the self and the other, *rather than fusion and fragmentation. The penis as a link represents both the separation and the link of the parental relationship, and forms the backbone of good mental functioning, which is bisexual functioning. (Birksted-Breen, 1996, p. 655, my emphasis)*

Thus, the *increase in the ability to dream* would provide access to the possibility of seeing, observing oneself, from the third position. The dream would imply the presence of both parents in the subject's mind: the maternal function of containing the patient, calming him down, and, at the same time, the paternal function of enabling a certain distance and, therefore, representation of this experience. It seems to me that the importance given to triangulation in increasing symbolic capacity is clear.

Focusing on psychopathology, André Green wrote a monumental article in 1975 called "The analyst, symbolization and the framework" (1975/1994), and although I will quote it again in the next topic, I mention it here because it relates to what I am commenting on. Referring to borderline patients, he argues that the implicit model for understanding them takes us back to the contradiction formed by the separation anxiety/intrusion anxiety pair. The effect of this double anguish is not on the problem of desire, as in neuroses, but on the formation of thought. It creates a blank in thought, an inhibition of the functions of representation.

He then describes the picture of *white psychosis*, in which the impossibility of thinking is created by a defective triangulation that takes place: a bad object, always present, invading, and an object seen as good, but inaccessible or weakly accessible. The first *prevents thinking because there is no absence,* and the second because it cannot be brought into personal space, nor can it be formed as an imaginary or metaphorical presence. It is a false triangulation, since the two are actually two parts of the same object, usually the maternal object. Green calls this "*bitriangulation*", that is, a triangulation in a dual relationship. A void is created in the ability to think, concentrate, and memorize, which is replaced by false thinking, such as ruminations, compulsive thoughts, or subdelirious ideas.

I could not close this section without briefly mentioning some invaluable contributions by René Roussillon (2013). Drawing on Freud,

Didier Anzieu and Piera Aulagnier, Roussillon proposes two basic levels of symbolization, the so-called primary and secondary symbolizations. Primary symbolizations are based on sensoriality and are inscribed from the relationship with a significant object in early childhood. They are inscribed as pictograms from the first interactions with primary objects. Although Roussillon starts from Freud's idea of mnemic traces, his description goes beyond the simple mark of the experience of satisfaction itself. These initial symbolizations record the encounter with the object as yet undifferentiated from the subject, containing parts of both the subject and the object. I believe that this is very close to the affective pictogram described by Piera Aulagnier. As well as being inscribed in the psyche, these primitive symbolic forms take part in the first non-verbal communications in the subject/object interaction.

Subsequently, these primary symbolizations are taken up again in the universe of language, naming the mnemic traces and thing-representations by linking them to the corresponding word-representations. This verbal link makes it possible to contain and transform the networks of affects and thing-representations in detail, having an impact on the associative chain. An integration between body and mind is created, in which the affects of a particular narrative, for example, are also expressed in mimicry and body posture. As Roussillon explicitly says, the subject

> *speaks with the word-representations, transmits, in his gestures, his mimicry, his postures, his actions, the thing-representations and representations that move them, expresses through his entire body the affects-representatives that accompany other forms of expression. (p. 16)*

In other words, in Roussillon's reference, secondary symbolizations integrate the whole range of sensory, affective, gestural, and mimic experiences with verbal signifiers, so that the verbal narrative is crossed by all the registers of the subject's most primitive experiences.

The aesthetic conflict

I dedicate a separate item – albeit a small one – to the question of the aesthetic conflict raised by Meltzer (1988/1995; Meltzer et al., 1986/1990), due to its originality, its relevance to the theme of symbolization and its formulation of questions that we should think about, even if we disagree with him. And also because it highlights the aesthetic dimension of psychoanalysis, inaugurated by Bion and developed later in this book. Some of the hypotheses put forward, veritable imaginative conjectures, if true, would revolutionize some of the basic concepts of psychoanalysis. I will quote some of his central ideas at length so as not to lose the aesthetic, poetic beauty of his thought.

Meltzer (1988/1995) advocates, with great poetic beauty, the centrality of aesthetic conflict in human development and creative thinking:

> *The ordinary beautiful, devoted mother presents to her ordinary beautiful baby a complex object of overwhelming interest, both sensual and infra-sensual. Her outward beauty, concentrated as it must be in her nipples and in her eyes, bombards him with an emotional experience of a passionate quality, the result of his being able to see these objects as "beautiful". But the meaning of his mother's behavior, of the appearance and disappearance of the breast and of the light in her eyes of a face over which emotions pass like the shadows of clouds over the landscape, are unknown to him . . . The mother is enigmatic to him . . . Even at the moments of most satisfactory communication, nipple in mouth, she gives an ambiguous message . . . He cannot tell whether she is Beatrice or his Belle Dame Sans*

> *Merci. This is the aesthetic conflict, which can be most precisely stated in terms of the aesthetic impact of the outside of the "beautiful" mother, available to the senses, and the enigmatic inside which must be construed by creative imagination. (p. 44)*

This centrality of the aesthetic conflict and its placement as the starting point of development have revolutionary implications, both in relation to Klein and Bion: they determine that creative thought, that is, the effort to give symbolic representation to the intense primitive emotional experience triggered by the beauty and mystery of the mother and the world, is activated in the *presence* of the object, and not by its absence, as Bion and Klein say.

As for Klein, Meltzer believes that it was a mistake to believe that it is only in the suffering and dramatic loss of the object of the depressive position, situated chronologically at a later point in development, that there is a "re-creation" of the object. He affirms that it was a linear structure of possession and loss that was formulated. He believes that it is in the experience itself, based on presence/absence and the Ps ↔ D oscillation, that creative thought is stimulated. He adopts and praises Bion's contribution of the Ps ↔ D oscillation for what it implies in terms of development, by replacing the diachronic notion with the notion of synchronic experiences of disintegration/integration. He seems to differ from Bion in the importance the latter gives to the absence of the object for the development of "thoughts proper".

He hypothesizes a fundamental inversion, suspecting that the starting point of development would be the aesthetic impact of the object on an attitude of the baby compatible with the depressive position and that later, as a defense to this conflict, the baby would use paranoid-schizoid mechanisms. He says this verbatim:

> *If, in fact, for the ordinary beautiful baby with his ordinary devoted beautiful mother, this aesthetic impact is what greets his emergence into the world outside the womb, then the aesthetic conflict and the depressive position would be primary for development, and the paranoid-schizoid secondary – the consequence of his closing down his perceptual apertures against the dazzle of the sunrise. (p. 51))*

Whether or not we agree with this hypothesis, it is, in any case, a stimulus for reflection and further proof of the complexity of the dawn of the human mind. To be faithful to the legacy of the scientific thought of Freud, Klein, Bion, among others, I think we should not – in search of an illusion of security – adopt premature positions around A or B, but rather exercise the creative potential of comparing A and B in order to broaden our horizon of understanding.

Although there is a difference between Bion and Meltzer (in terms of thought being stimulated in the absence or presence of the object), there are also points in common. In both authors, if there is an excess of projective identification, symbolization is impaired. In Bion, we have already studied how excessive projective identification impairs thinking. In Meltzer, a non-intrusive projective identification is also necessary so that the interior of the object is respected as an area of intimacy and intrusion does not occur. Only then will speculative thought, imagination, be stimulated in order to construct an image of the object's unknown interior. In the case of the intrusions described in *The claustrum* (Meltzer, 1992), we have symbolic equations, and not the creative thinking suggested in the description of the aesthetic conflict, since the fantasy of massive intrusion into the object is so intense that the sensation is of living concretely inside it, even conditioning the view of the world.

Advances in the understanding of symbolization and its implications for psychoanalytic technique

The theoretical changes brought about by Klein and later by Bion had a decisive influence on advances in the understanding of symbolization and various consequences for the technique. The fact that they worked with children and regressive patients (psychotic and borderline) in search of an understanding of very primitive anxieties brought them into contact with the problem of the constitution of the psychic apparatus and overcoming initial anxieties and, in case this did not happen, with the damage caused to the mental apparatus.

This is evident in Klein as early as 1930, in the Dick case, and also in Bion, who, from his earliest work on thinking, drew parallels with psychoanalytic care. Bion put the definitive emphasis on working on the container, and not so much on the content, especially in more compromised patients who attacked their thinking apparatus and that of the analyst in order to escape psychic pain (Bion, 1957/1988, 1959a/1988). He put the emphasis on the need for the analyst to "dream" and help the patient to "dream" their emotional experiences, or rather to symbolize these experiences. And Bion (1962b/1991) already warned of the possibility of the patient attacking symbolic creation (the third party that unites the two in the setting) – interpretation – which will be widely developed by numerous authors (Ferro, 1995, 1998; Ogden, 1996; Favalli, 1998).

Green (1975/1994), dealing with the changes of focus in psychoanalytic technique throughout its history, says that,

> *since it was born out of the experience of neuroses, psychoanalysis took thoughts of desire as its starting point. Today we can say that there are thoughts of desire because there are thoughts, if we give this term a very broad meaning that includes its most rudimentary forms. (p. 65)*

He then locates three movements in the evolution of psychoanalytic theory and technique: 1) the *patient's historical reality*: conflict, unconscious, representations of desire, fixations etc.; 2) *object relations*: when the importance of object relations was discovered, the mutual actions of the subject and the object began to be described. A lot of attention was paid to what happened in the object and the subject and little to the relationship, the link, until Bion said that what matters is its nature; 3) the *patient's mental functioning and the framework*. He then comments that in some patients we must analyze the container rather than the contained. However, he focuses the question not so much on the mental apparatus, but on the analytical framework, using Bion's concepts. He comments that it became necessary to analyze, in addition to the object relations developed in the analytical pair, the framework within which this took place.

Green describes clinical situations in which the analyst feels enveloped by an unclear atmosphere, which does not take on familiar visual or verbal forms and which develops following the pattern of drive motions, increase and relief, and that only then after a while, after a lot of mental effort, he manages to give meaning to that experience. The analyst had to carry out this work of symbolization because the patient has a weak structure that does not allow this experience to acquire meaning.

In normal psychic functioning (at the neurotic level), Green says almost verbatim that there is a vectorial tendency that goes from the drive to verbalization that makes it possible to form relations of correspondence between the various functions of the mind. A series of relations are created that refer to each other. These relations are not only of opposition (censorship), "but also of collaboration, since this is the way to move from one system to another, for example, from a latent content to a manifest one" (p. 77). These internal relations of symbolization ensure psychic continuity and discontinuity. This is what allows the patient, in the analytical work, to take the analyst for what he is and for what he is not, establishing what Baranger and Baranger (1961/1969) called the essential ambiguity of the analytical setting.

"In borderline structures, it is very difficult to establish the internal relations of symbolization because the various psychic materials are treated as 'things'" (Green, 1975/1994, p. 77). Dreams take on an evacuatory character; fantasies, a void-filling character; affects, a representation function; and acts are not intended to transform reality. All psychic functioning is impregnated with the model of the act. One of the consequences, I would say, is that the transference will lose its ambiguity (Baranger & Baranger, 1961/1969) and become a "thing in itself". The framework must be able to tolerate these extreme tensions and offer itself as a potential space to help develop what is not yet present.

Ferro (1995, 1998) develops the clinical application of the Bionian model in detail, with his ideas on unsaturated interpretations, the widening of the container and countless others that show the importance of "alphabetizing", to use one of his terms, the emotional experiences lived in the analytical field.

One author I would like to focus on a little more is Thomas Ogden (1996), although he has been studied in depth by Favalli (1998) in his enlightening work on the analytic field. The truth is that several contemporary psychoanalytic authors, such as Bion, Baranger, Ferro, and Ogden, have emphasized the importance of understanding the events of the session as a result of the interaction of the two minds in question in the psychoanalytic encounter: that of the patient and that of the analyst. In other words, certain material brought by the patient would be the result of countless tensions existing in the patient's mind and between the patient's mind and that of the analyst.

In summary, according to Ogden (1996), the psychoanalytic subject is created from various dialectical tensions. Its understanding depends on the possibility of articulating optics from different theoretical systems: the Freudian subject is constituted in the synthesis of the dialectical tension between the unconscious and the conscious; the Kleinian subject, in the result of the dialectical tension between the paranoid-schizoid and depressive positions (disintegration/integration) and the introjection/projective identification oscillation; and the Winnicottian subject, in the tension between existing and not existing, the I and the you, the subject and the object. What I like about Ogden is that he grasps all the complexity and richness of current psychoanalysis. He highlights the synchronic vision presupposed in Kleinian, Bionian, and Winnicottian theories, i.e. that the infantile and the adult, the psychotic and the neurotic, the primary and the secondary process, integration and disintegration persist in the mind simultaneously, in a permanent oscillation and constant conflict.

The subject is organized around the two axes, the synchronic and the diachronic. The importance of this vision for the theme of symbolization is that the here and now of the analytical session will come to be understood in a much more plastic and dynamic way. The analytic encounter will be understood as the meeting of two subjectivities that generate a third, intersubjective one, in the potential space *between* the patient and the analyst, that is, it is "the third area of experience that lies between I and non-I, between reality and fantasy . . . *It is in the space created between* these poles that symbols are created and imaginative activity takes place" (p. 50).

The first moment of the analytic encounter is marked by cross-projective identifications, confusion between I and not-I and the predominance of Ps. Experiences are lived concretely and often the only way to deal with them is by acting them out. Interpretation will come to be understood as a symbolic transformation, based mainly on the analyst's capacity for *rêverie,* but also on the patient's, of the intersubjective emotional experience created and lived in the space between the two. The possibility of representing it symbolically and, therefore, thinking of it allows for the reappropriation of individualities and the discrimination of self/non-self (Baranger & Baranger, 1961/1969; Ogden, 1996).

Interpretation understood in this way, as a symbol created between analyst and patient, fulfills the requirements studied so far to define what a true symbol is: it unites and at the same time distinguishes between analyst and patient; it enriches them both, since it adds meaning to them; it is created in the heat of the emotional experience lived between them and represents it; and, last but not least, it is structuring in the sense that it provokes a catastrophic reaction, forcing a re-accommodation of all previous knowledge. It is the third party that arises from the fertile relationship established between analyst and patient. Of course, once it has been formulated, we will have to see what the patient will do with this third party; whether it will be housed in a container where the L-link predominates, leading to the birth of yet another new idea and so on and so forth; or if it is enviously or destructively deprived of meaning, attacked, leading to emptying.

In patients with an impaired symbolic capacity, the first goal of the treatment will be for the analyst to "dream up" the raw experiences brought into the field, to "alphabetize" them, to give them a meaning, a symbolic representation, which will allow this function to develop in the patient. In patients whose symbolic capacity is preserved, or relatively preserved, the analytic experience will develop it even more, since it is in the essence of this experience to symbolically transform the emotions experienced.

References

Baranger, W., & Baranger, M. (1969). La situación analítica como campo dinámico. In *Problemas del campo psicoanalítico*. Kargieman. (Originally published in 1961)

Bick, E. (1991). A experiência da pele em relações de objeto arcaicas. In E. B. Spillius (Ed.), *Melanie Klein hoje: desenvolvimentos da teoria e da técnica* (Vol. 1). Imago. (Originally published in 1967)

Bion, W. R. (1988). Diferenciação entre a personalidade psicótica e não-psicótica. In *Estudos psicanalíticos revisados*. Imago. (Originally published in 1957)

Bion, W. R. (1988). Ataques ao elo de ligação. In *Estudos psicanalíticos revisados*. Imago. (Originally published in 1959a)

Bion, W. R. (1994). Scientific method. In *Cogitations*. Karnac. (Originally published in 1959b)

Bion, W. R. (1994). Dream-work-α. In *Cogitations*. Karnac. (Originally published in 1959c)

Bion, W. R. (1988). Uma teoria sobre o processo de pensar. In *Estudos psicanalíticos revisados*. Imago. (Originally published in 1962a)

Bion, W. R. (1991). *Aprendiendo de la experiencia*. Paidós. (Originally published in 1962b)

Birksted-Breen, D. (1996). Phallus, penis, and mental space. *International Journal of Psychoanalysis*, *77*(pt. 4), 649-657.

Britton, R. (1992). O elo perdido: a sexualidade parental no complexo de Édipo. In J. Steiner (Org.), *O complexo de Édipo hoje: implicações clínicas*. Artes Médicas. (Originally published in 1989)

Caper, R. (2002). Sobre a função alfa. In *Tendo mente própria: uma visão kleiniana do self e do objeto*. Imago. (Originally published in 1996)

Favalli, P. H. (1998). *O campo psicanalítico (considerações sobre a evolução do conceito)*. Dissertation for full membership of the Porto Alegre Psychoanalytic Society.

Ferenczi, S. (1992). O desenvolvimento do sentido de realidade e seus estágios. In: *Obras completas* (Vol. 2). Martins Fontes. (Originally published in 1913)

Ferro, A. (1995). *A técnica na psicanálise infantil – A criança e o analista: da relação ao campo emocional*. Imago.

Ferro, A. (1998). *Na sala de análise: emoções, relatos, transformações*. Imago.

Freud, S. (1969). Formulações sobre os dois princípios do funcionamento mental. In *Edição standard brasileira das obras psicológicas completas de Sigmund Freud* (Vol. XII). Imago. (Originally published in 1911)

Freud, S. (1969). Além do princípio do prazer. In *Edição standard brasileira das obras psicológicas completas de Sigmund Freud* (Vol. XVIII). Imago. (Originally published in 1920)

Gaburri, E., & Ferro, A. (1988). Gli sviluppi kleiniani e Bion. In A. A. Semi (Org.), *Trattato di psicanalisi*. Rafaelo Cortina.

Green, A. (1994). El analista, la simbolización, y la ausencia en el encuadre analítico. In *De locuras privadas*. Amorrortu. (Originally published in 1975)

Grinberg, L., Bianchedi, E. T., & Sor, D. (1991). *Nueva introducción a las ideas de Bion*. Tecnipublicaciones.

Klein, M. (1981). A importância da formação de símbolos no desenvolvimento do ego. In *Contribuições à psicanálise*. Mestre Jou. (Originally published in 1930)

Meltzer, D. (1979). *Os estados sexuais da mente*. Imago. (Originally published in 1973)

Meltzer, D. (1984). *Vida onírica: una revisión de la teoría y de la técnica psicoanalítica*. Tecnipublicaciones.

Meltzer, D. (1992). *The claustrum: an investigation of clautrophobic phenomena*. Clunie Press.

Meltzer, D. (1995). *A apreensão do belo*. Imago. (Originally published in 1988)

Meltzer, D. et al. (1979). *Exploraciones del autismo: un estudio psicoanalítico.* Paydos. (Originally published in 1975)

Meltzer, D. et al. (1990). *Metapsicología ampliada: aplicaciones clínicas de las ideas de Bion.* Spatia. (Originally published in 1986)

Ogden, T. (1996). *Os sujeitos da psicanálise.* Casa do Psicólogo.

Rezende, A. M. (1998). A relação sujeito-objeto no contexto do sétimo elemento de psicanálise: narcisismo-socialismo. *Revista Brasileira de Psicanálise,* 32(4), 781-794.

Roussillon, R. (2013). Las simbolizaciones primarias y secundarias. *Revista de Psicoanálisis de la Asociación Psicoanalítica de Madrid,* 69, 219-241.

Segal, H. (1982). Notas a respeito da formação de símbolos. In *A obra de Hanna Segal: uma abordagem kleiniana à prática clínica.* Imago. (Originally published in 1957)

Segal, H. (1993). Simbolismo. In *Sonho, fantasia e arte.* Imago. (Originally published in 1991a)

Segal, H. (1993). Espaço mental e elementos do simbolismo. In *Sonho, fantasia e arte.* Imago. (Originally published in 1991b)

Winnicott, D. W. (1975). Objetos transicionais e fenômenos transicionais. In *O brincar e a realidade.* Imago. (Originally published in 1951)

Winnicott, D. W. (1975). *O brincar e a realidade.* Imago. (Originally published in 1971)

Winnicott, D. W. (1979). La integración del ego en el desarrollo del niño. In *El proceso de maduración en el niño: estudios para una teoría del desarrollo emocional.* Laia. (Originally published in 1962)

Part II
Non-symbolizations and transformations in intimacy

6. Non-symbolizations: a metapsychological mapping of anti-symbols and "de-symbolizations"[1]

There have been significant changes in the way psychoanalysis has approached the question of the symbolic throughout its history. Firstly, there is a predominant concern with the study of symbolism; secondly, with symbolization, as I hope I have made clear in the previous chapters; and finally, with the losses in symbolic processes that end up creating situations of non-symbolization.

Contemporary psychoanalysis has been particularly concerned with studying limit situations in which symbolic processes have been damaged. André Green (2010) published a book, *The Work of the Negative*, in which he sets out to study the various forms of the negative, reviewing the contributions of psychoanalysis from this perspective. He studies everything from the best-known forms of the negative in psychoanalysis, repression itself, and the formation of the unconscious, to the less-studied forms, whether it is what cannot be symbolized or what has been symbolized but has been destroyed.

1 This chapter is based on and largely reproduces my article entitled: "From symbolizing to non-symbolizing within the scope of a link: from dreams to shouts of terror caused by an absent presence". *International Journal of Psychoanalysis*, 93(4), 837- 862, 2012.

In this chapter, I will focus on this form of negative: what could be called *de-symbolization* or *de-representation*. That which remains in the fourth sense of the negative described by Green (2010), that of *nothingness*. That which cannot exist in the mind, either as unrepresentable or de-represented. Something that does not appear in the mental in the form of symbolic material produced by the processes of transformation into alpha (Bion, 1962/1991). This negativity in the mental sphere is usually "positivized" in the territory of the body, conduct, or hallucination (Bion, 1962/1988, 1962/1991, 1965/2004).

I agree with Botella and Botella (2002) when they state that classical psychoanalysis has dedicated itself to the study of representations and their topography and that contemporary psychoanalysis has also studied non-representations and the unrepresentable, the negative in terms of representations. These experiences that remain in their negativity on the mental plane generate not only an impossibility of symbolization but also an impossibility of being "forgotten" (Alvarez, 1994), creating an apparent paradox. They remain present, in their raw state, creating a presentification of raw emotion that cannot be inserted into the unconscious mesch and worked through.

In this work, I will initially focus on the contributions of contemporary authors who have been more interested in the process of symbol production, symbolization, reaching its peak with the contributions of Bion (1957/1988, 1959/1988, 1959/1994, 1962/1988, 1962/1991, 1963/1988, 1965/2004). He studied the entire process of symbolic creation, from its first instants to the functioning of the thinking apparatus. Bion's greatest contribution was to place this whole process of symbolic creation taking place – and only being able to take place – in the warmth of a link. This gave rise to an important transformation in the concept of the analytical relationship and gave substance to the concept of the analytical field (Baranger & Baranger, 1961/1969; Ferro, 1995, 1998, 2007) and that of intersubjectivity (Ogden, 1996). I then intend to dwell a little more on the study of Bionian contributions that focus on the processes of non-symbolization, also studied by French authors (Green, 1975/1994, 1990, 1994, 2002/2008, 2010; Botella & Botella, 2002).

Within the multiplicity of situations in which symbolic processes may be impaired, in this work I also propose to detail some forms of the negative grid and link them to the clinic, especially a Bionian contribution, the negative of the symbol, the minus symbol. Insofar as the symbol, from a Bionian point of view (1965/2004), is the non-thing, because it represents the absence of the object, Bion conceptualizes that the destruction of the symbol creates the minus non-thing (–non-thing), which characterizes an absent presence.

Before I go any further, I would like to make a brief clarification. Because my theoretical inspiration is more closely linked to the Kleinian, post-Kleinian, and Bionian schools, I will predominantly use the concept of symbol, although at times I will use the term representation, but referring to the complex mental process of generating a new element, as described by Meltzer et al. (1995). This is because I will often use references from the French school, which commonly uses the concept of representation.

Thinking and links

Bion (1962/1991) is categorical in stating that an emotional experience cannot occur in isolation from a relationship. He masterfully describes the primitive relationship that exists between the baby and its mother, highlighting the primitive communication between the two. The mother, through her containment capacity and her *rêverie*, will receive her baby's emotional states, and her alpha function will allow her to transform these emotions into a meaningful utterance or gesture. In other words, through projective identification, the baby communicates a raw emotion to the mother and usually receives something transformed and meaningful back.

This shared activity is introjected by the baby, "in such a way that the container/contained apparatus is installed in the infant as part of the alpha function apparatus" (p. 123). In this way, the introjection of an object with a containment capacity and an alpha function will enable the subject to get in touch with his emotional life and transform it into alpha elements, thus expanding his mind. The development of the container occurs through the formation of a reticulum, in which the gaps are like vacuoles to be filled by thoughts and the threads that make up the mesh are emotion. The growing container/contained set provides the basis for an apparatus for learning from experience. Thus, from thoughts and the development of thoughts, comes the apparatus for thinking them. Learning depends on this apparatus being both integrated and flexible. This creates a mental state in which the individual can retain his knowledge and experiences and at the same time be prepared to reconstruct past experiences in the light of a new one.

Negativity in thinking: non-symbolizations

If symbol formation is the representation of the "truth" of emotional experience, we must study what happens when this "truth" needs to be distorted, attacked or destroyed by the psychic pain it causes or the unbearable meaning it carries. Here, we will have different psychopathological fates if the emotional experience is represented and repressed; represented and distorted; if there is no possibility of symbolization; or if there has been symbolization and its symbol has been destroyed. Evidently, when we enter the terrain of emotional experiences that could not be adequately symbolized, or those whose symbolization has been destroyed, we are in the terrain of trauma, which I will deal with later.

Meltzer makes important incursions into the territory of lies, concerned with understanding what he calls anti-symbols. He then describes his concept of *lies*:

> *The credibility of a lie depends not on its quantitative relation to the truth but on its structural or functional congruence, like symbols. That is, a lie must misrepresent the truth by employing* pseudo-symbols. *(Meltzer et al., 1986/1990, p. 86, my emphasis)*

Meltzer endeavored to follow the trail left by Bion, trying to develop the study of the negative grid, which is yet to be carried out more consistently in the future of psychoanalysis. This grid would encompass the destruction of meaning through the formation of lies or the cannibalization of alpha elements. He adds that we cannot consider that dreams always tell the truth: "The truth they tell is the treatment that emotional experiences receive in the depths of the mind; but truth is not always treasured here, for it is freighted with mental pain" (Meltzer, 1984, p. 101).

He also emphasizes the importance of delimiting which part of the personality is in charge of "directing" the dream and whether this part is interested in producing a truth, however painful, or a lie as a way of relieving psychic pain. In other words, here Meltzer refers to a part of the mind that actually forms "anti-symbols", that is, symbols with the opposite function to that which symbols have in the part of the personality that tolerates the pain of emotional truth. These would be abstract formations that aim to mask the truth, to generate lies in order to avoid contact with certain emotions that are unbearable to the subject, not only because of their intensity, but mainly because of their meaning.

I remember the dream of a narcissistic patient who was constantly attacking his and my analytical function of the personality to make contact with the psychic world. One day he dreamt the following:

> *I was at a party and heard a group of people talking about me. I'd come up to them and hear them saying that I couldn't be trusted, that I was like a sea full of reefs in*

> *which a boat was sailing peacefully and, when it least expected it, it would crash into the reefs and sink. I thought I had to warn you and ran away from the party. I ran and ran to get to your house, but you lived on a steep street and I was losing my strength. In the end I almost crawled, lost my strength and fainted.*

Well, here the dream was "directed" by the part of the personality committed to the truth to denounce the "lying", unreliable part of the self. But at the same time, it clarifies how much this function committed to the truth loses strength before it finds me.

In Meltzer's conception of the formation of lies, it is as if the alpha function formed the symbol, which, because it generates a considerable amount of psychic pain, would need to be covered with a cloak of lies. It is important to note that, in this situation, the symbol is created and not destroyed, but "only" covered with a "cloak of lies". Meltzer says: "the true symbol is not destroyed, but covered over, leaving the hope that it can once again shine through this covering and thus illuminate the mind from its penumbra" (Meltzer et al., 1986/1990, p. 116). Here we are still describing not the process of the symbol's destruction, but its falsification, the creation of the cloak of lies. We also need to understand what happens when the symbol is not formed or when it is destroyed.

Non-symbolization, attack on the alpha function and destruction of the symbol

In describing –K, a link constituted by not understanding (*misunderstanding*), Bion also moves through the territory of the negative. He considers envy to be one of the factors that lead to –K; it is the emotion that unites container and contained. Considering envy as the expression of the death drive, that which disconnects, it is understood that it does not lead to the creative production of something. In –K, the baby feels that the breast strips it of what is good and forces a worthless residue inside it. "The baby who started out afraid of dying ends up containing a nameless terror" (Bion, 1962/1991, p. 128). The negative container/contained relationship "presents itself as a superior object that asserts its superiority by showing flaws in everything" (p. 130). There is a hatred of any new development, as if it were a rival to be destroyed. The search for truth is met with destructive attacks. The contained are included in a container that strips them of value and deprives them of meaning. This envious divestment contrasts with the process of abstraction inherent in K's container/contained relationship. There is an inversion: –container/contained converts alpha elements into beta. In other words, the abstract is converted into things-in-themselves, unlike +container/contained. –K leads to a permanent "unlearning" (O'Shaughnessy, 1981/1990).

Delving deeper into the theme of attacks on the ability to represent experience, Bion goes on to describe situations in which what happens is not the production of the alpha element and its falsification, but the desperate destruction of the alpha function itself. In Chapter 5 of *Learning from experience*, Bion (1962/1991) describes a situation in which the baby, for fear of becoming aware of its jealous aggression, refuses to drink the milk offered by the breast. The baby, however, realizes that it will die this way. According to Bion, the baby, out of fear of death, resumes sucking as a result of a profound dissociation in its mind. It starts drinking milk so as not to die, but this experience of material satisfaction is dissociated from psychic satisfaction. "Envy, provoked by a breast that offers love, understanding, experience and knowledge, poses a problem that is solved by destroying the alpha function!" (p. 30).

Bion continues:

> *This split, enforced by starvation and fear of death through starvation on the one hand, and by love and the fear of associated murderous envy and hate on the other produces a state in which the patient greedily pursues every form of material comfort; he is at once insatiable and implacable in his pursuit of satiation. Since this state originates in a need to be rid of the emotional complications of awareness of life, and a relationship with live objects, the patient appears to be incapable of gratitude or concern either for himself or others... His pursuit of a cure takes the form of a search for a lost object. (p. 30-31)*

What Bion is describing is of the utmost relevance. He describes a situation in which because of envy, hatred, and fear of aggression, there is an attack on the alpha function. Once the symbolizing function is attacked, the subject is not aware of his envy and unbearable hatred, but neither can he enjoy the experience of satisfaction. The emotional experience of satisfaction cannot be transformed into alpha elements, oneiric thoughts, and then be felt and understood by gaining meaning from its mentalization, its insertion into the alpha reticulum. In *Cogitations*, Bion (1992/1994) returns to the subject by saying that, when there is a deficiency of alpha function, the patient may even be conscious, but cannot *become* conscious of certain emotional experiences, because he cannot *digest them*. These experiences remain as *undigested facts*, and only lend themselves to evacuation through the beta screen.

Despite material satiety, the patient remains mentally insatiable. There is an impossibility of feeling an experience of psychic satisfaction and the dissatisfaction, the hatred, become things in themselves, beta elements that only render themselves fit to be evacuated.

Bion's contribution seems essential to me, because he does not see the unrepresented or the unrepresentable as an "accident" in the weave of representations, a one-off experience that becomes unrepresentable and therefore traumatic. The attack on the alpha function creates chronic insufficiencies of mentalization, potentially generating "successive traumas."

This is a relevant contribution to the psychoanalytic technique. The patient who "cannot understand" may not simply be resisting, but resisting in a particular way (Bion, 1992/1994). Therein lies an essential difference between the typical neurotic's resistance, in which what is resisted is relegated to the unconscious, and the destruction of understandable meaning or the very capacity to produce meaning. Unless this is understood, this particular type of "resistance" can never be analyzed.

I would point out that in this type of "resistance" that brings, for example, an impossibility of enjoying and feeling satisfied with the results of the analysis – and of life's achievements – it is crucial to distinguish that what is being attacked is not the analyst, but a mental function of the patient. It is his symbolic function that is being compromised in that circumstance. Once the alpha function is attacked, those life experiences become dementalized (Meltzer et al., 1986/1990) in the protomental system, and one of the consequences is a life limited to an operative, almost machine-like, robotic functioning, with the subject unable to grasp and enjoy the emotional meaning of his experience. I would like to emphasize the enormous difference that this understanding entails in terms of classical psychoanalytic technique, in which many of these situations were understood and interpreted as an attack on the analysis and the analyst. Being able to understand them as an attack on the symbolic function represents a change of perspective with enormous clinical consequences.

There is yet another type of destruction in the field of symbolization that I would like to mention: that not of the symbolic function (alpha function), but of the symbol itself. In *Transformations*, Bion (1965/2004), in my opinion, makes a major contribution to the study of negativity in symbolization. In Chapter 7, he describes that the symbol marks the non-thing. In other words, where the symbol is, there was the thing, in a certain space and time. The symbol involves this spatial and temporal dimension, of past/present/future. It refers to something that has been somewhere, at some time, and could be there again at some point in the future. So, Bion imagines and postulates the –symbol, –contained, or –point in the nomenclature he proposes in *Transformations*. This means that this symbol has had its meaning destroyed for some reason, probably because it carries an unbearable meaning, a pain that cannot be felt.

Yet *this empty object that is created, devoid of meaning, will be eager to exist* (Bion, 1965/2004). This means that it will press to have some meaning attributed to it. This is why Bion says that this "is not a static object, it is a force that persists after having been annihilated" (p. 115). Using the grid as a reference, Bion proposes the following sign for this object: ←↑. He wants to signal that it is not static, it is a force that pushes toward the destruction of the symbol. Vertically, the arrow goes from abstraction to concreteness, and horizontally it goes through the columns, towards column 2, the column of lies. Here, from my point of view, Bion describes another type of attack on symbolization: what is attacked is the symbol itself, generating a –symbol; we are faced with *de-symbolization* or a *de-representation*.

In another work (Levy, 2005), I described this zone of non-symbolization as follows:

> *The image that comes to mind is of one of us approaching a canyon whose interior is hidden by a great mist. From there comes a frightening noise, an emptiness, a sinister mystery and we start trying to make sense of it, to create images of what might be there. It is almost as if a symbolic environment were created with the appearance of unconscious infantile fantasies that surrounded the void, like a vesicle with a permanent painful, frightening, and meaningless*

> *interior, but enveloped by a symbolic film. They would be attempts to symbolize an emptiness. (Levy, 2005, p. 10)*

Nevertheless, this image seems partially valid to me, because what Bion describes here is somewhat different and with worse consequences for the mind. According to him, this emptiness, this canyon, has a suction force that draws in whatever objects that pass by. It becomes destructive because in its eagerness to exist, it steals the meaning from other experiences. So, for example, if a patient has an intense psychic pain that cannot be felt, a pain whose meaning has been destroyed, any other experience in the patient's life will be used in an attempt to give it a meaning, and it may stop meaning what it really means.

Bion (1965/2004) states that this object to which we are referring, –point, –symbol or –contained, is "violent, envious, implacable, murderous, predatory, with no respect for the truth or people" (p. 116). Using a physics phenomenon as an image, it could be said that this object is a kind of "black hole" in the mind, important not only for its negativity, but also because of its power to suck in and destroy other possible symbolizations. It will be possible to better illustrate these concepts and the centrality of the analytical relationship in resolving these situations in the clinical material that will be presented.

Before moving on, I would like to propose a metapsychology of this structure (–symbol) that is created in the mind. This structure has: a topology, it is protomental, in the sense that it is outside the mental area insofar as it is no longer an alpha element. It has a genesis, in other words, it arises from the unbearability of the emotional experience; it has a dynamic, which is characterized by the movement I already described (below/above and left/right of the grid, typical of the de-symbolizations), producing pressure in the incessant search for meaning; and it has an economy given that it presents a constant suction force that brings in all the new symbols.

Botella and Botella (2002), in their valuable studies on the unrepresentable, describe zones of non-symbolization that would be a "void, a fracture in the fabric of representations" (p. 94), originating from neurotic infantile fantasies. This fracture, the non-representation, becomes noticeable through disturbances in thought, rather than in thought content. In Botella's language, a zone of psychic pain is created that goes beyond the possibility of figurability. They describe "a zone in which the violence of affects disorganizes the psyche" (p. 94). It would be a perceptive trait with no intelligibility. The authors say that it will be up to the psycho-neurosis to, *a posteriori*, give meaning to this zone of non-representation.

Perhaps an important difference between Botella's description and Bion's reference is that the English author, rather than pointing out the "violence of affects", tells us about a symbol, a symbolic utterance that had to be destroyed because of the meaning it carried. A construction was destroyed, and what we see are the noisy ruins of a destroyed civilization. They are active "ruins" that continue to produce more destruction. This omnipresent but shapeless negativity ends up being felt by the subject as a terrifying object, precisely because it has no form, no representation. This Bionian vision seems to me to describe more vividly the consequences in the patient's subjectivity of these non-symbolizations. There are two additions to Botella's description: firstly, it is not just a failure, but a failure that, by its nature, produces more destruction in the process of symbolization; secondly, this failure is felt by the subject as a terrifying object. It is a vivid description of the patient's subjective experience.

To summarize, Bion adds two situations in which non-symbolizations will be created: when the alpha function has been destroyed and when a symbolic utterance has been created and destroyed.

Regarding technique, patient and analyst, through a process of figurability (Botella & Botella, 2002) or *rêverie* (Bion, 1962/1991, 1965/2004), should be able to take in the raw emotions inscribed in the protomental system and transform them into symbolizations or representations that can be elaborated through their insertion into the symbolic network. Botella and Botella assert that by working with the patient as a double, the analyst, in a regressive state, gets closer to the hallucinatory pole, which allows them to work on the figurability that gives form to these unrepresented affects. From my point of view, Bion (1962/1988, 1962/1991) clarifies the mental mechanism through which this primitive communication occurs, which allows these raw emotions to be captured, which is projective identification for communicative purposes. But in both contributions, the analyst's mind plays a decisive role in the possibility of symbolizing these non-symbolizations.

Bion (1965/2004), however, warns us that in situations in which meaning has been destroyed, the patient may attempt to manipulate the psychoanalyst into making interpretations not to think about them and give meaning to the void, but to deny the absence of meaning and reassure themselves against the feeling of terror. In this situation, it is as if there is some understanding, when, in fact, the enunciations are a defense against the underlying terror.

Barros (2002; Barros & Barros, 2008) makes important contributions to the growing acquisition of meaning that occurs in the extended work of symbolization and also to the eventual obstructions to the evolution of the acquisition of meaning caused by traumatic situations. For the sake of space, however, I will not be able to dwell on the analysis of these rich contributions.

Non-symbolization and trauma

A few words on the question of trauma. An experience becomes traumatic whenever it cannot be symbolized (Botella & Botella, 2002) or when its representation has been destroyed (Winnicott, 1951/1975). Therefore, a situation is traumatic whenever it elicits emotions of an intensity or quality that are beyond the subject's capacity to cope at a given moment. Another fundamental aspect of this matter is the object's central role in creating the traumatic situation and its consequences for psychoanalytic practice. This incursion into the territory of trauma seems important to me because, in the psychoanalytic clinic, we often come across patients whose various traumatic experiences have caused a huge number of emotional experiences to be inscribed in a raw state, rendering them impossible to be worked through and, therefore, present in the analytic relationship.

In Winnicott's theory (1960/1982), the baby has a desire and the good mother, in a state he calls primary maternal care, presents and offers the object of desire at the appropriate time and place. In doing so, she fulfills the baby's omnipotence and gives it meaning, making the true self come alive. It is through the mother's strength and presence that the true self comes to life. The mother who is not good is centered on her own desire, she puts her gesture in the place of the baby's gesture and the baby, in order to survive, submits itself to her desire, giving rise to the false self as a pathology of character.

From this perspective, the basis for symbolic creation lies in the mother's capacity to present the object: the baby does something, a gesture, and the object appears. This "something" is the precursor to the symbol. But if the mother is not good, the baby does that "something" and the object does not appear. When the child does "something" and the object does appear, this appearance caused by the mother gives meaning to the baby's gesture: the meaning is created in interaction. The spontaneous gesture and the personal idea come from the true self, they represent the true self in action. Only the true self can create and be felt as real. From another angle, it can be said that the subject can recognize himself as having his own desire as a function of the presence of the mother who acknowledges this desire. We will see how, in traumatic situations, there is a rupture in this dynamic, with the other not only not acknowledging the subject's desire, but also introducing a strange, violent, sudden gesture that disrupts the very process of symbolization.

Winnicott (1967/1975) adds that babies whose mothers cannot look at them look at the mother and do not see themselves. Sometimes – as in the vignette I present you next – what is seen is a terrifying object that generates emotions that cannot be worked through. In normal situations, when the baby looks at the mother, it seeks and finds the meaning that should be there.

Specifically in relation to trauma, Winnicott (1965/1967) says that it is a failure related to dependency. It is what breaks the idealization of an object by the individual's hatred, reacting to the failure of that object to perform its function. It leads to a "loss of faith" and destroys the ability to believe. He goes on to say that it is the destruction of the individual's pure experience by a sudden, excessive, or unpredictable intrusion of real facts that causes the delusional hatred of the good object.

Bion (1962/1991) states that if the mother does not accept the projective identifications, or if she accepts them and panics along with the baby, the baby will receive back not only a fear of dying, but a *nameless terror*. Instead of creating a container object in the mind, capable of alpha transformations, an object is created in the inner world that "empties" what is good in the mind, strips it of meaning, and destroys baby-thoughts. We will see the dramatic repercussions of this type of object in the clinical vignette.

Winnicott refers to the constitution of the subject and the belief in a good object for healthy development. Ogden (2005/2010) points out that the feeling of *being* is based on the mother's ability to maintain the continuity of being through holding, and when the mother fails, trauma is created. Bion, we could say, talks about the constitution of the "thinker" and that when this is not adequately constituted, trauma is established. I think that Winnicott's and Bion's contributions are essential and complementary. In my opinion, the two authors talk about fundamental elements, although they are different in terms of the subject's constitution and the establishment of trauma when there are failures in this process.

The feeling of continuity of being and the ability to think are two different processes that run in parallel, like DNA helices that make up the chromosomes that enrich one another and are the foundation of the human subject. Could we say that one precedes the other? Is the subject constituted and then the thinker/dreamer? Perhaps so, but we do not think this diachronic approach is necessary. Perhaps it would be richer to develop the ability to imagine two complex processes occurring simultaneously, which, when we apply this model to psychoanalytic practice, allows us to broaden our possibilities of understanding what is happening with the patient and with us in the session.

With his various works on the theory of generalized seduction, Laplanche (1997) enters the debate on the importance of the other in the constitution of the subject's mind. He places the role of the other, the *foreigner*, at the center of the dynamics of the mind, starting with the foreigner inside the mind, that which is strange, mysterious and needs to be deciphered, which is the unconscious. For Laplanche, this is the psychic other. But this foreigner inside the subject would be placed there by another external foreigner. So, for Laplanche, the other, in his *foreignness*, sends enigmatic messages, both verbal and non-verbal, to the subject, which he, as a baby, has to learn to sort out and "translate" in order to assimilate into his own system. It is as if the adult is sending a signal to the child from his or her own unconscious that needs to be deciphered and translated. It is as if the adult were sending the child a signal from his own unconscious that needs to be deciphered and translated.

This intervention by the adult "other", with his sexual unconscious, is universal and goes beyond a specific circumstance. This is why the author constructed the theory of generalized seduction.

What is interesting for the discussion of the theme I propose to study in this work is that, in the encounter between the adult and the child, two universes collide: that of the real parents, with their own experiences, and that of the child. The child's universe is constructed by filling in, interpreting, and symbolizing what is shown, done, and offered to it. The child's fantasy will be built not on the other person's reality, nor even just on how it sees the other person; rather, it will be built especially on *the other person addressing the child*: "What does he want from me?"; "Why is he showing me this?"; "What is his intention in doing this?". I think that some traumatic situations are created because some of these signs, due to their violence, their intrusiveness, the helplessness they generate, become untranslatable and remain somewhere in the mind as foreign bodies, producing the most varied disturbances, as we shall see.

The issue of symbolization is at the heart of the problem of trauma. In fact, the issue of the impossibility of representing some experiences of helplessness that threaten the self with annihilation. In other words, we are beyond desire and fantasy; we are on the terrain of helplessness, of the threat of annihilation of the self. It is only secondarily that the ego tries to make sense of the sudden experience of danger and threat. These experiences become registered at a protomental level, in a raw state, incapable of transformation or working-through due to their inability to be articulated as psychic contents. Ultimately, they only serve to be evacuated: either in the somatic, or by acting outs, or in the real in the form of hallucinations.

Person and Klar (1994), from a different perspective although with some similar points of view, also believe that the marks left by forbidden unconscious fantasies and traumatic realities can be distinguished. They consider that unconscious fantasy and trauma are present in the mind in different registers. Fantasy descriptively exists in three registers: the conscious, the pre-conscious, and the unconscious; the codification of trauma, according to the authors, seems to be more complex. They comment that some memories of the traumatic situation can be repressed in the form of fear, guilt, shame, or humiliation, while other registers can be dissociated, in a vertical division, while repression operates in a horizontal division.

According to these authors, the vertical division of dissociation means that the dissociated material does not come into contact with other contents of the mind. It is as if there were an automatic "walling off" of the traumatic registers not only from the conscious mind, but also from the unconscious mental contents. This keeps whatever is stored unable to be articulated, "knitted" (Alvarez, 1994), elaborated together with the other unconscious phantasies.

Non-symbolizations in the analytical relationship

In the analysis room, Monica, like so many other occasions, would vociferously rant against the analyst in order to keep him at a distance. She was aggressive, oppositional, irritable, moody, at times depressed and at others desperate. Affects flowed freely in the session: she would turn her face away, look sullen, accuse, with her arms and legs crossed on the couch, "I'm not talking, it's no use!". My *rêverie* formed countless images in my mind. At first, a rather prosaic one, that of a very small, oppositional girl who refused to pee in the potty: she would not give me her *poo at all*! I kept asking myself if I was not "forcing" interpretations on the patient. I think sometimes I was. And when this happened, I would tell her that I thought she was pointing out that I had said too much and things that perhaps she did not want to hear or could not hear yet.

Monica was "sure" that the analysis would not work. At first, I attributed her resistance to previous failed treatments. Later, I realized that it was the result of a deep disbelief in her objects and the "certainty" that she would be betrayed, deceived. Her resistance stemmed from the almost delirious "certainty" that any object that approached her would not be able to resist being drawn into this "black hole" that transformed all of her life experiences into the same painful experience.

The fact is that we experienced intense, raw affects in the analytical field, which were dumped there, evacuated, waiting for a better symbolization.

The conflict between K and –K manifested itself almost constantly in Monica. A neurotic part of her personality symbolized the emotional experiences overflowing from the analytical field and another part destroyed this knowledge by referring to unthinkable situations. I will try to illustrate what I am talking about with two dreams.

When we started collecting the aforementioned infantile transference, she brought the following dream:

> *In the dream I was a little girl, in the house I used to live growing up. I was in the living room and through the windows there were flashes of light. I was curious to see what was outside the window, I would peek in and a very beautiful cathedral would appear. I approached the window, amazed, wanting to see that beautiful cathedral. But suddenly a cloud came towards the window and it was the image of a witch who wanted to come into my house. I got terrified and woke up.*

As well as symbolizing the image of a girl that we talked about in the sessions, it also symbolized her aesthetic conflict during the transference: when she saw me as an object that attracted her curiosity and seemed beautiful to her (Meltzer, 1988/1995) – in the sense of being attractive and arousing intense sensations and emotions – she was horrified because she felt that I was an invasive, uncontrollable, and frightening object. Perhaps that is why she needed to "take apart" everything I offered her in terms of understanding, as the following dream shows: "I had won a music box. But instead of opening it and listening to the music, I took it apart. Then I tried to put it back together and I couldn't."

We understood – and this last dream is a model that has been very helpful to us – Monica's active and present mental activity, in which, instead of using what I tell her to "listen, appreciate and think", she dismantles the mechanism into small pieces that are no longer useful for listening/thinking. As Bion (1959/1988) expressed, that-which-binds is attacked and turned into meaningless pieces. She did this not because of any particular destructiveness, but because of the horror she experienced, either when she approached me as an aesthetic object (Meltzer, 1988/1995), or because of the closeness to her internal world caused by the interpretation.

Here we can observe an aspect of what was mentioned earlier in terms of the pathology of symbolization: the reversal of the alpha function halfway through. The process of symbolic transformation of the emotional experience lived in the link begins, the representation is created ("the little music box she gets from the analyst"), but as this arouses unbearable feelings (the horror of the "certainty" that I will prove to be intrusive, uncontrollable and volatile like a cloud), the symbolization needs to be destroyed. To the point where, as will be seen later, it generates a mental void.

When she met me, Monica experienced intense emotions that she was able to transform partly, thanks to the poetic power of her unconsciousness, into beautiful images like those in her dreams, but the rest was discharged in action, by fighting with me, missing sessions etc. The dazzling cathedral and the terrifying witch are aesthetic elements, symbolic creations that aim to deal with the mystery of the intangible, the "traumatic" that comes from contact with the "other". The "other", the foreigner, whether internal (the id) or external (the object), permanently challenges the subject to construct images to give meaning to the mystery of the intangible. "What does he want from me?", Laplanche would say.

The unconscious has this poetic power to transform human emotions into visual or linguistic images. Artists have the creative talent to produce images that capture universal human emotions and generously make them available to the public so that they can be used to create powerful experiences. For this to happen, the ordinary person and the artist need to be able to tolerate the mystery, the not knowing, and creatively explore it in its various versions and vertices, through creative imagination.

Her analysis progressed, marked by the dramas she experienced in the analytical relation and her desperate attempts to relieve them by evacuating her psychic pain. Working-through was truncated by the destruction of the symbolizations most laden with unthinkable meaning for the patient at the time.

In the course of analysis with this type of patient, we see that the representations we have created, which account for their emotions and contain them, are repeatedly destroyed. Emotions that have acquired meaning through the process of symbolization conducted in analysis become proto-emotions again, returning to the state of a shapeless pain that needs to be evacuated. These symbolizations are the container of emotions, but the point is that they put the patient in unbearable contact with them. So the patient destroys them. What remains is a contained (proto-emotions) with no meaning and no container.

I think this is the possible evolution in patients of this type, who gradually build up symbolizations that express and contain their emotions, which they then need to destroy for not being able to bear this contact. I propose that these destructions of representations reproduce the primary object failure to contain unthinkable thoughts, due to their significance and the psychic suffering they arouse. Moreover, they cannot stand contact because they have to acknowledge – paradoxical as it may seem – the existence of the good object. They hate to see that the analyst has become a good object, capable of containing and creative in the sense that they are creating containing representations together with him and that they are depending on him to live better. Because, for them, depending on a good object is like depending on an "artificial ventilation", as a patient once told me. In other words, without it, the agony returns. So they hate the "ventilation".

We often succeed in this process, as Monica's dream illustrates:

> *I dreamt that I had fallen asleep during session and you were patiently sitting behind me, waiting for me to wake up. It was very curious because when I woke up the feeling was very good, it felt like you had been protecting me.*

I felt deeply moved, touched, and with a feeling of profound happiness. She was finally "waking up" from the "sleep" that prevented her from "seeing me" as someone who took care of her! She could finally perceive me as a good, caring object, without attacking her perception, her thoughts, and her thinking apparatus, after seven years of analysis. That voracious, implacable object (←↑Bion, 1965/2004), which I will detail later, had been vanquished, at least at that moment.

So, what is not symbolized in these patients, or is weakly symbolized, appears in its raw state, as beta elements that can only be evacuated. These are primitive, deeply painful emotions that need to be evacuated before they can even be felt through the acquisition of meaning, precisely because these meanings are unbearable. Perhaps experiences of abandonment, threat, helplessness and distrust. They lead to hatred of the object because they feel it is responsible for their suffering. Hatred, moreover, which often saturates the sessions and serves to give "meaning" to their shapeless emotions. These proto-emotions, since they are not symbolized, cannot be repressed, much less worked through. They cannot be understood as something from the past, nor can they be forgotten. They are present and suffocate the patient and his/her objects.

Some life situations become traumatic because of the intensity of the emotions involved and because they imply an intense threat to the integrity of the self. They contain a gesture from the object that is felt by the patient to be violent and unpredictable and goes beyond the individual's capacity for symbolization at the time. Sometimes, these experiences may even have been symbolized, but because there is no mind capable of containing them, of bearing them, because of their meaning, the symbol that represents them can be destroyed, creating a situation of –symbol (minus symbol). This creates an impossibility of inserting the emotional experience into the alpha reticulum, into the chain of symbolizations, and this makes the experience impossible to work through and constitutes a traumatic situation. If it were symbolized, we would be in the field of the usual neurotic fantasies.

I would like to highlight the quantitative and economic, as well as the qualitative, aspects involved. From the economic point of view, it is the intensity of the aroused excitations and their impossibility of being linked to representations that are traumatic. From the qualitative point of view, the quality of a given experience, due to its unpredictability, violence, and threat to the self, cannot be symbolized, and remains something meaningless, untranslatable.

As I mentioned earlier, I propose using Bion's (1965/2004) concept of –symbol (minus symbol), described in *Transformations*, for the symbol that has had its meaning destroyed because it is unbearable. An empty object is created, without meaning, which will be eager for existence. Bion proposes the following sign for this object: ←↑.

In Monica, the violence, the implacable, destructive character and disrespect for the truth or for people – referred to by Bion – of this non-symbolization appears, among other situations, in the patient's "certainties". Arrogantly, at the beginning and for much of the analysis, she "knew" that the analysis would fail, that I only had an economic interest in her, that her life would not change, that she was doomed to suffer. In other words, her raw emotions, which could evolve into despair, helplessness, fear, still formless, were chronically present in her life and in the analytical situation. In their eagerness to acquire a meaning, they "stole" the meaning of the other emotional experiences in her life: everything became the same thing. This object ←↑ is a source of pain, of terror, for it is a presence without meaning. Like a ghost, it is a terrifying, shapeless presence. A haunting that makes noises but has no shape cannot be seen and therefore cannot acquire any meaning. It is a negative presence. A minus presence (–presence). The negative of a presence that yearns to acquire meaning, even at the cost of destroying that of other experiences. From this came her certainty that nothing would work out in her life; all her objects would be frustrating, violent, and intrusive, names that his emotions were given throughout her analysis. I was unreliable; analysis would inevitably lead to another disappointment; she was doomed to failure etc. The "certainty" is already the presence of the voracious, superegoic, omnipotent object.

As Winnicott (1951/1975) states (which Green [1994] extensively studied), the negative is the only presence and is more real than the positive. Thus, everything is engulfed by the negative. In this famous work, Winnicott describes the case of a patient in which the separation from her parents in the war overwhelmed her capacity to wait and, therefore, he assumes that representation had been lost. Although Winnicott's clinical description is brilliant, it appears that he does not go into the microscopic description of this phenomenon of de-representation, as Bion does in his aforementioned works. It seems to me that Bion's magnifying glass is more powerful in describing the intimacy of the processes for generating and destroying thoughts. As I have mentioned earlier, I believe that, based on Bion's contributions, we can achieve a metapsychology of the processes of non-symbolization.

Final comments

In this chapter, I especially wanted to study the pathologies of symbolization. I focused on understanding these psychic structures that are not symbolized but are profoundly influential on the subject's mental state, and which we can call non-symbolizations.

If we understand topography as a detailed description of a location, it appears that since Freud there have been major changes in the understanding and conceptualization of the topography of the psychic apparatus. One was based on the study of the impossibility of symbolizing some experiences, which generate zones of non-symbolization in the psychic apparatus (Levy, 2003). In the subject's own psychic space, a zone was conceived that goes beyond what would be considered the mental proper, the protomental (Bion, 1962/1988, 1965/2004; Meltzer et al., 1986/1990).

Considering this expansion of the topography of psychic space, these structures, the non-symbolizations, seem to be situated on the border of the mind as protomental elements. These non-symbolic registers are elements endowed with great energy, pressing to be evacuated through action or through the somatic pathways, or by disturbing the creation of other representations. Their tremendous energy and dynamic quality of functioning as the equivalent of drives, in the sense of permanently imposing work on the mind, derive from the fact that they are not included into the chain of symbolizations and they are not worked through, nor can they be worked through without analytical work.

To summarize, perhaps we can say that it is possible to extend the negative grid in at least three situations.

1. The creation of anti-symbols through the activity of –K aims to mask the truth because of the psychic suffering it causes and the meaning it carries. They cover the symbol with a cloak of lies (Meltzer, 1988/1995). The symbol in this situation is not destroyed.

2. The attack on the symbol by the destruction of the meaning (–contained) creates in the mind not only a void in the symbolic web, as has been described, but an object (←↑; Bion, 1965/2004) that presents itself as a terrifying force in the mind, constantly and powerfully destroying the meaning of other symbols.
3. The attack on the alpha function creates a whole inability for the patient to be aware of his emotional life, condemning him to live an operative life devoid of satisfaction (Bion, 1962/1991).

Initially, Freud helped us to see the importance and strength of psychic reality organized from the unconscious, structured by symbolic processes. Psychoanalysis has evolved in an attempt to understand how these sparkling diamonds (Meltzer, 1988/1995), full of emotions and meanings, which are human symbolizations, are produced. Finally, psychoanalysis has also looked at situations in which patients have symbolic failures arising from attacks on their symbolic capacity, or because they have experienced situations that exceeded their capacity to symbolize them at the time. They present such specific issues in terms of disturbances in the system of representations that will require an appropriate technique. Among other things, these are patients who are so sensitized that sometimes the analyst must be able to contain the patient's undesirable emotions for a long time before they can be reintroduced by the patient through interpretations (Alvarez, 1994; Ferro, 1995, 1998; Ogden, 1996, 2005/2010).

References

Alvarez, A. (1994). Abuso sexual de crianças: a necessidade de lembrar e a necessidade de esquecer. In *Companhia viva: psicoterapia psicanalítica com crianças autistas, borderline, carentes e maltratadas*. Artes Médicas.

Baranger, W., & Baranger, M. (1969). La situación analítica como campo dinámico. In *Problemas del campo psicoanalítico*. Kargieman. (Originally published in 1961)

Barros, E. M. R. (2002). An essay on dreaming, psychical working out and working through. *IInternational Journal of Psychoanalysis, 83*(5), 1083-1093.

Barros, E. M. R., & Barros, E. L. R. (2008). *Reflexões sobre as implicações clínicas do conceito de simbolismo na vida onírica e sua relação com a perlaboração.* Paper presented at the Meeting on Meltzer promoted by the Brazilian Society of Psychoanalysis of São Paulo (SBPSP).

Bion, W. R. (1988). Diferenciação entre a personalidade psicótica e não-psicótica. In *Estudos psicanalíticos revisados.* Imago. (Originally published in 1957)

Bion, W. R. (1988). Ataques ao elo de ligação. In *Estudos psicanalíticos revisados.* Imago. (Originally published in 1959)

Bion, W. R. (1988). Uma teoria sobre o processo de pensar. In *Estudos psicanalíticos revisados.* Imago. (Originally published in 1962)

Bion, W. R. (1988). *Elementos de psicoanálisis.* Hormé. (Originally published in 1963)

Bion, W. R. (1991). *Aprendiendo de la experiencia.* Paidós. (Originally published in 1962)

Bion, W. R. (1994). Dream-work-α. In *Cogitations.* Karnac. (Originally published in 1959)

Bion, W. R. (1994). *Cogitations.* Karnac. (Originally published in 1992)

Bion, W. R. (2004). *Transformações: do aprendizado ao crescimento* (2a. ed.). Imago. (Originally published in 1965)

Botella, C., & Botella, S. (2002). *Irrepresentável: mais além da representação.* Criação Humana.

Ferro, A. (1995). *A técnica na psicanálise infantil – A criança e o analista: da relação ao campo emocional.* Imago.

Ferro, A. (1998). *Na sala de análise: emoções, relatos, transformações.* Imago.

Ferro, A. (2007). *Evitare le emozioni, vivere le emozioni*. Raffaelo Cortina.

Green, A. (1990). *Conferências brasileiras de André Green: metapsicologia dos limites*. Imago.

Green, A. (1994). El analista, la simbolización, y la ausencia en el encuadre analitico. In A. Ferro, *De locuras privadas*. Amorrortu. (Originally published in 1975)

Green, A. (1994). Para introduzir o negativo em Psicanálise. *Revista Brasileira de Psicanálise*, *28*(1), 25-38.

Green, A. (2008). *Orientações para uma psicanálise contemporânea*. Imago. (Originally published in 2002)

Green, A. (2010). *O trabalho do negativo*. Artmed.

Laplanche, J. (1997). A teoria da sedução e o problema do outro. *LAP*, *XIII*, 139-151.

Levy, R. (2003). A visão topográfica no processo psicanalítico: o irrepresentável. *Revista Brasileira de Psicanálise*, *37*(4), 1066-1077.

Levy, R. (2005). *Trauma e não-simbolização no campo analítico*. Paper presented at the 44th IPA Congress, Rio de Janeiro.

Meltzer, D. (1984). *Vida onírica: una revisión de la teoría y de la técnica psicoanalítica*. Tecnipublicaciones.

Meltzer, D. (1995). *A apreensão do belo*. Imago. (Originally published in 1988)

Meltzer, D. et al. (1990). *Metapsicología ampliada: aplicaciones clínicas de las ideas de Bion*. Spatia. (Originally published in 1986)

Meltzer, D. et al. (1995). Vicisitudes y fracaso de la simbolizacion. In *Clínica psicoanalítica con niños y adultos*. Spatia.

Ogden, T. H. (1996). *Os sujeitos da psicanálise*. Casa do Psicólogo.

Ogden, T. H. (2010). *Esta arte da psicanálise: sonhando sonhos não sonhados e gritos interrompidos*. Artmed. (Originally published in 2005)

O'Shaughnessy, E. (1990). A teoria do pensar de W. R. Bion e novas técnicas em análise de crianças. In E. B. Spillius (Ed.), *Melanie Klein hoje: desenvolvimentos da teoria e da técnica*. Imago (Originally published in 1981)

Person, E. S., & Klar, H. (1994). Establishing trauma: the difficulty distinguishing between memories and fantasies. *Journal of the American Psychoanalytic Association*, 42(4), 1055-1081.

Winnicott, D. W. (1967). *La familia y el desarrollo del individuo*. Hormé (Originally published in 1965)

Winnicott, D. W. (1975). Objetos transicionais e fenômenos transicionais. In *O brincar e a realidade*. Imago. (Originally published in 1951)

Winnicott, D. W. (1975). O papel da mãe e da família no desenvolvimento emocional infantil. In *O brincar e a realidade*. Imago. (Originally published in 1967)

Winnicott, D. W. (1982). Distorção do ego em termos de verdadeiro e falso *self*. In *O ambiente e os processos de maturação: estudos sobre a teoria da desenvolvimento emocional*. Artes Médicas. (Originally published in 1960)

7. The void and the prostheses-thoughts

I will provide a quick introduction to what I think about the so-called pathologies of emptiness, based on authors who are fundamental to me, and then I will dwell a little more on the concept of "prostheses-thoughts", trying to articulate it with the aforementioned pathologies.

I believe that the pathologies of emptiness began to be studied more emphatically in psychoanalysis when authors became interested in the process of symbolization, of creating symbols, of developing the ability to think about them, and the interference of the death drive in this process. Right from the start, we must think that if, on the one hand, certain experiences are negated in the system of representations or in the symbolic fabric, creating symbolic voids, object voids, on the other hand, they are "positivized" somewhere else: either in the proto-mental system, or in the soma, or in the act (Levy, 2010, 2012, 2017).

Very early on in his work, Freud took an interest in the question of death in human life. As an example, as early as 1913, in *Totem and Taboo* (1913/1980), he claimed that man, in a certain point in its history, starts civilization with the creation of primitive laws, taboos and, prohibitions, in order to curb sexual and aggressive impulses which, if unrestrained, would become a threat to community life. This would have been the beginning of civilization: from the threat of sexuality and violence, individuals unite around laws and regulations that curb the individual's drives, ultimately their violence. In 1930, in *Civilization and its discontents* (1930/1969), he returned to the theme of the repression of aggression and the risk of war. In 1932, in his famous dialog with Einstein entitled "Why war?" (1932/1969), he again deals with the destructiveness of man. Of course, we could go on quoting several other passages from his work in which he deals with this theme.

More specifically in relation to the topic we are dealing with now – the representation or lack of representations of experiences within the sphere of the mind – I believe that, after describing the death drive in *Beyond the Pleasure Principle* (1920/1969), when introducing the second topic model in *The Ego and the Id* (1923/1969), Freud develops the idea that there is a *quantum* of unrepresented elements in the sphere of the self that may or may not be represented. In other words, he describes the id as an archaic, primitive unconscious, immersed in the soma and pre-representational. In this outstanding work, he makes clear his view that the id is a kind of huge unconscious, part of which is the repressed Ics, but the rest are records of some kind waiting to be inserted into the sphere of the self.

Although the theme of destructiveness and the symbolic inscription or not of experiences in the mind had already been studied by Freud, I believe that, especially since the contributions of Winnicott and Bion and, later, André Green (1994), a great impetus has been given to a more in-depth, detailed study of the work of the negative in the process of symbolization. Of course, this was followed by enormous contributions derived from these two currents, English psychoanalysis and French psychoanalysis. In addition, many contemporary authors, from other regions and also from Brazil and Latin America, have "drunk" from both sources and generated new contributions that are also original, such as Ogden, Ferro, Civitarese, Roussillon, Botella and Botella, Levine, Barros and Barros, Cassorla, Hartke, Marucco, just to name a few and not to continue doing an injustice by not mentioning the others.

Winnicott, both in his classic work "Transitional objects and transitional phenomena" (1951/1975) and in his no less important contribution, "The Fear of Breakdown" (1963/1994), describes situations in which it is impossible to retain a representation in the absence of the object, creating a representational void that leads the patient to cling to the negative, to the lack, because this is felt to be more real than the object's presence; and other situations of non-representation of primitive agonies, when the primary auxiliary object, the mother, or its substitutes, failed to help the subject represent them as an experience of the self. These primitive agonies remain unrepresented, real "black holes" in the experience of the self, threatening to suck out its integrity, which is experienced as a fear of breakdown. The (re)living of this experience in the analytical relationship becomes necessary so that the patient can integrate it into his self, into his representational system, so that it acquires a form and a name and finally ceases to be an absent presence, as I described in the article "From symbolizing to non-symbolizing within the scope of a link: from dreams to shouts of terror caused by an absent presence" (Levy, 2012). This fear of breakdown is felt as a fear of death. What is rich and paradoxical about Winnicott's statement is that this death "has already happened", but it has not been experienced… It has remained outside the experience of the self and is now sought by the subject in order to be able to experience it fully.

This tension between life and death and the possibility of symbolizing or not symbolizing the subject's experiences is also dealt with in a masterly way by Bion in Chapter 5 of *Learning from experience* (1962/1991). In it, Bion describes situations in which the baby, for fear of experiencing certain emotions arising from contact with the object, refuses to drink the milk offered by the breast. The baby, however, realizes that it will die this way, and, out of fear of death, resumes sucking as a result of a profound dissociation in its mind. It starts drinking milk so as not to die, but this experience of material satisfaction is dissociated from psychic satisfaction. Difficulty of experiencing these primitive emotions "poses a problem that is solved by destroying the alpha function" (p. 30). This splitting of the mind and the destruction of the alpha function produces a mental state in which the subject will seek physical, material comfort, but will feel chronic dissatisfaction due to the impossibility of representing the emotional experience of satisfaction. To free himself from the emotional complications involved in grasping life and relating to living objects, the subject is thrown into a robotic, operative life, living like an undead person relating to inanimate objects. It would be a kind of death in life.

Green has also made valuable contributions to understanding the pathologies of emptiness and the tension between death and life in mental functioning. As just one more example, in his book *Life narcissism, death narcissism* (1988), Green describes the essential situation in which fusion with an idealized object, as a defense against the separation and absence of the primary object obtained in life narcissism, is no longer within reach. What is sought, then, is no longer unity with this idealized object, but nothingness, emptiness, a reduction of tensions to the zero level that would be the approach of psychic death.

With this quick overview, I just wanted to illustrate how some thinkers of psychoanalysis inaugurated and how much they have developed the study of these pathologies in which there are voids arising from attacks on symbolic functions, processes of disconnection and devitalization, de-objectification, linked in some way to the action of the death drive, which result in experiences of boredom, emptiness, death, despair, psychic starvation etc.

Let us focus now on a clinical situation which, on the one hand, illustrates what I am describing, but on the other, aims to make a small contribution to understanding the mental functioning of these patients. I apologize to those who already know some aspect of João's clinical material.

João is a patient who came to me in the middle of his adolescence: obese, smelling of nicotine, addicted to alcohol, cocaine, and marijuana and totally disinvested of his school life. He spent his time in the underworld, either because he had involved himself with drug dealers or because of his sexual compulsion, which led him to frequent the most sordid brothels. He exuded something deadly. He was also addicted to websites that shared extremely violent material, where he would visit during his tedious nights when he was not engaged in situations that risked his physical integrity. In this context of multiple addictions, I often wondered if João was not actually addicted to the search for excitement which, as Rosenberg (2003) describes, in these patients aims to fill an object void. The deadly characteristic of this form of masochism described by this author replaces the search for the longed-for object with the search for excitement, which determines this deadly character.

However, I will not go into the details of his analytical process and the technique I used to work with him, nor all the challenges posed by the tensions of the analytical field. I will go into detail about the technique of working with these patients in the next chapter, where I thoroughly describe what I called the creation of scaffolding for thinking with patients with these zones of negativity in which real holes are created in the symbolic fabric due to the impossibility of representing certain experiences. In the next chapter, I describe the "prostheses-thoughts" the patient uses in a frustrated attempt to fill the symbolic voids when he cannot yet dream about his primitive anxieties of helplessness, abandonment, and loneliness.

In any case, before we were able to help him develop the "thinkability" of what had previously been unthinkable, João had been stuck in periods in which evacuation predominated as a way of expelling unthinkable emotions from the psyche, generating fractures in his symbolic fabric or voids that were never filled; finally, we reached a moment when he seemed to be looking for ways of figuring out these anxieties; and perhaps we were beginning a moment in which he himself could create images that would allow him to contain and think about unthinkable emotions, as Barros has described in detail in various works (2002, 2006; Barros & Barros, 2008).

I understand that the hallucinatory transformations in which he would "turn into" a dangerous terrorist in several social media he inhabited, the fear of dying that he instilled in persons in countless social situations, the multiple addictions to various drugs, the dreams and prosthetic thoughts were "noisy positivations" that aimed to cover up, fill in, hide the representational and object voids derived from inconsistent object relations. The primal agonies – the fear of dying, of disintegrating – that were not adequately symbolized caused a turbulence that paradoxically, as Winnicott describes, led him towards death in life and literal death. We had to experience the fear of death together, of his and our breakdown, so that João could finally live more fully. And so, after much turmoil, he came into my office and played a song for us to listen to together. It was *Viva la vida* by Coldplay!

References

Barros, E. M. R. (2002). An essay on dreaming, psychical working out and working through. *International Journal of Psychoanalysis* 83(5), 1083-1093.

Barros, E. M. R. (2006). Afeto e imagem pictográfica: o processo de constituição do significado na vida mental. In J. R. Avzaradel, *Linguagem e construção do pensamento*. Casa do Psicólogo.

Barros, E. M. R., & Barros, E. L. R. (2008). *Reflexões sobre as implicações clínicas do conceito de simbolismo na vida onírica e sua relação com a perlaboração.* Paper presented at the Meeting on Meltzer promoted by the Brazilian Society of Psychoanalysis of São Paulo (SBPSP).

Bion, W. R. (1991). *Aprendiendo de la experiencia*. Paidós. (Originally published in 1962)

Freud, S. (1980). Totem e tabu. In *Edição standard brasileira das obras psicológicas completas de Sigmund Freud* (Vol. XIII). Imago. (Originally published in 1913)

Freud, S. (1969). Além do princípio do prazer. In *Edição standard brasileira das obras psicológicas completas de Sigmund Freud* (Vol. XVIII). Imago. (Originally published in 1920)

Freud, S. (1969). O ego e o id. In *Edição standard brasileira das obras psicológicas completas de Sigmund Freud* (Vol. XVIII). Imago. (Originally published in 1923)

Freud, S. (1969). O mal-estar na civilização. In *Edição standard brasileira das obras psicológicas completas de Sigmund Freud* (Vol. XXI). Imago. (Originally published in 1930)

Freud, S. (1969). Por que a guerra? In *Edição standard brasileira das obras psicológicas completas de Sigmund Freud* (Vol. XXII). Imago. (Originally published in 1932)

Green, A. (1988). *Narcisismo de vida, narcisismo de morte*. Escuta.

Green, A. (1994). Para introduzir o negativo em psicanálise. *Revista Brasileira de Psicanálise*, *28*(1), 25-38.

Levy, R. (2010). Adolescence: the body as a scenario for non-symbolized dramas. In M. Aisenstein, & E. R. Aisemberg (Eds.), *Psychosomatics today: a psychoanalytic perspective*. Karnac.

Levy, R. (2012). From symbolizing to non-symbolizing within the scope of a link: From dreams to shouts of terror caused by an absent presence. *International Journal of Psychoanalysis*, *93*(4), 837-862.

Levy, R. (2017). *Intimidade: o dramático e o belo no encontro e no desencontro com o outro. Keynote paper* at the IPA Congress, Buenos Aires.

Rosenberg, B. (2003). *Masoquismo mortífero e masoquismo guardião da vida*. Escuta.

Winnicott, D. W. (1975). Objetos transicionais e fenômenos transicionais. In *O brincar e a realidade*. Imago. (Originally published in 1951)

Winnicott, D. W. (1994). O temor ao colapso (breakdown). In *Explorações psicanalíticas*. Artes Médicas. (Originally published in 1963)

8. The polyphony of contemporary psychoanalysis: creating scaffolding for thinking[1]

Whenever I set out to study a topic relating to man's symbolic processes, I remember Cassirer's (1944/1997) brilliant assertion that man should not be called a rational animal, but rather a symbolic animal. Man's mental functioning, as we all know, is not dominated by rationality, but by the symbolic system he creates and which irremediably mediates his relationship with the world. He formulates an interesting image to help us reflect on this: he observes that it would not come as a surprise to find a group of humans dancing around a tree to summon rain, but you would never see a pack of dogs doing so! To put it another way, what marks out human behavior is not its rationality, but its immersion in the world of symbolism, fantasy, thought, and language.

Naturally, when Cassirer (1944/1997) refers to the human symbolic system, he means thought, language, the fine arts and scientific theories, not to mention the contributions of psychoanalysis concerning the unconscious. For psychoanalysis, the construction of the symbol starts from unconscious activity. Depending on the theory used, its construction will be understood as either stemming from

1 This chapter is a slightly modified version of: The polyphony of contemporary psychoanalysis: the multiple languages of man. *International Journal of Psychoanalysis, 100*(4), 656-673, 2019.

the re-transcriptions of unconscious desire in the psychic apparatus derived from pulsional activity (Freud, 1915/1969) or from the intersubjective encounter with the other, as developed by Bion (1962/1991, 1965/2004) and Winnicott (1951/1975) and will be constructed throughout the course of this chapter. Although the conception of what a symbol is differs between philosophy and psychoanalysis, I believe that some of the ideas from philosophy can be used to reflect on the theme of language and its development.

André Green (1990) argues that we should understand the psyche as an intermediate formation in the dialog between the body and the world, which according to the French author is brutal, as it confronts the tyrannical demands of the body with the restrictions imposed by the world of culture. This intermediate formation referred to by Green, the psyche, is in fact the human symbolic system, which constitutes the human essence as understood by psychoanalysis.

From a philosophical point of view, Walter Benjamin (1921/2013) considers that any manifestation of human mental life can be conceived as language. Thus, man lives immersed in countless languages: the language of the act, the language of dreams, the language of the visual arts, music, poetry, and the language of words articulated within a grammatical structure, the discursive language (Langer, 1941/1989) itself.

Susanne Langer (1941/1989), also from a philosophical perspective, has a different view. She believes that language is a special mode of expression, consisting of a specific vocabulary and syntax. Its elements, the words, have a fixed meaning to the extent that they can be translated into other languages. She understands that other symbolic forms that convey meaning – the visual forms (presentational symbolism, for example) – have other laws that govern them. Therefore, she believes that language in the strict sense would only be discursive language and that, although we refer to other means of non-verbal representation as language, this is loose terminology.

I believe that it is precisely this looseness mentioned by Langer that makes Benjamin's conceptualization interesting for our purposes. For us psychoanalysts, it is essential to understand the various manifestations of man's symbolic system, or its flaws, insofar as it communicates, or fails to communicate, meanings that we want and need access to.

Benjamin (1921/2013), nevertheless, goes further and adds that the linguistic essence of man is his naming language, different from all other languages in the animal world. The lion expresses its instinctive disposition and essence by roaring. Man expresses his linguistic essence by naming. Man creates a thing by naming it. Psychoanalytically, it might be more accurate to say that man creates the thing when he represents it. Of course, as Bion had already said, the thing itself precedes man, thought precedes the thinker, but, paradoxically, for thought to exist it needs the thinker. The unconscious, for example, existed before Freud, but by discovering and naming it, it came to exist in culture and science.

Among the countless languages of man, I am interested in studying "the languages" that we have to embrace and use when we practice psychoanalysis in our offices. I put "languages" in quotation marks because I am talking about language in the sense of the multiple expressions and manifestations of man's emotional life, not necessarily as an organized system of symbolic representations. And when I refer to the "language of the act", I am actually creating a figure of speech, knowing that the action of evacuation is not a language in itself, but a discharge of unrepresented or weakly represented emotions that can acquire meaning if they find a transforming container.

Although, even in the philosophy of language, the perspective of the interpreter who gives meaning to what is uttered by the speaker (Marinho, 2006) has been taken into account, psychoanalysis has made a decisive contribution by grasping the fact that meaning is constructed in the space between two subjects. Bion contributed by developing the notion that meaning is born in the baby's mind from the container/contained relationship, mediated by maternal *rêverie*; and Winnicott brought the idea that the mother, in primary maternal care, presents the object of the baby's need, giving meaning to its gesture. Contemporary authors have broadened this notion: Ogden (1996) with his conceptualization of the intersubjective third; Ferro (1995, 1998, 2011) with the "alphabetization" of "betalomas" through the creation of characters by the analytical pair; and Green (2002/2010) with his assertion that psychoanalysis has become interested in the role that the exchanges between the analysand and analyst play in the evolution of the treatment and the mutual influences of the analytical pair. In other words, as Bion said, *the unity of man is the pair*.

Based on these contributions, contemporary post-Bionian and post-Winnicottian psychoanalysis is working on a new model, which does not imply discarding other models. In this new way of working, the transformative (Ferro, 2011; Levine, 2012), the analyst's mind plays a decisive role in the possibility of symbolizing the non-symbolizations arising from traumatic experiences, in which raw emotions were inscribed in the protomental system, unable to be inserted into the fabric without analytic help (Levy, 2012b), or even in broadening the mind to new meanings and new visions of the world. This is why the analyst must sometimes be able to contain the patient's unwanted emotions for a long time before they can be reintroduced by the patient through interpretations (Alvarez, 1994; Ferro, 1995, 1998; Ogden, 1996, 2005/2010).

From the perspective of language, in the contemporary model, we are often speaking of the creation/construction of meanings, or even of language, and not only in the sense of revealing existing meanings, or translating one language into another, even though we often work using this model.

Ogden (2012) comments very pertinently that contemporary psychoanalysis is much more interested in how we think than in the content of what we think. And the way we think manifests itself in and through language. In other words, language translates the way of thinking and the vicissitudes of thinking. However, at the same time, language is how we intervene to try to help the patient achieve transformations in their thinking apparatus (Bion, 1962/1991). Language, then, has the dual characteristic of reflecting the way of thinking and of being a tool for transformation, which, I believe, depends on the *rêverie* of the analytic pair. As Ogden (2005/2010) puts it,

> *In his* effort to say something to the patient that is true to the conscious and unconscious emotional experience that is occurring in the analytic relationship at any given moment, *the analyst has inevitably, inescapably, entered into a struggle with language itself. (p. 26, emphasis in original)*

As awareness of our mental states is mediated by words, we need words to "know" about our feelings, in the Bionian sense of knowing through experience (transformations of O → K), but we cannot "say" a feeling, we can only express how it is. As Bion observed, an emotion can only be "felt" and, when we talk about it, we are already talking about transformations of that emotion. And metaphorical language is often what best translates how we feel.

I think that the contemporary analyst must essentially be a "polyglot", who can listen to and understand the different languages that are present in the analytical field and which will reflect the different levels and modes of thought that are constantly alternating. Verbal language is, in fact, an epiphenomenon of this whole process of underlying symbolic forms and is just one of the languages present in the analytical field, perhaps the most superficial and limited. This possibility of listening and letting different languages permeate oneself is perhaps something similar to what the child analyst is used to doing. The analysis will aim to help the patient evolve from primitive or absent symbolic forms to more abstract forms, including the possibility of creating oneiric images with their high evocative power. The difficulty of being able to dream about one's experiences can last for a long time during analysis. This topic has been studied by several contemporary authors (Cassorla, 2010; Sapisochin, 2013; Barros, 2002, 2006; Barros & Barros, 2008; Ogden, 2005/2010, 2012) from our environment and from other latitudes.

So, among other things, in this chapter I set out to study the language of the unsymbolized, the *non-dream* in the words of Cassorla (2005, 2014), how it expresses itself, how we can listen to it, dream it, and name it. Because naming is in the essence of what is human (Benjamin, 1921/2013; Bion, 1962/1991). However, thinking with Bion (1970/1993) and Meltzer (1988/1995), we will notice that our asymptotic goal is not just to name the thing, but to seek a language with presentational connotations (Langer, 1941/1989), rather than discursive, to be able to grasp the complexity of human emotions. Langer states that discursive language is a poor means of expressing our emotional nature. "It merely names certain vaguely and crudely conceived states, but fails miserably in any attempt to convey the ever-moving patterns, the ambivalences and intricacies of inner experience" (p. 107). Although I approach the theme in such a way that it seems that less symbolized and more symbolized forms of expression evolve diachronically over the course of an analysis, in fact they can alternate synchronously.

I will start from listening to the language of the non-symbolic to the construction of symbolic forms through the use of scaffolding for thinking, including the analyst's capacity for *rêverie* and his ability to metaphorize the patient's communication and the experience of the analytic pair. I will detail the technique of creating what I am calling "scaffolding for thinking" since it seems to me that this is a key element of psychoanalysis today. It is psychoanalysis, this great process of symbolization, that will allow the historicization, the narration of the patient's life. Otherwise, there is the eternal presentification of experience, the "murder of time", according to André Green (2000/2002).

The language of the cry for an absent presence

In this section, I am referring to patients who come to analysis with symbolic insufficiencies, without constancy in their representations of the self or its objects. Patients who need to evacuate many emotions before they even feel them, because they cannot symbolize them and therefore cannot contain them. They are patients whose "container" is insufficient.

These are patients who, as well as having multiple addictions, have a symptomatology that is basically expressed in their behavior, with self-mutilation, exposure to risky situations, violent actions etc. Often, these acts are intended to evacuate feelings of helplessness, fragility, impotence, fear of dying, which cannot be contained, transformed symbolically, and therefore elaborated psychically.

At the first moment of analysis, these unrepresented or weakly represented feelings cannot be accessed directly precisely because the patient does not yet have a psychic container capable of containing these emotions and thereby symbolizing them.

In this mental functioning, the way to deal with unbearable emotion is to evacuate it by acting it out; the threat, the helplessness, the fear of dying, the despair are put on a dramatic stage instead of being felt, dreamt, and spoken. I hear this language almost as if it were a dramatization in which a cry is heard: "I'm furious, I'm desperate, I'm afraid to die, save me!". I emphasize that I construct this meaning in my mind from its evacuation. The idea here is that emotions, anxieties – whether unsymbolized or weakly symbolized – true beta elements, when evacuated from the mind for being unbearable, can be a primitive form of communication, as if they could find a transforming container. Bion (1962/1991) points out that the evacuation of beta elements through projective identification can be a form of primitive communication between the baby and the mother, or between patient and analyst, provided that, using their *rêverie*, they become containers for these non-symbolic elements.

The problem we face in this type of analysis is that, precisely because the patient cannot bear these emotions, which are unthinkable, they are evacuated in the form of behavior, in the body – which is what suffers – or they are split off and projected. And forcing their reintroduction prematurely or forcing their "thinkability" would only recreate a traumatic situation.

These raw emotions, unthinkable because they are unsymbolized or weakly symbolized, or because they lack a psychic container to support them, can also give rise to narcissistic retreats, true transformations into hallucinosis (Bion, 1965/2004), because there, in the retreat, they feel powerful and invulnerable. This way, feelings of helplessness and fragility disappear. Some patients browse the internet for sites of extreme violence or live cannibalism. These remind of the excitement addictions described by Rosenberg (2003). In them, the search for an object is replaced by the search for excitement, which aims to fill the object void.

Other patients, fascinated by the addition to the world of violence that "evacuates" the feeling of fragility and powerlessness, create, for example, false identities on the web as if they were dangerous terrorists so that, through these characters, they can feel strong, violent, and frightening. They are often dominated by a form of magical thinking (Ogden, 2012), which has the function of protecting them from the anguish of helplessness and fear that are as yet unnamed and totally evacuated, or projected, often onto the analyst himself. We are constantly surprised, since we fear that the patients will be violent, or that they will be killed, or even arrested. When they "step into" these characters, their thoughts become almost delirious, making the atmosphere of the session extremely tense. Sometimes their immersion in these characters is so intense and concrete that they even think about making bombs, going to fight in Afghanistan, Syria… They experience intensely the mania and hypomania that Ogden (2012) describes, and in this state, they do not feel fragile, helpless and in need of a caring object; they feel powerful and menacing.

In order to make these raw emotions "thinkable", work on the transitional becomes an important resource. A technique that has been widely developed by authors such as Antonino Ferro, François Richard, among others, it allows the creation of what I have called "scaffolding for thinking". It involves using the characters brought to the session to "analyze" them in the transitional space (Winnicott, 1951/1975) – neither the inner world nor the outer world – and to construct the meaning of certain actions or needs without referring directly to the patient, which would not be bearable.

Through the emotional atmosphere shared in the session, we can build some understanding about the emotional life of these patients' "doubles". It is often possible to analyze the patient's feelings of abandonment and impotence – split off and projected onto these "doubles" who "attend" the analysis room – through the patient's narrative.

Following the example of what is done in child analysis, it is possible to take those "friends" as characters in a game (Ferro, 1995, 1998), since there, in that intermediate space, the patient tolerates "analyzing" those emotions. Often, the patient does not tolerate any kind of allusion to himself – for example, saying that "the terrorist is an aspect of him" does not make any sense to him, he simply *is* that character, there is no room for metaphors – but he does tolerate the analysis of the character in the intermediate space and so, in that intermediate space, it is possible to expand his symbolic chain and his psychic container. Gradually, we can create or expand the network of signifiers, or an alpha reticulum in Bion's words, which allows them to contain and think about their own emotions, which were initially unthinkable. This expansion of the symbolic chain through work in the transitional space is already a form of scaffolding for thinking.

We must understand that we have to be able to live with this violence that is split off and evacuated or projectively identified in the friends for a very long time. The presence of this violence in these patients' lives probably has as much to do with expressing their hatred of the objects they felt abandoned by, as it does with making them feel stronger and more powerful. Furthermore, it may also indicate how they felt treated by their objects.

In these situations, it takes a lot of containment and transformation into alpha of the various countertransferential experiences raised by the relational field that analyst/patient share. Often, this occurs at the cost of containing premature interpretative interventions, as described by Bolognini (2004, 2005). We are talking here about Bion's concept of negative capability (1962/1991, 1970/1993), where the analyst tolerates the anguish of the absence of understanding or even the absence of interpretation by respecting the patient's capacity to tolerate mental pain.

I would like to re-emphasize how tormenting and laborious these moments of analysis are when we "listen" to the language of the act and the "cry" (where more abstract symbolic forms are absent or have been destroyed because they would express unbearable emotions and fantasies) but at the same time, paradoxically, the noises emanating from their ruins are present. In another work (Levy, 2012b), I attempted to describe the metapsychology of non-symbolizations and used the metaphor of terror in which one feels a formless, terrifying presence that makes noises but has no image. So, in the tormenting work with these patients, as we want to and must be close to them in order to get to know them without being able to rely too much on associative discourse, we allow ourselves to be penetrated by their emotions, we are "dragged" to unsuspected worlds and experience some of the horrors of human misery. With many patients, for example, I have "known" the sordidness of the most miserable brothels, the promiscuous parking lots of the red-light districts where people have sex standing up, live torture websites – and many other situations I could list – with all the nausea, disgust, and fear they caused me. With them, every session we had to wait with apprehension to see "who" would arrive: the torturer, the gang "leader", the gambler, or who knows who else.

In regressive patients, the borderline cases, we can see that it is *as if* the process developed in two stages. Richard (2001), based on Winnicott, names them the transitional time and the interpretative time itself. By transitional, we mean the time in which the interventions are situated between the patient's internal and external realities; in the characters that are brought and created in the session; in which the analyst's presence and gaze are more important than his interpretative acuity. Today, perhaps, I can be more precise. More than two times, diachronically speaking, they are two ways in which the pair works, synchronously, in which, at times, containment and work in the transitional predominate, while at others the interpretative itself predominates.

I want to emphasize that this work in the transitional is what allows the expansion of the patient's symbolic fabric, a profound work of containment and transformation carried out in the analyst's mind that produces effects in the patient. The process of transforming and metaphorizing the performances and characters in the field takes place in the analyst's mind and remains there for a long time so as not to cause indigestion in the patient's thinking apparatus, preventing these understandings from being transformed into new beta (or bizarre) elements that need to be eliminated again (Ferro, 2011). I say this so that it does not appear to be a non-psychoanalytic moment, of passivity on the part of the pair. Perhaps it is a process similar to that described by Cassorla (2010) when he says that the analyst's implicit alpha would prepare the patient to have the psychic conditions to relive the trauma in a non-traumatic way.

In "Wilma's Wounds", Stéfano Bolognini (2005) helps his patient to transform her real wounds, bodily memories of her traumatic history, into symbolic wounds, memories in the author's words, through what he calls an elaborative psychic coexistence with a competent, present and available object.

Winnicott (1969/1975, 1971/1975) emphasizes the importance of the analyst being able to wait and hold back interpretations, especially in severely disturbed patients, in borderline cases. He says so in his 1969/1975 work:

> *it is only in recent years that I have become able to wait and wait for the natural evolution of the transference arising out of the patient's growing trust in the psychoanalytic technique and setting, and to avoid breaking up this natural process by making interpretations. It will be noticed that I am talking about the making of interpretations and not about interpretations as such. It appalls me to think how much deep change I have prevented or delayed in patients in a certain classification category by my personal need to interpret. If only we can wait, the patient arrives at understanding creatively and with immense joy, and I now enjoy this joy more than I used to enjoy the sense of having been clever. (p. 121-122)*

I emphasize once again that waiting and holding back does not mean being passive and inert from the point of view of psychoanalytic transformations. This is very close to what Ogden (2012) comments when he says that he listened to his patient and "did not want to run the risk of ending the hallucination with premature understandings" (p. 206). In this sense, perhaps we can say that the analyst must be able to respect the language in which the patient is able to communicate, to understand it, to allow oneself to be permeated by it, and to make use of that language, seeking more symbolic forms through scaffolding for thinking, which is what I am proposing.

Towards the language of images and dreams

After building up a solid symbolic fabric through work in the intermediary – and also through the work of constructing meaning through regular psychoanalytic interventions – we can be surprised by a significant increase in the ability to dream, whether it is dreaming in the literal sense of dream production during sleep, in the Bionian sense, or continuously "dreaming" emotional experiences, in the Meltzerian sense.

Sometimes, in between the "language of the cry" and the "language of the dream", we find what I have called "prosthetic-external-thoughts". To illustrate it, I will use the clinical situation of a borderline patient, already mentioned in a previous chapter.

> *João arrives at the session telling me that he is tired because last night, before going to sleep, he watched a video about a genocide that took place in a Middle Eastern city, recorded live. Very real. "It's a violent movie, you know. People, children, being killed live, shot in the head. Not many people can watch these scenes. You have to be strong. I don't know why, but I get electrified, I can't stop watching, but then I lay down and couldn't sleep."*
> *I feel nauseous and revolted by his description, but I begin to make imaginative conjectures. Many associations come to me, with theories, models, images. Could it be his addition to the excitement by which he replaces the object void in the solitude of the early morning? Would it be his sadism and violence? But he tells me about a genocide. A genocide of children. What genocide is he talking about? Is he telling me*

> *about a tragedy of childhood, a primitive one, in which his head/mind was destroyed, a psychic death?*

The video of this genocide and infanticide is perhaps an prosthesis-external-thought that captures him because it serves the purpose of giving figurability to his still unthinkable primitive tragedy. As several colleagues have already described (Barros, 2006; Marinho, 2006; Junqueira Filho, 2006; Avzaradel, 2006), the image serves, through the connection between the various elements represented there, to create a scene that is charges with a high density of emotions. Although he did not create these images, he adhered to them additively because they suited him.

Prosthesis-thoughts are images offered by culture, through websites or video games, to which the patient adheres compulsively, additively. These images capture these patients because they serve to give figurability to primitive tragedies that are still unthinkable by the patient himself.

I would like to propose the following concept: when the mind does not yet have enough alpha function to symbolize a certain emotion, or when it has not yet formed a container capable of containing certain thoughts (loaded with unthinkable emotions), nor a thinker capable of thinking certain thoughts, the subject can addictively cling to prosthetic thoughts, which are images offered by culture, because they depict tragedies unthinkable for the subject at the time. I believe that many addictions to violent video games may have this basis.

I do not believe that the attraction to these prosthesis thoughts occurs because they are associated by meaning with repressed unconscious fantasies. Rather, I suggest that they attract, magnetize, precisely because they serve to give figurability to non-symbolic elements, to registers that are not symbolized, or insufficiently symbolized, embedded in the mind, and that remain generating symptoms typical of traumatic situations. I believe that in severely disturbed patients, in whom symbolic failures and insufficiencies in the symbolic function are present, this use of symbolic prostheses can precede, with the help of psychoanalytic treatment, the ability to dream about their emotional experiences; almost as if it were halfway between the evacuation through the passage to act and the ability to dream.

I think it is possible to articulate this with Freud's assertion (1920/1969) that the dream of traumatic neuroses differs from the dream as a manifestation of repressed desires. In the dreams of traumatic neuroses, Freud states from his metapsychological perspective, the subject aims to reproduce the traumatic situation in order to try to retrospectively cope with the excess of stimulus that created the trauma. In the opinion of the creator of psychoanalysis, it aims to produce the preparatory anguish that was lacking at the traumatic moment and to connect, to symbolize, an amount of unbound excitation, obeying the repetition compulsion.

Were the images of the destruction of this Middle Eastern city – and those images from websites showcasing extreme violence – "prosthesis-dreams" of the traumatic situation? João, like so many other patients, had been trapped in periods in which evacuation predominated as a way of expelling unthinkable emotions from the psyche; we were at a moment when he seemed to be looking for forms that would give figuration to these anxieties; and perhaps we were beginning a time when he himself could create images that would allow him to know and think about emotions that were not thinkable, as Barros has described in detail in a number of works (2002, 2006; Barros & Barros, 2008). Avzaradel (2006), with the collaboration of various authors (Marinho, Junqueira Filho, Barros, and others), also makes relevant contributions to the theme of images.

I would like to make a small digression to differentiate what I am proposing from the concept suggested by Celia Fix Korbivcher (1999, 2001, 2004) in her important work on autistic transformations. I understand that the author argues that, when experiencing certain anxieties of death and disintegration, in order to avoid feeling them, some subjects transform these anxieties (Bion, 1965/2004) into concrete bodily sensations to which they adhere to obtain relief. If we think in terms of Bion's grid, it would be a movement in the ↑ direction, in other words, in the direction of concretization, of the sensory, in order to avoid thinking. What I am proposing, the prosthetic-thoughts, are quite the opposite. They would be "scaffolding" for thinking; attempts to evolve in the direction ↓ of the grid, i.e. from the concrete to thinking, via the image.

What is important for this chapter, what is essential, is that these pre-symbolic images can, through the analyst's *rêverie*, be taken as metaphors for the patient's inner world. This process of metaphorization, in which the analyst's mind plays a fundamental role, is essential for the patient's psychic growth. Without it, these visual signifiers, whether they are images from video games or videos, sometimes from ultra-violent websites, or humanitarian massacres, remain only portraits of these tragedies.

Menezes (2013) makes an important contribution in this regard. He recalls that, in "Constructions in Analysis" (1937/1969), Freud comments that he doubts that any psychic structure can be completely destroyed: something of its essence is preserved. Freud adds that if the analysis is "carried out correctly, we produce an assured conviction of the truth of the construction which achieves the same therapeutic result as a recaptured memory" (p. 300). I would add the idea of Meltzer et al. (1986/1990) that emotion is the first manifestation of the "meaning" of an experience and symbolic meaning is its working through, being the result of a work of symbolization. Therefore, it is possible that even if the symbolic meaning has been attacked, destroyed or never built, the meaning of the experience remains in the ruins of this register, which will be in search of a signifier and a meaning, as I tried to study in another article (Levy, 2012b).

The destroyed symbols, or the unsymbolized primitive marks, seem to have a *signifying potential* (some meaning) capable of being enriched in their presentification in the field and, through analytical work based on the analyst's or the pair's *rêverie*, gaining a name and becoming thinkable. Until they gain meaning, these ruins emit terrifying noises (Levy, 2012b), cries that are heard in the actions or in the repeated presentification in the field of raw emotions.

Rosolato (1985) describes primitive records of some basic human experiences which he calls *demarcation signifiers*. The demarcation signifiers would be visual elements that register very primitive experiences of human experience (presence/absence; pleasure/displeasure; good/bad; inside/outside) and constitute units that will make up more complex symbolic representations and structures until they are articulated with linguistic signifiers, with words. Something that is different from (but reminds of) the alpha elements described by Bion. It is suggested that they would be like photograms of a celluloid film whose sequence creates the narrative of the movie. Insofar as these primitive signifiers demarcate the meaning of experience (Meltzer), their quantities are themselves signifiers. The more frustrating or gratifying experiences in object relations, the more signifiers of one kind or another are waiting for symbolic constructions to give them appropriate meanings.

If we use this conceptualization for subjects with any kind of symbolic insufficiency, these demarcation signifiers, loaded with primitive emotions, proto-emotions, will be noisily waiting for more complex symbolic constructions to give them meaning. These signifiers being similar to alpha elements, we would be talking about very primitive registers, or remnants of them, but already symbolic. In another paper (Levy, 2012a), I suggested, based on Bion, Meltzer, and other authors, the existence of even more primitive, protomental registers at the somato-psychic boundary.

In good evolutions, we are gradually surprised by feelings of profound impotence, threat, and loneliness that appear in the form of dreams dreamt by the patient himself during the analysis. They begin to make contact with what was unthinkable, sometimes deeply paranoid and depressive feelings. Like another patient of mine, who at this point in the process, dreamt: "I was lost at night in a very violent area of Rio de Janeiro, very distressed, not knowing where to go. But I had the impression that assassins or gangs of drug dealers would appear at any moment".

Epilogue: the language of achievement

From the moment the patient is able to contain, transform, and dream about their heaviest emotional experiences, without having to evacuate them in the form of acts or addictions, the process of internal symbolization and working-through is underway. We can then observe symbolic constructions with increasing abstraction, which are accompanied by changes in the patient's conduct and social life. Often, they achieve a stable love relationship, healthier and less toxic links.

Little by little, we were able to name what was happening to the patient, and a container (Bion, 1962/1991) – or a sketch of one – was already being built up that was a little more capable of containing his violence and his unbearable proto-emotions. Verbal language is gradually taking precedence. Of course, each patient and each analytical pair will have greater or lesser capacity to reach more abstract and metaphorical levels of language. Or perhaps we could also speak of moments in the analysis in which more (or less) rich and meaningful formulations are reached.

I agree with Ferro's (1995) statement that the analysis of some patients ends where that of others begins. That is to say, we have a gradient of capacity for mentalization and symbolic expression that goes from the raw concreteness of non-symbolized emotions to poetry, and each analysis, each analytical pair, will have its limitations. Bion (1963/1988), with his grid, maps out all these levels of symbolic abstraction. How far a given pair can go is not known *a priori.*

If, on the one hand, being able to speak, to name, to put into words is important, on the other, we must be alert to the pitfalls of language. In a lecture entitled "Evidence", Bion (1976/2000) comments that words are like coins which, if used in excess, can lose their value and become worn out. For this reason, the analyst must always seek the language of achievement (Bion, 1970/1993). This depends on the analyst's negative capability to endure the absence of understanding until a formulation emerges that enunciates the emotion of the field.

Why does Bion use Keats' poem at the opening of his text on the language of achievement?

I believe that Susanne Langer (1941/1989) helps us to think about this issue. She tells us that although discursive language is the most appropriate for formulating complex logical thoughts, it is poor at expressing human subjectivity and the complexity of emotions. Presentational, poetic, metaphorical language, rich in linguistic images, is often the language that manages to capture the richness of the most unsuspected human passions and fantasies.

Little by little, we may be surprised to see the patient, who was previously only able to communicate through the "language of the cry", acting intensely, finally communicating in a highly evocative metaphorical language. For example, by saying "Yesterday I felt like an abandoned, lost baby", without the analyst ever having referred to him in this way. And, in turn, the analyst will also respond in metaphorical language, for example, saying, "When you feel frustrated and scared at a party, you behave like a terrorist leader so as to make everyone scared...".

Discursive language is made up of a succession of ideas and concepts that are articulated one after the other. The "language" of images, or linguistic, metaphorical images, has the power to simultaneously evoke various complex, emotionally charged, which would be empty if we were to describe them, one by one, with discursive language. A metaphor, through the disarticulation it makes between the word and its original meaning and the rearticulation to a new meaning (Searle, 1995/2002; Menezes, 2013) created by the pair, is shared by the pair, enriching the understanding of the patient and the analyst. And the richness of this type of joint creation by the analytical pair, as in a squiggle game, seems to be the expression in words of the *intersubjective third* conceptualized by Ogden (1996).

For all these reasons, many of us believe that candidates should have less theoretical seminars and more contact with the visual arts, literature, and theater. This would be a way of expanding the aesthetic vocabulary of future analysts so that they could signify a wider range of human experiences.

In the transformative model of analytic work (Ferro, 2011; Levine, 2012), the goal is to listen to the polyphonic languages present in the analytic field through the analyst's capacity for *rêverie* at first, but also that of the patient (as I have tried to show throughout this chapter), and to transform them to broaden and modify the patient's view of themselves and their inner and outer world. We will pass through primitive stages of thinkability until we reach, if possible, richer and more complex forms of language.

Even if we are not poets, nor are our patients, we often achieve this quality of language. Perhaps it could be said that we should look for a language capable of providing an aesthetic experience, in other words, capable of connecting with the emotion at play and awakening the desire to know more.

References

Alvarez, A. (1994). Abuso sexual de crianças: a necessidade de lembrar e a necessidade de esquecer. In *Companhia viva: psicoterapia psicanalítica com crianças autistas, borderline, carentes e maltratadas*. Artes Médicas.

Avzaradel, J. R. (2006). *Linguagem e construção do pensamento*. Casa do Psicólogo.

Barros, E. M. R. (2002). An essay on dreaming, psychical working out and working trough. *International Journal of Psychoanalysis*, *83*(5), 1083-1093.

Barros, E. M. R. (2006). Afeto e imagem pictográfica: o processo de constituição do significado na vida mental. In J. R. Avzaradel, *Linguagem e construção do pensamento*. Casa do Psicólogo.

Barros, E. M. R., & Barros, E. L. R. (2008). *Reflexões sobre as implicações clínicas do conceito de simbolismo na vida onírica e sua relação com a perlaboração*. Paper presented at the Meeting on Meltzer promoted by the Brazilian Society of Psychoanalysis of São Paulo (SBPSP).

Benjamin, W. (2013). Sobre a linguagem em geral e sobre a linguagem do homem. In *Escritos sobre mitos e linguagem*. Editora 34. (Originally published in 1921)

Bion, W. R. (1988). *Elementos de psicoanálisis*. Hormé. (Originally published in 1963)

Bion, W. R. (1991). *Aprendiendo de la experiencia*. Paidós. (Originally published in 1962)

Bion, W. R. (1993). *Attention and interpretation*. Karnac. (Originally published in 1970)

Bion, W. R. (2000, Sept.). Evidência. *Revista de Psicanálise da Sociedade Psicanalítica de Porto Alegre*, *7*(2) (Originally published in 1976)

Bion, W. R. (2004). *Transformações: do aprendizado ao crescimento* (2nd ed.). Imago. (Originally published in 1965)

Bolognini, S. (2004). Um bar no deserto. Simetria e assimetria no tratamento de adolescentes difíceis. *Revista Brasileira de Psicanálise*, *38*(2):259-269.

Bolognini, S. (2005). As feridas de Vilma. *Revista de Psicanálise da Sociedade Psicanalítica de Porto Alegre*, *12*(3), 515-526.

Cassirer, E. (1997). *Ensaio sobre o homem: introdução a uma filosofia da cultura humana.* Martins Fontes. (Originally published in 1944)

Cassorla, M. S. R. (2005). Considerações sobre o sonho a dois e o não sonho a dois no teatro da análise. *Revista de Psicanálise da Sociedade Psicanalítica de Porto Alegre*, *XII*(3), 527-549.

Cassorla, M. S. R. (2010). Função-alfa implícita do analista, trauma e enactment na análise de pacientes borderline. *LAP*, *XXIV*, 61-78.

Cassorla, M. S. R. (2014). Em busca da simbolização: sonhando objetos bizarros e objetos iniciais. *Revista Brasileira de Psicanálise*, *48*(1), 141-153.

Ferro, A. (1995). *A técnica na psicanálise infantil – A criança e o analista: da relação ao campo emocional.* Imago.

Ferro, A. (1998). *Na sala de análise: emoções, relatos, transformações.* Imago.

Ferro, A. (2011). *Viver as emoções, evitar as emoções.* Artmed.

Freud, S. (1969). Suplemento metapsicológico à teoria dos sonhos. In *Edição standard brasileira das obras psicológicas completas de Sigmund Freud* (Vol. XIV). Imago. (Originally published in 1915)

Freud, S. (1969). Além do princípio do prazer. In *Edição standard brasileira das obras psicológicas completas de Sigmund Freud* (Vol. XVIII). Imago. (Originally published in 1920)

Freud, S. (1969). Construções em análise. In *Edição standard brasileira das obras psicológicas completas de Sigmund Freud* (Vol. XXIII). Imago. (Originally published in 1937)

Green, A. (1990). *Conferências brasileiras de André Green: metapsicologia dos limites.* Imago.

Green, A. (2002). *El tiempo fragmentado.* Amorrortu. (Originally published in 2000)

Green, A. (2010). Introducción al pensamiento clínico. In *El pensamiento clínico.* Amorrortu. (Originally published in 2002)

Junqueira Filho, L. C. U. (2006). In J. R. Avzaradel, *Linguagem e construção do pensamento.* Casa do Psicólogo.

Korbivcher, C. F. (1999). Mente primitiva e pensamento. *Revista Brasileira de Psicanálise,* 33(4), 687-707.

Korbivcher, C. F. (2001). A teoria das transformações e os estados autísticos: transformações autísticas: uma proposta. *Revista Brasileira de Psicanálise,* 35(4), 935-958.

Korbivcher, C. F. (2004). A mente do analista e as transformações autísticas. *Revista Brasileira de Psicanálise,* 39(4), 113-130.

Langer, S. (1989). *Filosofia em nova chave.* Perspectiva. (Originally published in 1941)

Levine, H. (2012). Criando analistas, criando pacientes de análise. *LAP, XXVI,* 207-224.

Levy, R. (2012a). Dando "pensabilidade" ao impensável: criando "andaimes" ao pensar em adolescentes com transtornos severos. *Revista Brasileira de Psicanálise,* 46(3), 78-89.

Levy, R. (2012b). From symbolizing to non-symbolizing within the scope of a link: from dreams to shouts of terror caused by an absent presence. *International Journal of Psychoanalysis,* 93(4), 837-862.

Marinho, N. (2006). Mente e significado: a avaliação filosófica de Marcia Cavell da teoria psicanalítica. In J. R. Avzaradel, *Linguagem e construção do pensamento.* Casa do Psicólogo.

Meltzer, D. et al. (1990). *Metapsicología ampliada: aplicaciones clínicas de las ideas de Bion.* Spatia. (Originally published in 1986)

Meltzer, D. (1995). *A apreensão do belo.* Imago. (Originally published in 1988)

Menezes, L. C. (2013). A linguagem e a potência da metáfora no trabalho de interpretação e de construção na análise. *Revista Brasileira de Psicanálise*, *47*(2), 49-54.

Ogden, T. O. (1996). *Os sujeitos da psicanálise*. Casa do Psicólogo.

Ogden, T. O. (2010). *Esta arte da psicanálise: sonhando sonhos não sonhados e gritos interrompidos*. Artmed. (Originally published in 2005)

Ogden, T. H. (2012). Sobre três formas de pensar: o pensamento mágico, o pensamento onírico e o pensamento transformativo. *Revista Brasileira de Psicanálise*, *46*(2), 193-214.

Richard, F. G. (2001). *Le processus de subjectivation a l'adolescence*. Dunod.

Rosenberg, B. (2003). *Masoquismo mortífero e masoquismo guardião da vida*. Escuta.

Rosolato, G. (1985). *Elements de l'interpretation*. Gallimard.

Sapisochin, G. (2013). Second thoughts on Agieren: listening to the enacted. *International Journal of Psychoanalysis*, *94*(5), 967-991.

Searle, J. R. (2002). *Expressão e significado: estudo da teoria dos atos de fala*. Martins Fontes. (Originally published in 1995)

Winnicott, D. W. (1975). Objetos transicionais e fenômenos transicionais. In *O brincar e a realidade*. Imago. (Originally published in 1951)

Winnicott, D. W. (1975). O uso de um objeto e relacionamento através de identificações. In *O brincar e a realidade*. Imago. (Originally published in 1969)

Winnicott, D. W. (1975). Interrelacionar-se independentemente do impulso instintual e em função de identificações cruzadas. In *O brincar e a realidade*. Imago. (Originally published in 1971)

9. Truth and the aesthetic dimension of psychoanalysis[1]

I begin this chapter by transcribing the notes I took at the end of a session with a patient years ago.

> *I ended the session with tears in my eyes because we had had such tense emotional experiences analyzing her relationship with her sister. Is the truth beautiful, as Meltzer says inspired by the English poets? She always presented an image of her sister as an arrogant, snobbish, vain person. But now another view of her was emerging: a suffering person, scarred by the early abandonment she had suffered from her parents, as she had been sent to be raised by another family for many years. And the two of us, my patient and I, were thrilled to see the new vision she had of her sister, a vision that emerged creatively through a dream she had brought me and through our work in the session. We shared the emotion of building a new, beautiful image of the sister. Beautiful because it seemed truer to us than the previous one. We were moved not only by the new image we had built of her sister but by the beauty of the analytical work capable of such fertility.*

1 A substantial part of this text was published in: Revista de Psicanálise da Sociedade Psicanalítica de Porto Alegre, 26(1), 61-83, 2019.

Where did that feeling of truth come from? What was the relationship between beauty and truth? What was "true" about it? So is the question of truth still important for psychoanalysis? What truth are we talking about?

At the 2016 Congress of French-Speaking Psychoanalysts, while listening to landscape architect and poet Paul Andreu (2016) talk about the relationship between light and materials in an architectural work, I was reminded of the analytical relationship (Levy, 2017). He said that there needs to be a "dansity" between these elements, a possibility for light and materials to *dance* with each other, to interact, to interpenetrate, so that something alive can come out of it. I also remembered the relationship with our patients when Andreu, talking about his creative process, emphasized the importance of the temporal dimension, of allowing oneself to be flooded, submerged and suddenly discover that something emerges; "that's where the truth is", he said. This is what happens in the analytic relationship. We need to have this "dansity" with our patients, to have a living interaction, to allow ourselves to be submerged in the emotional experience with them, in a mental state that is closer to the oneiric than to the secondary process, welcoming their communications, of all kinds, to make something emerge thanks to our analytic function, so that something living is born, a new understanding that differentiates the two participants in the analytic pair (Ithier & Levy, 2014).

The passage quoted belongs to my work on "Intimacy" (Levy, 2017), in which I make a correlation between our experience as psychoanalysts and the description of a creative experience, one of contact with "truth" in another area of human activity, namely architectural creation. In other words, there seems to be a type of experience of truth, common to various human domains, which unifies various elements of the human experience – cognition, emotion, language – and which provides a particular type of experience that we could call aesthetic experience.

What does aesthetic experience have to do with the theme of truth and lies in psychoanalytical practice? And has it always been like this?

We will see that psychoanalysis, throughout its history, has always sought tools to establish the truth of what happens in the psychoanalytic clinical experience (Civitarese, 2018), even if these tools have changed over time, as we will see next. One of the major changes has been to accept that we no longer work with the notion of an absolute truth, the Truth, but rather the truth that is possible for a given analytic pair. Not all truth can be told. Bion helped us to understand that only part of the truth can be told, the other part can only be lived (Civitarese, 2018).

The question of truth and its epistemological contexts

We can begin to study the theme of truth from at least two angles: the search for scientific truth, that is, how science, and psychoanalysis in particular, has occupied itself with trying to grasp the "truth" of the subject's mental functioning; and also the feeling of being true, of existing, and relating to objects that are also true, but we will see that one vertex is directly related to the other.

In several areas of science, truth has been conceptualized in different ways: truth as "agreement" between the judgment and its object (Aristotle quoted in Heidegger, 1927/2001) in the empirical sciences; truth as coherence in the formal sciences; truth as symbolic consensus in the human sciences (Rezende, 1997); but perhaps it was Heidegger (1927/2001) who placed the human subjectivity at the center of the search for and creation of truth and clearly expressed the idea that truth for the subject lies at the center of a relation in which one discovers and is discovered.

In Chapter 2, I commented on symbolization (Levy, 2000) which, as Cassirer defines it, is the *abstract space* characteristic of man; it has nothing to do with the space of the senses. It is a symbolic space, constructed through the apprehension of abstract relationships between things. Geometry is a typical example of this space. The concept of truth changes, because in it we are not dealing with the truth of things, but with the truth of propositions and judgments. As we will see later, this concept of truth has greatly influenced the concept of psychoanalysis, since what is sought is psychic truth, the psychic meaning of a given event, and not necessarily that which can be apprehended through the senses, through the world of things.

Classical psychoanalysis, influenced by the epistemological context of its time, positivism, considered truth especially as agreement and coherence. It is possible to infer the epistemological model underlying Freud's clinical attitude and his theoretical formulations. In other words, in Freud, the search for truth was implicitly carried out, for example, by the search for agreement between the proposition – the interpretation – and the unconscious, which was there given, formed, waiting to be discovered and revealed by the objective observer, the analyst. Childish desire, seen almost as a natural fact, had to correspond to the interpretation made or the dynamic understanding constructed.

We must understand this Freudian stance in its historical context. In the early days of psychoanalysis, Freud, in his eagerness to turn it into a natural science, believed that psychoanalytic facts should correspond to real facts experienced in the subject's infancy (Hanly, 1992/1995) or inscribed in their biology, in their body. There should be real facts in the patient's "lived history" that correspond in some way to the oneiric productions and neurotic symptoms brought to the analyst.

Physics (Rezende, 1999), I would say Newtonian, is the prototypical science in epistemology for this search for truth by correspondence. In this type of scientific stance, the working hypothesis must necessarily correspond to a real fact, which endows it with veracity. Thus, the result of a Newtonian physics equation about the force of gravity, for example, must always correspond to a real phenomenon. An apple thrown from a certain height should always take the same time to reach the ground if the experiment is carried out on Earth, where the force of gravity is a constant.

Freud, in pursuit of scientific realism (Hanly, 1992/1995), often took this epistemological stance. The most illustrative example is the classic analysis of the Wolf Man. In interpreting the dream with the wolves, Freud, like a true historian/detective involved in reconstructing a historical event, rebuilds the "real scene" that should certainly have taken place, from his point of view at the time. It was the search for almost absolute correspondence. He postulates that the Wolf Man not only witnessed his parents having sex but even tried to determine their position and the time it happened. Although Freud also used other scientific criteria, for example, truth by coherence (Hanly, 1992/1995), this "objectivity" seemed essential for psychoanalysis to be able to claim a place as a science. In this context, then, the psychoanalyst would be the one seeking to reconstitute the objective truth of the facts, a process called reconstruction.

As I have already said, Freud also used another criterion of "truth", truth by coherence, typical of the mathematical sciences. In it, one always looks for coherence between the two sides of a mathematical equation. $2 + 3$ must always equal 5 ($2 + 3 = 5$ or $2 = 5 - 3$). For example, dream interpretation consisted of looking for coherence in oneiric thoughts, which had lost it through condensation and displacement (Hanly, 1992/1995). In this way of gauging the truth, oneiric thoughts had to be consistent with the manifest dream, as long as it was understood what kind of deformation the thoughts had undergone.

If we have to consider Freud's historical context, we cannot debate Freud's contributions outside their epistemological context either. Ilya Prigogine (1996), Nobel Prize winner in Chemistry and director of thermodynamics research institutes in Belgium and the United States, talks about the changes that have taken place in contemporary science. He says that the concept of chaos has changed our formulation of the laws of nature. Newtonian science, which was deterministic, believed that once the initial position was known, any past or future position of the trajectory could be predicted using its laws. He comments that there was an almost "legalist" attitude, as if nature had to submit to immutable laws created by man, as if it were possible to reduce nature to a set of laws. It was an attempt to put the human point of view into a divine perspective. As we have seen before, the principle of causality, for example, which was important in Freudian conceptualization, established that it was essential to establish the cause of the phenomenon that was being analyzed, as if it were possible to establish a causal linearity from the initial fact to the current phenomenon.

This began to change when Einstein wrote, "the direction and time of elementary processes are determined by chance". Prigogine claims that we are at a new moment in science, we must revise our laws of nature, probability has to be included, certainties are diminishing. It is good to see how much psychoanalysis – which in the last century presented itself as deterministic – is in line with the most current scientific stance, especially since the contributions of Bion, Winnicott, Baranger and Baranger, and others. In particular, Bion, creating the notion of Ps ↔ D oscillation, states: firstly, that order (D – depressive position) emerges from chaos (Ps – paranoid-schizoid position) and that immediately after ordering itself, it returns to Ps, the chaos; secondly, that ordering occurs from an almost casual phenomenon which is the selected fact; and, thirdly, that there is no single direction in growth, it occurs with permanent and constant oscillation, and that chaos is part of the mind, of all minds, of patients and analysts, creating a permanent instability. This principle contradicts some outdated psychoanalytic positions that the analyst is a kind of faithful custodian of order and unshakeable maturity.

Edgar Morin (1996), president of the Association for Complex Thinking in Paris, comments that when we say that a thought is complex, it means that difficulty will always be present. We would like to avoid complexity and have simple thinking, but complexity exists when there is an entanglement of actions, interactions, and feedbacks. And isn't that precisely what happens in the analytical field? He says that there is another complexity that comes from random phenomena that add uncertainty to thought. Morin states that the universe is the result of a dialog between order and disorder, in other words, two logics that are totally heterogeneous and that reject each other. And it is this dialog between order and disorder that produces the organizations of the universe.

Furthermore, especially from the 1930s onwards, Heisenberg (1930/2013) described the principle of indeterminacy, in which he established that: at the subatomic level it is impossible to determine the position of particles and whether they consist of mass *or* energy. In fact, they are both mass *and* energy and occupy an indeterminate space. Moreover, the new paradigm understands that the observer inevitably interferes in the phenomenon being observed. It is the end of the naive empiricism that greatly influenced psychoanalysis when the psychoanalyst was believed to be a cold mirror merely reflecting the patient's image. This new paradigm in physics reveals the complexity with which phenomena have come to be understood and we can imagine what this has meant in terms of understanding mental functioning.

Once again, it is important to emphasize how much current psychoanalysis is in tune with this more current notion of scientific thinking, which combines chaos and complexity into the search for knowledge, overcoming deterministic thinking. This model understands the observer as being part of the field of observation and, inevitably, interfering in it. This definitively removes the psychoanalyst from his classic position of an observer of what was in the patient's mind. The analyst is not only affected by the patient's emotions and fantasies but also directly affects the relational field.

If complexity and uncertainty are part of our daily practices, what about the question of truth in psychoanalysis? How do we do without the certainty of positivist, deterministic practice?

Before moving on, I want to point out that while Freud, on the one hand, used the criterion of truth by correspondence and coherence from his positivist epistemology, on the other hand, paradoxically, as Civitarese (2018) rightly affirms, he was one of the brilliant thinkers who eroded the foundations of positivism. Freud's concept of *Nachträglichkeit*, of *après-coup*, for example, does this. If the past can be re-signified and re-inscribed, this means that the past can change. This is implicit in the concept that the observer changes the observed; and even more, as Freud admits that the same subject, different at another time, gives new meaning to their past.

Truth as an encounter with the other and with oneself

The work of Bion (1962/1991, 1963/1988, 1965/2004, 1970/1993) is precisely about the process of knowing the "truth" of the emotions experienced in human links, in which emotion is the connecting element. How do you make contact and know (K) what is going on in your own mind or in the mind of another? How does a new thought emerge from the emotional experience lived in the link with the other? How do you get closer to the "truth" of the other or of yourself? Truth here is understood as an enigma, imminent revelation (Ungar, 2000).

This was another of Bion's great contributions: all the effort he made throughout several of his books (Bion, 1963/1988, 1970/1993) to warn us about the importance of the analyst freeing himself from his certainties, eliminating his memories, practically blinding himself, in order to be able to see the truth of the patient, of the shared experience in the analysis room. In "Evidence" (Bion, 1976/2000), he goes so far as to state that "*there is an inexhaustible pool of ignorance about which we base ourselves on – and that is all we have to base ourselves on*" (p. 275). The negative capability, to be able to tolerate not knowing, to "walk in the dark", to live with uncertainty, came to be proclaimed as the way to reach the potential truth of oneself and the other. And since the truth that interests us from a psychoanalytic point of view cannot be apprehended by the senses, but only by a cultivated, developed, educated intuition (Civitarese, 2018), the analyst's training, the development of his containment capacity and his tolerance of doubt and uncertainty became even more essential.

By placing emotions as a connecting element between human beings, Bion determines that they will be central to accessing and understanding the subjective experience of self and other. As we will see next, the fact that emotions acquire this centrality in the knowledge of subjective life will imply a new dimension to psychoanalysis, namely its aesthetic dimension. Although words, verbal language, remain important for understanding subjective life, not least because they are "pierced" by emotion, Bion will say that the way to get closer to the subjectivity of the other is to "become the other", not to "be the other", to lose one's identity (Grotstein, 2005/2010).

This process of building the "truth" of the other and of oneself, as we are seeing, is neither simple nor permanent in the psychoanalytic experience, since this "truth" will not always be tolerated by the patient, or by the analyst, or by both.

As I discussed in another paper (Levy, 2017), the experience of coming into contact with oneself, with the "truth" of one's subjective intimacy, can be frightening, because, on the one hand, it brings the subject closer to the infinite, unknown void of their unconscious (Bion, 1965/2004), and, on the other, in the case of the analytical experience, it often brings him into contact with projected, repressed, displaced and refused desires and fantasies, defensive processes. These processes have already been extensively described by Freud, Klein, and countless psychoanalytical authors. Thus, the subject resists being himself, living his ultimate reality, which Bion refers to as the O.

According to Bion (1965/2004), in order for the analyst to grasp the patient's truth, O, it is necessary to become O, to symmetrize. To become O is to share an emotional experience with the patient. Once you become O, you can make representations of O. The mind, in the K-link, permanently makes representations, versions of O. Here we can see how the notion of truth is built on an emotional link between subject and object and that at the heart of this search is the subject's emotional experience. I think that we are facing another form of search for truth, a more contextualized, more circumstantial one, called by Rezende truth by symbolic consensus.

Bion, in *Attention and interpretation*, markedly influenced by Kant (Sandler, 2000), considers that the ultimate truth of the subject, which he calls O, is in itself unknowable, in other words, what psychoanalysis tries to know, the inner reality of the patient, is in itself unknowable. We can try to know something about it through the representations we make of it. Bion makes it clear, then, that what we can achieve is to make representations of this ultimate experienced truth. In this sense, Grinberg, Bianchedi and Sor (1991) tell us:

> *Bion maintains that every thought, once formed, is false if we compare it with the "truth" of the fact it formulates. What varies is the degree of falsity, and here it will be necessary to discriminate between truth and lie, or rather between falsehood and lie. (p. 110)*

No matter how much the representation "represents" the truth, it will always have some degree of falsity, as it is not the thing itself, it only represents it. The mind, then, has a permanent symbolizing function that seeks to create for itself representations, versions, of the realities with which it is confronted, feeling them as "truths".

Thus, in a more intersubjective vision, the construction of truth necessarily includes the other. From an intersubjective point of view, truth is built in the link: in order for the subject to recognize himself, including as someone who desires, he needs to be seen as such. It is because the mother looks at the baby as someone with a desire of its own that it can recognize itself as such. In other words, it is in otherness that the feeling of "selfhood" is built (Ogden, 1996). If the subject is not allowed to be the master of his or her own desire, if the mother gets upset, for example, if it expresses its desire, the baby may renounce it and adopt the mother's desire as its own, giving rise, as has already been said, to the false self. In contrast, then, the true self would be the one in which the subject's desire can be recognized as such.

In this context, the aim of analytical work, of interpretation, is to help the patient become himself. It could be said that when patients become themselves, they can have an experience of intimacy, of truth with themselves. This emotional experience, precisely because it is intolerable, is often unsymbolized or weakly symbolized, split off and expelled from the mind, either by projective identification, or by actions with evacuative purposes (Levy, 2012a; Ruggiero, 2007), or in the soma (Bion, 1962/1991; Aisenstein, 2004, 2009), or in hallucinatory activities (Bion, 1962/1991; Ithier, 2016).

In the analytical field, however, this emotional experience (at first intolerable to the patient), in order to be known, understood, and later worked through (Barros, 2002; Barros & Barros, 2008), must exist, evolve into some container, as described by Ogden in a number of works (1996, 2005/2010) and also by Ferro (1998, 2011), among others. If the analyst is willing and can contain it, the emotion refused by the patient (although present in the field, or projectively identified in the analyst) can evolve in him, the analyst. He will become the patient's emotion, or the one generated in the field by the encounter between the two, allowing him to get to know it intimately. At this point, we might say that the analyst is having an experience of intimacy with some aspect of the patient's self and, in this way, will be able to make contact with the patient's "truth".

As I will illustrate next, when the analyst accepts the patient's projective identifications, he experiences to a certain extent a denial of his own individuality, as if he were no longer himself at that moment in order to "become" what the patient is not able to be at that moment. It is expected, though, that in a second moment, the analyst will be able to recover himself, recover his ability to think, his analytic function, and transform that experience into an understanding that will become an "analytic object" (Ogden, 1996), a bearer of psychoanalytic meaning produced intersubjectively.

This process of constructing the truth in the analytic experience raises yet another issue. After the analyst has welcomed emotions, fantasies, or wild thoughts (Bion, 1977/1997) through his *rêverie*, allowed them to evolve within himself and even be understood by him, i.e. had contact with the "truth" of his patient's subjectivity, when does he share them with the patient? When will the patient have a container to reintroject them?

In another work (Levy, 2012a), I also studied the need to create *scaffolding for thinking*, to help the patient build a symbolic container network that can receive back aspects that have been previously evacuated without de-structuring himself. This way, he will ultimately be able to know the "truth" of aspects of himself that were previously unbearable. The possibility of waiting has been one of the most valuable developments in contemporary psychoanalysis: waiting for the patient's time, when he will be able to think and accept previously unthinkable thoughts.

Winnicott also makes essential contributions to the understanding of the constitution of the subject in the intersubjective relationship with the other. He makes important additions to the understanding of how the subject, in the relation with the object, apprehends and has his "truth" apprehended by the other.

Claiming to be influenced by Lacan, Winnicott (1967/1975) asserts the importance of the other, initially the mother, in the constitution of the subject. He states that the precursor of the mirror is the mother's face. Very skillfully he comments that when the baby looks at the mother's face, it sees itself, to the extent that the English author coined the phrase: "when I look, I am seen; so I exist" (p. 157). The mother who manages to "look" at the baby becomes like what she sees there. The baby's sensation gains meaning on the mother's face. It is in this interplay, of showing oneself and being seen, that the subject's self-image is built, which will become the "truth" about oneself. In other words, in intimate human relationships, we see ourselves, we find our "truth" in the faces of others. Winnicott goes on to say that babies whose mothers cannot look at them, will look at their mothers and will not see themselves.

We see here how Winnicott, along with Bion, also made important contributions, thinking about psychoanalysis from the complexity of the constitution of the human being. Along with the ideas of these English authors, who laid solid metapsychological foundations for the intersubjective dimension of psychoanalysis, the theory of the analytic field developed by the Baranger couple (1961/1969, 1964/1969) further substantiated the understanding of what happens when two subjects with their subjectivities meet in the analysis room.

Ogden (1996) enriches this Winnicottian conception by saying that when the child sees itself in the mother's face, a dynamic of existence/non-existence is created in which the mother, while recognizing and identifying with the baby's inner state, disappears and allows the baby to see itself as another. The infant puts itself in the mother's place and sees itself as another. For our topic here, it is important to point out that it is in this dynamic of decentring oneself that the subject takes itself as an object (of knowledge) and knows itself, its "truth", and recognizes itself as a real, existing subject.

Winnicott (1967/1975) made another relevant contribution to the subject of truth in his work on the transitional object, when he stated that, in relation to it, an "agreement" is established between the mother and the child whereby they accept that "it is and it is not" the mother. The transitional object will be taken to be the real mother, knowing that it is not. We will see later how important this is in contemporary technique.

As we have seen, the contact and approximation of two subjectivities through an emotionally charged link is a complex and paradoxical process. On the one hand, there are the aforementioned exchanges, the communication pathways *between two subjects,* while on the other hand, it is also necessary to live with the idea that, ultimately, the interior of the other is intangible, inaccessible, to the point that Meltzer (1971/1994) states: "The great solipsistic loneliness of all humans suffer rests in the impossibility of knowing – really feeling – some other human's emotions" (p. 186). All we can do, with a lot of effort, is to conjecture (Meltzer, 1988/1995), make contact through our *rêverie* or our intuition (Bion, 1962/1991, 1965/2004; Ogden, 2005/2010; Ferro, 1995, 1998; Civitarese, 2014, 2015), our empathy (Bolognini, 2008, 2016), our work as a double (Botella & Botella, 2002), opening our minds to try to take in something of the other's subjectivity.

Returning to the importance of emotion in the encounter with the other and its centrality in the task of knowledge, Meltzer, in several works (1971/1994, 1988/1995; Meltzer et al., 1986/1990), describes the enchantment and wonder in this approximation, but also the fear and anguish. He considers contact with the object to be an aesthetic experience, insofar as its meaning, its nature, is indicated by the intense emotions and sensations it arouses, and not by reason. I will return to the issue of truth and aesthetic experience soon.

Truth and the aesthetic experience

Freud (1919/2010), in his work "The Uncanny", writes that aesthetics is the area of knowledge dedicated to studying "the theory of the qualities of feeling" (p. 329). He points out, nevertheless, that psychoanalysts work in other areas of psychic life and do not deal with "subdued emotional activities which, inhibited in their aims" (p. 329), which are the material of aesthetics. However, he makes a reservation, pointing out that the psychoanalyst may eventually become interested in an area of aesthetics, as would be the case with the analysis and the study of the "uncanny". Again, Freud was concerned with characterizing psychoanalysis as an objective science, but, as we will see in more detail later, psychoanalysis, especially after Bion and Meltzer, has changed in this aspect. It is no longer just interested in the qualities of feeling but understood that feeling is one of the first ways of knowing the "truth" of experience.

At the beginning of his work, particularly in *Learning from experience* (1962/1991) and some earlier works from his epistemological period, Bion describes an almost mechanical-rational process of acquiring knowledge about emotional experience, through its symbolic representation. However, the later Bion, especially after *Transformations* (1965/2004), began to consider intuition and emotion as the first category of knowledge of reality, characterizing knowledge as an aesthetic experience. At many points, he is inspired by English poets, making a link between truth and beauty, quoting Keats, for example, saying that "beauty is truth, truth beauty" (Keats, 1819).

Later, Meltzer (1988/1995) gives his masterly description of the aesthetic conflict. An ordinary beautiful baby looks intrigued, fascinated, seduced, and enchanted at his ordinary beautiful mother. Passion and sensuality exude from both sides of this relationship. He, the baby, the prince, is looked at with love, fear, irritation, sensuality, and mystery by his majestic mother. And she, the great fairy, is likewise looked at, admired, feared, desired, loved, hated, by the wonderful ordinary baby, enchanted by her beauty – in the sense that it floods him with sensations and bombards his sensoriality – but intrigued by the mystery of her inner self, which is unapprehensible to the senses. This is the aesthetic conflict.

Meltzer places the aesthetic conflict as the starting point of development, postulating that it remains so throughout life, as an essential element of mental growth. From this point of view, creative thought is constituted in the effort to give representation to the "other" and the enigmatic of its intangible interior. The presence of the object and its mystery puts the mind to work, to create symbolic forms that represent something of the emotional experience. In other words, this dual element, a presence that is intensely rich in sensory stimuli, which is why it is beautiful, breathtaking, and in mystery, due to the unreachable, unattainable nature of the object's interior, is essential to the development of speculative imagination, of creative thought.

This would be a poetic function of our unconscious (Meltzer et al., 1986/1990; Civitarese, 2014), in that it creates images, whenever possible, that contain the emotion of the encounter with the other. Or, if these emotions are unbearable, they can be evacuated from the mind through action, defensive projective identification, or hallucinations. In other words, here, the emotion experienced in the encounter with the other is the starting point for the process of knowing the truth of that experience. In Meltzer's opinion, emotion gives meaning to the experience and its meaning is built in a long process of symbolic construction which, in the analytical situation, viscerally involves the analyst.

This approach, which places emotion at the center – and as a link – of the subjective experience between two subjects and the unconscious with the poetic task of constructing images full of meaning that translate this emotionality, constitutes the aesthetic dimension of psychoanalysis.

The aesthetic experience of the meeting with the other includes an infinite palette of emotions of all kinds: admiration, enchantment, horror, wonder, fear. They all activate the conflict between the positive links L (*love*), H (*hate)* and K (*knowledge)* and the negative ones –L, –H and –K (Meltzer, 1988/1995). For the topic at hand, that of truth, this means that some emotions will be unthinkable because they are intolerable at a given moment, so the anti-links will be activated, obstructing the process of knowing the truth of that experience.

In other words, in this theoretical approach, it is clear that the "truth" that will be built, whether about what happens inside the object or what happens in the relationship with the other, will be the meaning that the subject attributes to these experiences. The "truth" about the other and oneself will be linked to the emotion experienced and the meaning attributed to it, much more closely linked to the aesthetic experience and the world of meanings than to the world of things and facts.

In a paper called "Giving 'thinkability' to the unthinkable: creating 'scaffolding' for thinking in adolescents with severe disorders" (Levy, 2012a), I studied precisely the process of constructing symbolic representation and the unthinkable, unsymbolized, or weakly symbolized emotional experiences. I then studied the various "languages" that circulated in the analytical field (Levy, 2015) until we arrived, at least at times, at the language of achievement (Bion, 1970/1993), which is able to convey and evoke intense emotions in the analytical relationship and portray the truth of our experience.

As I mentioned in the chapter on the polyphony of psychoanalysis, in the moments of the analytical process when João could not think, could not make contact with some aspects of his subjectivity, I used the resource of working on the transitional (Levy, 2015). As described by Ferro (1998) and Civitarese (2015), and as is done in the analysis of children, I treated his adventure partners and the high-risk situations to which he exposed himself as his doubles. I took those characters who somehow carried some aspect of him, or feelings of abandonment, fear of dying, hatred of parental objects, and I "analyzed" them right there, in the intermediate space. In other words, not even in João's inner world, nor in the outer world, but in that transitional space described by Winnicott (1951/1975). There, João tolerated making contact with those aspects of himself, broadening the range of representations around these emotions, and with this we expanded his symbolic network, his container.

For the subject of this chapter, the question of truth, I would like to emphasize that when we worked in the transitional, we knew that those characters were and were not João; we knew that what we "analyzed" about their emotions and motivations was and was not true; I believe we also knew that we were developing an "as if" between us with the aim of gradually bringing us to a greater and tolerable truth in relation to himself, that was still unthinkable at that time. Being able to tolerate this paradox without asking the unanswerable question "is this true or not" is essential to work with this technique.

In this sense, Civitarese (2018) highlights something that seems important to me: this psychoanalytic model that works with the gradual construction of the possible truth, inspired by Bion and Winnicott especially, is the one that has most developed the ability to live with uncertainty, with doubt, walking in the "dark", taking the psychoanalyst out of that almost omniscient, authoritative position of "knowing" and imposing a "truth" on the patient, with the traditional saying: "*Actually*, what you're telling me is this, this and this!".

So, in this post-Bionian psychoanalytic model, in which emotion is understood to be the link between subject and object, the psychic "truth" valid for that pair, at that moment, is constructed intersubjectively by the analyst/patient pair and what is sought is no longer factual truth, but psychic truth. What is sought is the meaning of the emotional experience in progress and, in this sense, as the symbolic representation of emotions is built, there is an expansion of the network of symbols, of the container.

The sensation of "truth" in the aesthetic model comes from the fact that knowledge of the experience in progress begins not only with emotion and intuition – and not with reason – but also with the experience of being with each other (*atonement*). The two participants in the experience share the sensation that a given utterance makes sense. More than that, what is felt is confirmed by reason. The feeling of truth also derives from other unifications and correlations. Bion believes that the unconscious/conscious binocular vision is fundamental, for what is felt in the unconscious is corroborated by conscious perception. The sense of truth, then, is built on multiple connections and consensualities that take place: between the two subjects involved in the experience; between emotion and reason; between subjective experience and language; between conscious and unconscious; and, finally, between body and mind (Civitarese, 2018). That is why it is an aesthetic experience: knowledge begins with emotion and continues with its connection/confirmation by thought and language, which are inextricably linked, generating a consensus.

We can assume that in this process the life drive prevails, generating different types of links in psychic life between the various instances and functions of the self and also in the relationship with the other. This predominance of the life drive is probably what generates the feeling of harmony and beauty. Contrary to what happens when the death drive prevails, causing discontinuity, disconnection, attacks on links, disharmony, generating a mismatch between the various functions of the self.

As already mentioned, Rezende (1999) refers to this experience of truth as truth by symbolic consensus. Civitarese (2018) will say that this is a social truth, as it is shared with the other, or with others, somewhat along the lines of what Bion described about narcissism *versus* social-ism.

Going back to the beginning of this chapter, my patient and I reconsidered the image of her sister through several linking processes: the dream she brought to the session and our associations, which evolved in a process of increasing enrichment as if it were a *squiggle game* (Winnicott, 1968/1994). We shared the emotion of being faced with something new and much truer than the previous image of the sister, perhaps because the previous image took into account defensive narcissistic aspects of the sister, leaving suffering aspects of her life split off and excluded.

Monica and the aesthetic dimension of psychoanalysis

For the purposes of this chapter, I would like to refer back to the clinical case in Chapter 6. I am going straight to two of her dreams, repeating them to make it easier for the reader, as I believe they illustrate her difficulty in tolerating the "truth" that shone through. Furthermore, the conflict between K and –K manifested itself almost constantly in Monica.

A neurotic part of the personality symbolized the emotional experiences overflowing from the analytical field and another part destroyed this knowledge by referring to unthinkable situations that I will illustrate below.

> *In the dream I was a little girl, in the house I used to live growing up. I was in the living room and through the windows there were flashes of light. I was curious to see what was outside the window, I would peek in and a very beautiful cathedral would appear. I approached the window, amazed, wanting to see that beautiful cathedral. But suddenly a cloud came towards the window and it was the image of a witch who wanted to come into my house. I got terrified and woke up.*

As well as symbolizing the image of a girl that we talked about in the sessions, it also symbolized her aesthetic conflict during the transference: when she saw me as an object that attracted her curiosity and seemed beautiful to her (Meltzer, 1988/1995) – in the sense of being attractive and arousing intense sensations and emotions – she was horrified because she felt that I was an invasive, uncontrollable, and frightening object. Perhaps that is why she needed to "take apart" everything I offered her in terms of understanding, as the following dream shows: "I had won a music box. But instead of opening it and listening to the music, I took it apart. Then I tried to put it back together and I couldn't."

We understood – and this last dream is a model that has been very helpful to us – Monica's active and present mental activity, in which, instead of using what I tell her to "listen, appreciate and think", she dismantles the mechanism into small pieces that are no longer useful for listening/thinking. As Bion (1959/1988) expressed, that-which-binds is attacked and turned into meaningless pieces. She did this not because of any particular destructiveness, but because of the horror she experienced, either when she approached me as an aesthetic object (Meltzer, 1988/1995), or because of the closeness to her internal world caused by the interpretation.

When she met me, Monica experienced intense emotions that she was able to transform partly, thanks to the poetic power of her unconsciousness, into beautiful images like those in her dreams, but the rest was discharged in action, by fighting with me, missing sessions etc. The dazzling cathedral and the terrifying witch are aesthetic elements, symbolic creations that aim to deal with the mystery of the intangible, the "traumatic" that comes from contact with the "other". The "other", the foreigner, whether internal (the id) or external (the object), permanently challenges the subject to construct images to give meaning to the mystery of the intangible. "What does he want from me?", Laplanche would say.

The unconscious has this poetic power to transform human emotions into visual or linguistic images. Artists have the creative talent to produce images that capture universal human emotions and generously make them available to the public so that they can be used to create powerful experiences. For this to happen, the ordinary person and the artist need to be able to tolerate the mystery, the not knowing, and creatively explore it in its various versions and vertices, through creative imagination.

Final comments

Was Monica really that tantrum-throwing girl who so often "showed up" at the sessions? Was her mother a witch? Are these her "historical truths"? Or am I the witch, as I assumed? Both hypotheses may be true; these images are from both her past and present. Above all, these images are Monica's symbolic constructions, inhabitants of her inner world, whose meaning we understood from our experience in the analytical field. And at the same time as these constructions seemed true to us, they have the capacity to undergo new symbolic transformations, adding more meanings that were at first absolutely unknown and unthought of. They contain aspects of her current and past experiences and are also open to new inquiries, in other words, they must be able to contain a certain amount of mystery. And this is the mystery we must embrace: that the revealing element also contains mystery.

Here we may have to face a paradox. We know from Bion (1962/1991) and Meltzer (1988/1995) that the mind needs to know, to name, that this is its nourishment, and that this is what expands it towards the infinite. At the same time, we need tolerate not knowing (Bion, 1962/1991), the mystery (Meltzer, 1988/1995) and sustain the refusal to know (Laplanche, 1992). We must know and at the same time tolerate that this knowledge, these "truths", are approximations to the thing itself, to O. And more than that, we must tolerate the idea that reality remains intangible and always possesses a dose of mystery to be conjectured. In the same vein, William James (quoted by Ogden, 2015) argues that "thought is the lie we tell ourselves so that we can sleep more comfortably with all that will be mystery – reality, emotions, ourselves" (p. 433). Along the same lines, Benjamin Ogden (2015) hopes that psychoanalysis is not waiting for an analyst who will reveal the truth, but for one who will "*replenish the stores of mystery*" (p. 443) because it is mystery that stimulates our imagination.

The encounter with the aesthetic object produces an intense emotional experience that sets in motion creative thinking and the expansion of the mind, or, when the emotion is unbearable, an evacuative attitude based on acting out. As a result of the above, I agree with Gabriela Goldstein (2019) when she says that "aesthetic experience and analytical treatment can operate as an opening to working-through, to another way of thinking and to new knowledge" (p. 20).

References

Aisenstein, M. (2004). O doloroso enigma, enigma da dor. *Revista de Psicanálise da Sociedade Psicanalítica de Porto Alegre*, *11*(1), 35-49.

Aisenstein, M. (2009). *Les exigences de la représentation*. Paper presented at the XXX Congrès des Psychanalystes de Langue Française.

Andreu, P. (2016). *L'espace, poétiques et perspectives*. Conference at the 76th Congress of French-speaking Psychoanalysts, Brussels.

Baranger, W., & Baranger, M. (1969). La situación analítica como campo dinámico. In *Problemas del campo psicoanalítico*. Kargieman. (Originally published in 1961)

Baranger, W., & Baranger, M. (1969). El "insight" en la situacion analítica. In *Problemas del campo psicoanalítico*. Kargieman. (Originally published in 1964)

Barros, E. M. R. (2002). An essay on dreaming, psychical working out and working trough. *International Journal of Psychoanalysis*, *83*(5), 1083-1093.

Barros, E. M. R., & Barros, E. L. R. (2008). *Reflexões sobre as implicações clínicas do conceito de simbolismo na vida onírica e sua *relação com a perlaboração.* Paper presented at the meeting on Meltzer promoted by the Brazilian Society of Psychoanalysis of São Paulo (SBPSP).

Bion, W. R. (1988). Ataques ao elo de ligação. In *Estudos psicanalíticos revisados.* Imago. (Originally published in 1959)

Bion, W. R. (1988). *Elementos de psicoanálisis.* Hormé. (Originally published in 1963)

Bion, W. R. (1991). *Aprendiendo de la experiencia.* Paidós. (Originally published in 1962)

Bion, W. R. (1993). *Attention and interpretation.* Karnac. (Originally published in 1970)

Bion, W. R. (1997). *Taming wild thoughts.* Routledge. (Originally published in 1977)

Bion, W. R. (2000, Sept.). Evidência. *Revista de Psicanálise da Sociedade Psicanalítica de Porto Alegre, 7*(2) (Originally published in 1976))

Bion, W. R. (2004). *Transformações: do aprendizado ao crescimento* (2. ed.). Imago. (Originally published in 1965)

Bion, W. R. (2004). *Transformações: do aprendizado ao crescimento* (2. ed.). Imago. (Originally published in 1965)

Bolognini, S. (2008). *A empatia psicanalítica.* Freud's Company.

Bolognini, S. (2016). *The humanizing function of contemporary psychoanalytical empathy* [video]. Lecture held at the Sigmund Freud Museum, Billrothhaus, Vienna. Retrieved from: https://youtube/rjzpA8QZrWk.

Botella, C., & Botella, S. (2002). *Irrepresentável: mais além da representação.* Criação Humana.

Civitarese, G. (2014). *I sensi e l'inconscio.* Borla.

Civitarese, G. (2015). *O inconsciente inacessível e a rêverie como um caminho para a figurabilidade.* Conference presented at SPPA, Porto Alegre.

Civitarese, G. (2018). Truth as immediacy and unison: A new common ground in psychoanalysis? Commentary on essays addressing 'Is truth relevant?'. In *Sublime subjects: aesthetic experience and intersubjectivity in psychoanalysis*. Routledge.

Ferro, A. (1995). *A técnica na psicanálise infantil – A criança e o analista: da relação ao campo emocional.* Imago.

Ferro, A. (1998). *Na sala de análise: emoções, relatos, transformações.* Imago.

Ferro, A. (2011). *Viver as emoções, evitar as emoções.* Artmed.

Freud, S. (2010). O inquietante. In *Obras completas* (Vol. 14). Companhia das Letras. (Originally published in 1919)

Goldstein, G. (2019). *A experiência estética: escritos sobre psicanálise e arte.* Triângulo Graf. Ed.

Grinberg, L., Bianchedi, E. T., & Sor, D. (1991). *Nueva introducción a las ideas de Bion.* Tecnipublicaciones.

Grotstein, J. S. (2010). "Transidentificação projetiva": uma extensão do conceito de identificação projetiva. In *Um facho de intensa escuridão: o legado de Wilfred Bion à psicanálise.* Artmed. (Originally published in 2005)

Hanly, C. (1995). *O problema da verdade na psicanálise aplicada.* Imago. (Originally published in 1992)

Heidegger, M. (2001). *Ser e tempo* (Vol. 1). Vozes. (Originally published in 1927)

Heisenberg, W. (2013). *The physical principles of the Quantum Theory.* Dover (Originally published in 1930)

Ithier, B. (2016). Contemporary conversations: the arms of the chimeras. *International Journal of Psychoanalysis, 97*, 451-478.

Ithier, B., & Levy, R. (2014). A função paterna na cena primitiva interpretativa. *Revista de Psicanálise da Sociedade Psicanalítica de Porto Alegre, 21*(3).

Keats, J. (1819). *Ode on a Grecian urn.* Retrieved from: www.keats--poems.com

Laplanche J. (1992). *Novos fundamentos para a psicanálise.* Martins Fontes.

Levy, R. (2000). *Do símbolo à simbolização: uma revisão da evolução teórica e suas repercussões sobre a técnica psicanalítica.* Dissertation for full membership of the Psychoanalytic Society of Porto Alegre.

Levy, R. (2012). Dando "pensabilidade" ao impensável: criando "andaimes" ao pensar em adolescentes com transtornos severos. *Revista Brasileira de Psicanálise, 46*(3), 78-89.

Levy, R. (2015). A polifonia da psicanálise contemporânea. In *Diálogos psicanalíticos contemporâneos: o representável e o irrepresentável em André Green e Thomas H. Ogden.* Escuta.

Levy, R. (2017). *Intimidade: o dramático e o belo no encontro e no desencontro com o outro.* Keynote paper at the IPA Congress, Buenos Aires.

Meltzer, D. et al. (1990). *Metapsicología ampliada: aplicaciones clínicas de las ideas de Bion.* Spatia. (Originally published in 1986)

Meltzer, D. (1994). Sincerity: a study in the atmosphere of the human relations. In A. Hahn (Ed.), *Sincerity and other works: collected papers of Donald Meltzer.* Karnac. (Originally published in 1971)

Meltzer, D. (1995). *A apreensão do belo.* Imago. (Originally published in 1988)

Morin, E. (1996). Epistemologia da complexidade. In D. F. Schnitman (Org.), *Novos paradigmas, cultura e subjetividade.* Artmed.

Ogden, B. (2015). O risco da confissão verdadeira. In T. S. Candi (Org.), *Diálogos psicanalíticos contemporâneos: o representável e o irrepresentável em André Green e Thomas Ogden.* Escuta.

Ogden, T. H. (1996). *Os sujeitos da psicanálise.* Casa do Psicólogo.

Ogden, T. H. (2010). *Esta arte da psicanálise: sonhando sonhos não sonhados e gritos interrompidos.* Artmed. (Originally published in 2005)

Prigogine, I. (1996). O fim da ciência? In D. F. Schnitman (Org.), *Novos paradigmas, cultura e subjetividade*. Artmed.

Rezende, A. M. (1997). *Investigação em psicanálise: uma procura da verdade*. Lecture given at the Ribeirão Preto Meeting, commemorating the centenary of Bion's birth.

Rezende, A. M. (1999). *A questão da verdade na investigação psicanalítica*. Papirus.

Ruggiero, I. (2007). Autodestrutividade na adolescência: entre a repetição e a elaboração. *Revista de Psicanálise da Sociedade Psicanalítica de Porto Alegre*, *14*(2).

Sandler, P. C. (2000). *A apreensão da realidade psíquica: as origens da psicanálise na obra de Kant*. Imago.

Ungar, V. (2000). Transferência e modelo estético. *Psicanálise*, *2*(1), 155-177.

Winnicott, D. W. (1975). Objetos transicionais e fenômenos transicionais. In *O brincar e a realidade*. Imago. (Originally published in 1951)

Winnicott, D. W. (1975). O papel da mãe e da família no desenvolvimento emocional infantil. In *O brincar e a realidade*. Imago. (Originally published in 1967)

Winnicott, D. W. (1994). O jogo do rabisco. In *Explorações psicanalíticas*. Artes Médicas. (Originally published in 1968)

10. The construction of the experience of intimacy in the analytical process through aesthetic experience: transformations in intimacy[1]

Though all our knowledge begins with experience, it does not follow that it all arises out of experience.
Kant (1787/1999, p. 53)

One could say that this chapter and the previous one are two sides of the same coin, because intimacy and the construction of truth, in the aesthetic dimension of psychoanalysis, are totally intertwined. In the previous chapter, I used some clinical and personal experiences to illustrate the issue of constructing the possible truth about emotional life; in this one, I will use them to focus on the vertex of constructing the experience of intimacy in the analytical session.

Studying and writing about intimacy in psychoanalysis is perhaps the most human thing we can do, because ever since we emerge from our mother's womb, the utmost experience of inhabiting and sharing another's body, we seek the reassuring warmth of an intimate

1 Much of this text comes from the author's main conference at the 50th International Congress of the IPA, held in Buenos Aires in July 2017, entitled "Intimacy: the Drama and Beauty of Encountering the Other". The text was subsequently published in national and international journals.

link with another human being for the rest of our lives, a process described beautifully by Eizirik (2016). In other words, the search for – or flight from, in pathology – intimate links runs throughout human life, because, as Bion (1978-1980/1992) said, "the human being is an animal that depends on a partner" (p. 95).

Throughout this search, throughout the entire life cycle, the body undoubtedly plays a central role in experiences of intimacy. As well as inhabiting the mother's body during pregnancy, at birth the human subject continues to share the intimacy of the mother's body, feeding on it and in it. Furthermore, primitively, the mother helps the baby to get to know its own body and to build an image of it and of itself as a subject, that is to say, she helps it to begin an intimate contact with itself. In adolescence, familiarity and intimacy with one's own body has to be rebuilt, just like in old age, when the body becomes fragile and inevitably deteriorates. With regard to sexuality, in adolescence and adulthood, the body once again takes on an essential role in the search for sexual intimacy between lovers, between couples, in the search for pleasure, warmth, and procreation. I think the cycle ends when the positions are reversed, and the children gratefully help their ageing parents, even with bodily care: they become their parents' fathers and mothers.

The experience of intimacy is an emotional one. I think that writing about this fits in with the psychoanalytic approach that has set out to study human emotionality, understanding that emotion indicates the initial meaning of the experience with the object and that meaning is constructed through a long process of symbolization that involves containment and symbolic transformation, from the most primitive symbolic elements to the most abstract, including language.

Allow me to digress. The human mind is perhaps one of the most complex systems in the universe. In order to grasp it, psychoanalysis, during its 120 years of existence, has created various theoretical models in an attempt to deal with such complexity. Possibly none of them alone can encompass the universe of the human mind. Identifying oneself more with one of them does not invalidate the others, and I even believe that in psychoanalytic practice we can navigate through several of them, depending on the clinical situation. Through clinical illustrations, I hope to be able to clearly show how I think about and work with intimacy in the clinical practice.

Bion placed emotional experience, human emotionality, and its symbolization at the core of the expansion of the mind. If, for Freud, the expansion of the psyche was driven by libido, Klein tied the locomotive of development to sadism (Petot, 1991). Then along comes Bion and states that loving (L – *love*) or aggressive (H – *hate)* emotional experiences will only lead to the expansion of the mind if they are subordinated to knowledge (K – *knowledge*); in other words, if they can be known, thought out (Bion, 1962/1991, 1965/2004; Hartke, 2007; Levy, 2012b; 2015; Barros, 2002; Barros & Barros, 2008), thus making K almost tantamount to drive. As a consequence of this approach, despite the recognition that life and death drives and their derived unconscious fantasies remain in the background, attention has been focused on the emotions experienced in the encounter with the object, on relations with objects and their destinies, especially in the post-Bionian psychoanalytic current.

What is done with emotion? Is it contained and symbolized? Is it evacuated? Is its meaning distorted? Is it symbolized, but then its symbol is attacked and destroyed?

I agree with Meltzer et al. (1986/1990) in saying that the challenge of psychoanalysis is to transform the analytical relationship, initially contractual, into an intimate one. For them, human life basically consists of three types of relationship: occasional, contractual, and intimate. In the first two, we function in an operative, adaptive, protomental, mechanical mode, performing activities for which we have been trained, and automatically repeating them. In intimate relationships, the situation is different. These are relationships involving emotional experiences that can lead to the expansion of the mind, to mental growth, through a prolonged work of containment and symbolization of the emotions in progress. We must, however, conceptualize what the truly intimate moments are in the analytic relationship, in the relational field that is generated therein (Baranger & Baranger, 1961/1969; Ogden, 1996), because, as we shall see, not all of them will correspond to experiences of intimacy between the pair.

Before I go any further, I want to clarify that when I refer to the analytic relation, I understand that *this* includes Freud's (1912/1969) concept of transference, as reminiscences of the past and the result of identifications (Freud, 1923/1969), and Klein's (1952/1985) concept of transference, as externalization of the internal world. This also includes the concepts of countertransference as thought up by Heimann (1949) and Racker (1960). I think that the concepts of the analytic field (Baranger & Baranger, 1964/1969) and the intersubjective third (Ogden, 1996) add to the notion that the transferential and countertransferential experiences of a given analytic pair generate something new, the shared fantasy of the field and the analytic third.

Furthermore, I hope to be able to address this very subjective, intimate experience without losing its richness and subtlety, or falling into an impoverishing technicality. I also propose to face, as much as possible, the inevitable limitation of words for describing complex and profound emotional situations.

Intimacy and the aesthetic dimension of psychoanalysis

In the scene mentioned in the previous chapter, which took place at the 2016 Congress of French-speaking Psychoanalysts, while I was listening to landscape architect and poet Paul Andreu (2016) talk about the relationship between light and materials in an architectural work, I was reminded of the analytical relationship. He said that there needs to be a "dansity" between these elements, a possibility for light and materials to *dance* with each other, to interact, to interpenetrate, so that something alive can come out of it. I also remembered the relationship with our patients when Andreu, talking about his creative process, emphasized the importance of the temporal dimension, of allowing oneself to be flooded, submerged and suddenly discover that something emerges; "that's where the truth is", he said. This is what happens in the analytic relationship. We need to have this "dansity" with our patients, to have a living interaction, to allow ourselves to be submerged in the emotional experience with them, in a mental state that is closer to the oneiric than to the secondary process, welcoming their communications, of all kinds, to make something emerge thanks to our analytic function, so that something living is born, a new understanding that differentiates the two participants in the analytic pair (Ithier & Levy, 2013). As will be seen in detail later on, this type of experience already implies an intense and necessary intimacy for the creative and analytic process.

The work of Bion (1962/1991, 1963/1988, 1965/2004, 1970/1993) is precisely about the process of knowing the "truth" of the emotions experienced in human links, in which emotion is the connecting element. How do you make contact and know (K) what is going on in your own mind or in the mind of another? How does a new thought emerge from the emotional experience lived in the link with the other? How do you get closer to the "truth" of the other or of yourself? Truth here is understood as an enigma, imminent revelation (Ungar, 2000).

Intimate comes from the Latin *intimus,* which is the superlative of inside, i.e. as inside as possible. Intimacy, then, means having contact with one's interior or another person's interior. Bion refers to "becoming the other", in the sense of getting as close as possible to the other's emotional experience, and not "being the other", losing one's own identity (Grotstein, 2005a/2010). He portrayed the phenomenon of intimacy, with himself or with the other, like it never had been done before. "He transformed psychoanalysis into a practice of obtaining and experiencing intimacy" (Grotstein, 2005b/2010, p. 325).

Another essential contribution by Bion (1962/1991) to the understanding of how intersubjective exchanges take place was to modify Melanie Klein's (1946/1978) seminal concept of projective identification. He makes a fantastic theoretical leap concerning Klein's concept when he describes realistic projective identification, with communicative purposes. In other words, infants and human beings in general can communicate their emotions to others by unconsciously projecting them onto the other, without excessive splitting up.

The description and conceptualization of the process of communicating raw emotions via projective identification, their reception, and symbolic transformation by the object have had a revolutionary effect on psychoanalysis, as they have several implications. The first is that the baby's subjectivity is constituted and/or expanded through the mediation of the mother's subjectivity and her psychic functions, just as the mother's emerging subjectivity is constituted by that of the new baby. The second, directly related to the first, is that the object acquires a new status: it is now considered to perform functions that constitute and expand the subject's subjectivity. The third, along with the Winnicottian contributions that I will address later, is that thrusts psychoanalysis definitively into the paradigm of complexity (Prigogine, 1996; Morin, 1996).

This will also have consequences for the way intimacy is understood in the analytical process, since we can assert that, just as the mother has access to the baby's intimate subjective experience and enables the baby to "know" itself, the analyst will be able to share the emotional experience with the patient, getting to know them and helping them. This opened up a whole new path in psychoanalysis, its intersubjective dimension, and inaugurated a new psychoanalytic model, the transformative (Ogden, 2012; Ferro, 1998; Levine, 2012, 2016), in which Baranger's notion of the analytic field (1961/1969, 1964/1969), expanded by Ogden (1996, 2005/2010), Ferro (1998), Cassorla (2010) and others, assumed a central place.

Winnicott (1967/1975) also made essential contributions to understanding the constitution of the subject in the intersubjective relationship with the other, approaching it based on the dynamic of the presence/absence of the other. In turn, Winnicott's notion that the subject's subjectivity is constructed depending largely on the gaze of the other is enriched by the ideas of Ogden (1996). He says that when the child sees itself in the mother's face, a dynamic of existence/non-existence is created in which the mother, while recognizing and identifying with the baby's inner state, disappears and allows the baby to see itself as another. The infant puts itself in the mother's place and sees itself as another.

As we have seen, the contact and approximation of two subjectivities through an emotionally charged link is a complex and paradoxical process. On the one hand, there are the aforementioned exchanges, the de-centering of one subject regarding the other, the communication pathways *between two subjects,* while on the other hand, it is also necessary to live with the idea that, ultimately, the interior of the other is intangible, inaccessible, to the point that Meltzer (1971/1994) states: "The great solipsistic loneliness of all humans suffer rests in the impossibility of knowing – really feeling – some other human's emotions" (p. 186). All we can do, with a lot of effort, is to conjecture (Meltzer, 1988/1995), make contact through our *rêverie* or our intuition (Bion, 1962/1991, 1965/2004; Ogden, 2005/2010; Ferro, 1995, 1998; Civitarese, 2014, 2015), our empathy (Bolognini, 2008, 2016), our work as a double (Botella & Botella, 2002), opening our minds to try to take in something of the other's subjectivity.

Since the 1970s, André Green (1975/1988) – along with the Botella couple (2002) and Roussillon (2013), among other French psychoanalysts – have also been part of the psychoanalytic movement that aimed to understand the process of psychic growth that results from the exchanges between patient and analyst. He wrote:

> *the real analytic object is neither on the patient's side nor on the analyst's, but in the meeting of these two communications in the potential space which lies between them, limited by the setting which is broken at each separation and reconstituted at each new meeting. (p. 54)*

Unfortunately, for a lack of time and space, I will not be able to expand on these rich contributions.

Returning to the importance of emotion in the encounter with the other and its centrality in the task of knowledge, Meltzer, in several works (1971/1994, 1988/1995; Meltzer et al., 1986/1990), describes the enchantment and wonder that lie in this approximation, but also the fear and anguish. He considers contact with the object to be an aesthetic experience, insofar as its meaning, its nature, is indicated by the intense emotions and sensations it arouses, and not by reason.

The beauty of his description of the aesthetic conflict is such that it cannot be repeated enough. An ordinary beautiful baby looks intrigued, fascinated, seduced, and enchanted at his ordinary beautiful mother. Passion and sensuality exude from both sides of this relationship. He, the baby, the prince, is looked at with love, fear, irritation, sensuality, and mystery by his majestic mother. And she, the great fairy, is likewise looked at, admired, feared, desired, loved, hated, by the wonderful ordinary baby, enchanted by her beauty – in the sense that it floods him with sensations and bombards his sensoriality – but intrigued by the mystery of her inner self, which is unapprehensible to the senses (Meltzer, 1988/1995). This is the aesthetic conflict.

Once again, we see the importance of emotions and sensations mobilized by the encounter with the other, by the presence of the object. An area of negativity is also highlighted, which would be the mystery of the other's interior, unknowable; it can only be built imaginatively by the speculative imagination, true creative thought. I like the idea of Meltzer et al. (1986/1990) and Civitarese (2014) that this would be a poetic function of our unconscious in that it creates images, whenever possible, that contain the emotion of the encounter with the other. This is the aesthetic dimension of psychoanalysis: knowing through the symbolic creation of representations that contain and reflect the emotions experienced in the encounter with the other.

The analytical situation has the virtue of providing a territory for the expression of the language of emotionality experienced by the analytic pair in an intimate relationship. The convergence of the oneiric material with the direct emotional experience in the transference and the process of construction-reconstruction of past relationships challenges the patient and the analyst to find precise verbal forms which describe the experience of understanding and being understood (Meltzer, 1971/1994). And this possibility of being aware of oneself and of the shared experience depends largely on the sincerity that the subject is capable of; it depends on the subject being able to accept, contain, and acknowledge the emotion that is being experienced. Evidently, this also happens in the analyst's mind. The possibility of becoming aware of the emotional experience taking place in the session depends on his mental openness to accept the shared emotions, his containing capacity, and his sincerity. It will also depend on his tiredness, the type of transference, personal stress etc. (Meltzer, 1971/1994).

Is it possible to define a gradient of intimacy?

In an attempt to be more precise in characterizing experiences of intimacy, perhaps we could define a spectrum of experiences of object relations – and even of the relationship with oneself – that would go from one extreme representing a mental state of autistic isolation to another, a mental state of narcissistic fusion, running through a gradient of intimate experiences. I propose the following diagram, inspired by Meltzer and Bion:

Autistic isolation ↔ … Intimacy … ↔ Narcissistic fusion

With this diagram and its bidirectional arrows, I suggest that there is a dynamic oscillation between these various positions and that in human relationships we move through mental states in which we are more or less available for intimate relationships. I also suggest that we can have different degrees of intimacy with the other and with ourselves. This does not prevent us, in pathological situations, from moving, for example, directly from a state of narcissistic fusion to autistic dismantling, depending on the anxiety and the defenses against it.

As Bion said, the meeting of two subjectivities provokes a storm of emotions that demand immense efforts on the mind. The range of emotions is almost infinite: passion, love, hatred, erotic desire, the desire to know, envy, fear, guilt, separation anxiety, fear of rejection, contempt, attraction, repulsion, admiration, and we could go on naming *ad infinitum*. The defenses against intolerable emotions can be distributed along the same spectrum illustrated in the diagram: they can range from autistic defenses and their consequent dementalization (Korbivcher, 2001; Civitarese, 2015) to narcissistic states, with their omnipotent and narcissistic object relations, in which the subject, through intrusive projective identification, appropriates the other, or uses the other to evacuate his undesirable aspects (Meltzer, 1973/1979, 1992; Rosenfeld, 1987/1988). At either extreme, the boundaries of the self are blurred or lost, the notion of otherness is lost, as well as the possibility of having experiences of intimacy. We could also assume that, in order to be able to have an intimate relationship with oneself, to know one's own inner self, the subject cannot be in a state of mental functioning in which either autistic or projective defenses predominate, since both prevent the subject's contact with his emotional life.

In order for there to be a genuine experience of intimacy in an object relationship, it seems to be necessary for the pair, apart from sincerity regarding the emotions experienced, to maintain the limits of the self and the notion of otherness (Minerbo, 1993), and for the sense of identity not to have been overly affected. Variations in intimacy do not have to do with the intensity of the psychic pain but with the degree to which it is accepted (Meltzer, 1971/1994). From the perspective of aesthetic conflict, intimacy could be defined as the capacity to tolerate the turbulence arising from the object's presence, without autistically avoiding contact or omnipotently merging through projective and intrusive identifications.

The problem is that in the analytical encounter, initially at least, the analyst comes across patients who, to defend themselves from suffering, have given themselves over to narcissistic organizations, or have pathological identifications. The challenge will be to find out how to turn this encounter into an intimate one. The analytic pair must be brave enough to face the psychic pain that is inevitable when the pair proposes intimate, sincere contact. Analysis is a process of discovery, driven not only by the patient's unconscious but also by our own. We rely upon the help of our internal objects – all those with whom we have had deep relationships, our original objects, our own analysts, supervisors, patients, and the internalized analytical method and setting, our theories – and we give ourselves over to them believing that they will help us when we need it.

For us too, however, the intense emotional contact of analysis can often be painful, causing us to resist it. If we have the necessary willingness, courage, and sincerity, in a mental state close to oneiric, based on the conscious and unconscious emotional experience with the patient, we can feel intuitions. Or it may happen that in our unconscious, images, metaphors, or words will present themselves that best contain the emotional experience we have seen, or that we will have to produce them oneirically through our capacity to dream. Therein lies, I believe, the psychoanalyst's creativity.

The times of intimacy

As we have seen, the intimate emotional encounter guided by emotion between two subjects is a rich, complex phenomenon that constitutes man. I would now like to widen the scope we are using to describe the experience of intimacy in the analytical field. I suggest we try to follow, just for study purposes, the times in which it develops – in practice, the process is much more complex and ineffable.

The intimate experience with oneself can be frightening because, on the one hand, it brings the subject closer to the infinite, unknown void of his unconscious (Bion, 1965/2004) and, on the other, in the case of the analytical experience, it often brings him into contact with projected, repressed, displaced and refused desires and fantasies, defensive processes. These processes have already been extensively described by Freud, Klein, and countless psychoanalytical authors. Thus, the subject resists being himself, living his ultimate reality, which Bion refers to as the O (1965/2004).

In this context, the aim of analytical work, of interpretation, is to help the patient become himself. It could be said that when patients become themselves, they can have an experience of intimacy, of truth with themselves. This emotional experience, precisely because it is intolerable, is often unsymbolized or weakly symbolized, split off and expelled from the mind, either by projective identification, or by actions with evacuative purposes (Levy, 2012a; Ruggiero, 2007), or in the soma (Bion, 1962/1991; Aisenstein, 2004, 2009), or in hallucinatory activities (Bion, 1962/1991; Ithier, 2016).

In the analytical field, however, this emotional experience (at first intolerable to the patient), in order to be known, understood, and later worked through (Barros, 2002; Barros & Barros, 2008), must exist, evolve into some container, as described by Ogden in a number of works (1996, 2005/2010) and also by Ferro (1998, 2011), among others. If the analyst is willing and can contain it, the emotion refused by the patient (although present in the field, or projectively identified in the analyst) can evolve in him, the analyst. He will become the patient's emotion, or the one generated in the field by the encounter between the two, allowing him to get to know it intimately. At this point, we might say that the analyst is having an experience of intimacy with some aspect of the patient's self. I suggest that this could be a moment in the process of intimacy.

As I will illustrate next, when the analyst accepts the patient's projective identifications, he experiences, to a certain extent, a denial of his own individuality, as if at that moment he ceases to be himself to "become" what the patient is unable to be at that point.

It is expected, though, that in a second stage of intimacy, the analyst will be able to recover himself, his ability to think, his analytic function, and transform that experience into an understanding that will become an "analytic object" (Ogden, 1996), a bearer of psychoanalytic meaning produced intersubjectively. Often, however, the analyst is simply prompted by projective identifications to function in a certain way, losing his capacity for *rêverie* and transformation into alpha, and may even, in some situations, depend on the patient to recover it, as I believe the following situation illustrates.

> *In one of his sessions, Bob, a rather competitive patient, told me what a spectacular quartet he, his wife, and their twin sons were, superior to other families. They were wonderful parents, and their twins were simply fantastic! Each of the twins would complement each other. One would excel in the humanities, the other in the exact sciences, etc. That irritated me, it seemed pretentious, exhibitionist, they were creating an "as if" situation, and I thought "poor children...". Well, the next thing I knew, I was talking about child development, children's needs, the first child etc., based on my experience working with children and adolescents, with a "I'll put you in your place" feeling!*

> *The other day, Bob told me that he went to the movies and saw a film about an important historical trial in which the judge stepped out of his impartial role and gave a speech in which he revealed his anger at the defendant. The defendant felt totally helpless because he felt he hadn't been given a fair trial. The patient makes various associations, but for our purposes here, I understood that Bob had been able, by recalling the film, to "dream" what had been acted out by me the day before: I had stopped being his impartial, neutral analyst/judge, I had abandoned the analytical attitude, and he had felt this as abandonment, a withdrawal from analyzing him because of his arrogance.*
>
> *In fact, instead of welcoming and transforming his projective identifications, I acted out in the session this set of raw emotions that invaded our relational field, competing with him and showing him I was "knowledgeable"; it was certainly an enactment (Cassorla, 2014). At that moment, I had lost my internal setting, which could be restored through Bob's rêverie and his understanding of me, and it was he who was able to "dream up" the raw emotions of the link by bringing that memory of the movie to the session. Perhaps we could say that Bob's memory is what Bion called a "dream-like memory".*

Going further in the description of the experience of intimacy, I suggest a new moment in which, if the analyst believes that the patient is already able to contain this projected part of the self, the analyst can interpret it so that the patient can experience it and recover part of his lost subjectivity.

I imagine yet another situation in the construction of the experience of intimacy, because, depending on how the pair's work goes, if they continue to evolve in the emotional experience present in the analytical field, learning about it and living it, without excessive projective identifications, they could perhaps live an experience of shared intimacy. This is perhaps what we could call a "true intimate experience" – if we allow ourselves such freedom with language – since the two subjects are separate, with their sense of otherness preserved, each being themselves, but sharing an emotional experience present in the analytical field.

It occurs to me that there may be an additional moment in the times in the experience of intimacy that I would refer to as *deferred intimacy*. After the analyst has welcomed emotions, fantasies, or wild thoughts (Bion, 1997) through his *rêverie*, allowed them to evolve within himself and even be understood by him, i.e. had close contact with the patient's subjectivity, when should he interpret them? When will the patient have a container to reintroject them? In another work (Levy, 2012a), I also studied the need to create *scaffolding for thinking*, to help the patient build a symbolic container network that can receive back aspects that have been previously evacuated without de-structuring himself. This way, the patient will ultimately be able to gain intimacy with his unbearable aspects. The possibility of waiting has been one of the most valuable developments in contemporary psychoanalysis: waiting for the patient's time, when he will be able to think and accept previously unthinkable thoughts.

This whole process of building an intimate experience with oneself and the possibility of sharing it with others is typical of and can only occur in the analyst's office. In other life situations, the subject either has intimate experiences and enriches their psychic world, or they do not and remain impoverished. It is the analytic relationship, with its necessary degree of high emotional density, which can use the need for and fear of intimate experience for the purposes of treating the patient.

Of course, the description of the times of intimacy that I have given is only possible for theoretical, academic purposes, because, as we will see in the clinical cases, the experience of all this is much more complex, mysterious, and ineffable, and much of it is only understood *après-coup*. In the heat of the analytical session, we are guided by intuition and enlightened by the concepts we carry within us, and both are necessary and indispensable.

Billy, escaping from and conquering intimacy

> *I'm with Billy in my office as I regularly do, four times a week. He is a middle-aged man, at the beginning of his analysis, with no children. Suddenly, I feel an unusual precordial pain of a certain intensity. I get distressed and fantasize that I might be getting a heart attack. Immediately I begin to speculate: "What do I do? Do I tell him I'm sick? But he's a narcissist, with no regard for anyone else, not even for his family or his wife... He'll treat me with contempt. But what if I don't tell him and I die? Imagine the trauma I'll cause him... I should tell him." While I'm lost in my thoughts, Billy interrupts me: "Ruggero, are you there? How awful, I thought you might have died.".*
>
> *I was struck by the level of intimacy we shared at that moment. Although, at first, I was absorbed in my pain and wondering what I would do, I soon realized, based on his statement, that we were sharing the same emotional experience of death during the session. I had a somatic hallucination, a sensory experience of "heartache" and, thanks to an absolutely unconscious rêverie, it had evolved into preconscious and conscious daydreams that were shared with my patient, initially non-verbally.*
>
> *I realized that our experience in the field was probably associated with Billy's recent attacks on our analytical relationship, which were relatively frequent, even though*

> *he appeared to be extremely cordial, with a boyish face, which sometimes made me wonder if he wasn't the legendary American western gunslinger Billy the Kid. I interpreted that his fear that I might have died might have come from what he had recently told me, that mine was a second-rate work, that I deserved to be working in an office on the outskirts of town, which could have caused me unbearable "heartache".*
>
> *Billy gets emotional, recalling a scene from his teenage years, and starts to cry. He was at the table with his family, when they still lived on their small rural property, and he had started an argument with his father, telling him that he was a failed mediocre man because the property had never expanded. It remained just like when he had inherited it from his own father, Billy's grandfather. The father got up from the table, went out onto the porch, and started crying. Billy recalls that, on seeing the scene, he felt triumphant. I was struck again by his violence, but somewhat relieved since now, with his crying, he seemed to be getting back to his senses. He had remembered, which etymologically means "to bring back to the heart" (recordar, in Portuguese). I believe that at this moment, differentiated, separated, with our sense of otherness preserved, we intimately shared another feeling, that of sadness, which had taken hold of Billy when he realized his violence towards his father.*

I think this situation illustrates how much our subjectivities constituted each other. My experience of the session was constituted by our encounter, in the same way as Billy's experience, generating a highly complex field fantasy.

I had probably felt "in my heart", in an initially somatic experience, the fury of his parricidal attacks, which were probably weakly symbolized and therefore presented themselves through the transformation into hallucinosis (Bion, 1965/2004). Thinking back, I believe that the experience of death and helplessness that I felt during the session was an expression of Billy's even more primitive unsymbolized emotional experiences. In Chapter 6, I studied how these non-symbolized, de-symbolized or weakly symbolized emotional experiences become present in the analytical field. It is interesting to think how much the construction of the patient's intimacy with his pain depends on our capacity to tolerate such pain, to give it a home, to welcome it, and provide it with symbolic form, so that only then can the patient feel it through our giving it back to him in a form that he can tolerate. And think about how much intimacy there is in all this is.

Moreover, the "heartache" and feeling of helplessness probably resonated with my experiences concerning my own father, because years later I realized that at that time my father had already undergone or was about to undergo heart surgery. Ithier (2016) makes an important contribution in this field, describing how, in the analytical encounter, the affinities of the patient's and analyst's primitive, unsymbolized traumatic experiences allow images – and also somatic feelings – that carry the emotion of that experience to emerge in the analyst's mind in a hallucinatory experience. If we expanded the concept of the traumatic to include any unsymbolized experience – not just primitive ones – it would be possible to include more recent experiences that also lack better symbolization.

At first, Billy and I shared a feeling of concern for my life, and then, following his associative flow, we shared his sorrow. I think these were really intimate experiences we had. Although he was evacuating some emotions in me, we were able to contain and transform the emotions we shared.

During this session, Billy and I evolved towards experiences of intimacy, but this was not always the case. A narcissistic functioning predominated in him, and so he used me and his most intimate objects to evacuate his feelings of helplessness, inferiority, and castration. I could engage in intimate contact with his experience of smallness and often felt small and powerless as an analyst. Mistrust would underlie my almost chronic countertransference with him, as I often felt that, because of his anguish, he was trying to manipulate me. He told me several dreams that revealed how manipulative and untrustworthy he really felt towards me, but also others in which he showed his desire to get closer to me. Those dreams, however, mobilized homosexual anxieties in him, which he greatly feared, so he was very afraid of having experiences of psychoanalytic intimacy.

Final comments

The moments in which there is this possibility of experiencing the emotion together with the patient are not so common in an analytic treatment. Still, they bring enormous pleasure when we attain them. Perhaps it is due to the fact that we once again feel so close to another human being, the pleasure of the paradox of "being at one with, but separate" (Winnicott, 1958/1975).

These moments of unison, though, are the ones that allow us to access their intimacy and ours, in an embodied way, with body and mind integrated into an inseparable unity, and they will enable us to experience truth and beauty outside exclusively rational parameters, constituting a true aesthetic experience. However, due to the intensity of the emotional experience and the necessary annulment of our identity at some point in this process, with all the psychic work it demands of us, we frequently defend ourselves against this experience and conduct the analytical process, unfortunately, in an uninspired fashion that is closer to thinking than to feeling. Bion (1965/2004) would say that we are working more from the perspective of *learning about* than of *becoming*, thereby resulting in work that is less rich and beautiful than it could be. Fortunately, when we tolerate the experience of emotional intimacy, poetry often occurs.

References

Aisenstein, M. (2004). O doloroso enigma, enigma da dor. *Revista de Psicanálise da Sociedade Psicanalítica de Porto Alegre*, *11*(1), 35-49.

Aisenstein, M. (2009). *Les exigences de la représentation*. Paper presented at the XXX Congrès des Psychanalystes de Langue Française.

Andreu, P. (2016). *L'espace, poétiques et perspectives*. Conference at the 76th Congress of French-speaking Psychoanalysts, Bruxelas.

Baranger, W., & Baranger, M. (1969). La situación analítica como campo dinámico. In *Problemas del campo psicoanalítico*. Kargieman. (Originally published in 1961)

Baranger, W. & Baranger, M. (1969). El "insight" en la situacion analítica. In *Problemas del campo psicoanalítico*. Kargieman. (Originally published in 1964)

Barros, E. M. R. (2002). An essay on dreaming, psychical working out and working trough. *International Journal of Psychoanalysis*, *83*(5), 1083-1093.

Barros, E. M. R., & Barros, E. L. R. (2008). *Reflexões sobre as implicações clínicas do conceito de simbolismo na vida onírica e sua relação com a perlaboração*. Paper presented at the Meeting on Meltzer promoted by the Brazilian Society of Psychoanalysis of São Paulo (SBPSP).

Bion, W. R. (1988). *Elementos de psicoanálisis*. Hormé. (Originally published in 1963)

Bion, W. R. (1991). *Aprendiendo de la experiencia*. Paidós. (Originally published in 1962)

Bion, W. R. (1992). *Conversando com Bion: quatro discussões com W. R. Bion – Bion em Nova Iorque e em São Paulo*. Imago. (Originally published in 1978-1980)

Bion, W. R. (1993). *Attention and interpretation*. Karnac, (Originally published in 1970)

Bion, W. R. (1997). *Taming wild thoughts*. Karnac.

Bion, W. R. (2004). *Transformações: do aprendizado ao crescimento* (2. ed.). Imago. (Originally published in 1965)

Bolognini, S. (2008). *A empatia psicanalítica*. Freud's Company.

Bolognini, S. (2015). Vinculos y intimidad. *Revista Peruana de Psicoanálisis, 16*, 11-20.

Bolognini, S. (2016, May 21). *The humanizing function of contemporary psychoanalytical empathy* [video]. Lecture at the Sigmund Freud Museum, Billrothhaus, Vienna. Retrieved from: https:// youtube/ rjzpA8QZrWk.

Botella, C., & Botella, S. (2002). *Irrepresentável: mais além da representação*. Criação Humana.

Cassorla, M. S. R. (2010). Função alfa implícita do analista, trauma e enactment na análise de pacientes borderline. *LAP, XXIV*, 61-78.

Cassorla, M. S. R. (2014). Em busca da simbolização: sonhando objetos bizarros e objetos iniciais. *Revista Brasileira de Psicanálise, 48*(1), 141-153.

Civitarese, G. (2014). *I sensi e l'inconscio*. Borla.

Civitarese, G. (2015). *O inconsciente inacessível e a rêverie como um caminho para a figurabilidade*. Conference presented at SPPA, Porto Alegre.

Eizirik, C. (2016). Intimitá, ciclo vitale e relazione analitica. *Rivista di Psicoanalisi, LXII*(2).

Ferro, A. (1995). *A técnica na psicanálise infantil – A criança e o analista: da relação ao campo emocional*. Imago.

Ferro, A. (1998). *Na sala de análise: emoções, relatos, transformações*. Imago.

Ferro, A. (2011). *Viver as emoções, evitar as emoções*. Artmed.

Freud, S. (1969). A dinâmica da transferência. In *Edição standard brasileira das obras psicológicas completas de Sigmund Freud* (Vol. XII). Imago. (Originally published in 1912)

Freud, S. (1969). O ego e o id. In *Edição standard brasileira das obras psicológicas completas de Sigmund Freud* (Vol. XVIII). Imago. (Originally published in 1923)

Green, A. (1988). O analista, a simbolização e a ausência no contexto analítico. In *Sobre a loucura pessoal*. Imago. (Originally published in 1975)

Grotstein, J. S. (2010). "Transidentificação projetiva": uma extensão do conceito de identificação projetiva. In *Um facho de intensa escuridão: o legado de Wilfred Bion à psicanálise*. Artmed. (Originally published in 2005a)

Grotstein, J. S. (2010). Epílogo. In *Um facho de intensa escuridão: o legado de Wilfred Bion à psicanálise*. Artmed. (Originally published in 2005b)

Hartke, R. (2007). *Repetir, simbolizar e recordar*. Paper presented at the 45th IPA Congress, Berlin.

Heimann, P. (1949). *On countertransference*. Paper presented at the 16th International Psychoanalytical Congress, Zurich.

Ithier, B. (2016). Contemporary conversations: the arms of the chimeras. *International Journal of Psychoanalysis*, 97, 451-478.

Ithier, B., & Levy, R. (2013). La fonction paternelle dans la scène primitive interpretative. *Revue Française de Psychanalyse*, 77(5), 1571- 1576.

Kant, I. (1999). *Crítica da razão pura*. Nova Cultural (Originally published in 1787)

Klein, M. (1978). Notas sobre alguns mecanismos esquizoides. In *Os progressos da psicanálise*. Zahar. (Originally published in 1946)

Klein, M. (1985). As origens da transferência. In *Inveja e gratidão e outros trabalhos*. Imago. (Originally published in 1952)

Korbivcher, F. C. (2001). A teoria das transformações e os estados autísticos. Transformações autísticas: uma proposta. *Revista Brasileira de Psicanálise*, *35*(4), 935-958.

Levine, H. (2012). Criando analistas, criando pacientes de análise. *LAP*, *XXVI*, 207-224.

Levine, H. (2016). *A situação epistemológica fundamental: a realidade psíquica e as limitações da teoria clássica*. Conference presented at SBPRJ.

Levy, R. (2012a). Dando "pensabilidade" ao impensável: criando "andaimes" ao pensar em adolescentes com transtornos severos. *Revista Brasileira de Psicanálise*, *46*(3), 78-89.

Levy, R. (2012b). From symbolizing to non-symbolizing within the scope of a link: from dreams to shouts of terror caused by an absent presence. *International Journal of Psychoanalysis*, *93*(4), 837-862.

Levy, R. (2015). Insight e elaboração. In C. L. Eizirik, R. W. de Aguiar, & S. Schestatsky (Orgs.), *Psicoterapia de orientação analítica: fundamentos teóricos e clínicos* (3. ed.). Artmed.

Meltzer, D. (1979). *Os estados sexuais da mente*. Imago. (Originally published in 1973)

Meltzer, D. (1992). *The claustrum: an investigation of claustrophobic phenomena*. Clunie Press.

Meltzer, D. (1994). Sincerity: a study in the atmosphere of the human relations. In A. Hahn (Ed.), *Sincerity and other works: collected papers of Donald Meltzer*. Karnac. (Originally published in 1971)

Meltzer, D. (1995). *A apreensão do belo*. Imago. (Originally published in 1988)

Meltzer, D. *et al.* (1990). *Metapsicología ampliada: aplicaciones clínicas de las ideas de Bion*. Spatia. (Originally published in 1986)

Minerbo, M. (1993). Intimidade e formas de intimidade. *Revista Brasileira de Psicanálise, 27*(2), 223-248.

Morin, E. (1996). Epistemologia da complexidade. In D. F. Schnitman (Org.), *Novos paradigmas, cultura e subjetividade.* Artmed.

Ogden, T. H. (1996). *Os sujeitos da psicanálise.* Casa do Psicólogo.

Ogden, T. H. (2010). *Esta arte da psicanálise: sonhando sonhos não sonhados e gritos interrompidos.* Artmed. (Originally published in 2005)

Ogden, T. H. (2012). Sobre três formas de pensar: o pensamento mágico, o pensamento onírico e o pensamento transformativo. *Revista Brasileira de Psicanálise, 46*(2), 193-214.

Petot, J. M. (1991). *Melanie Klein* (Vol. I). Perspectiva.

Prigogine, I. (1996). O fim da ciência? In D. F. Schnitman (Org.), *Novos paradigmas, cultura e subjetividade.* Artmed.

Racker, H. (1960). *Estudios sobre técnica psicoanalítica.* Paidós.

Rosenfeld, H. (1988). *Impasse e interpretação.* Imago. (Originally published in 1987)

Roussillon, R. (2013). Las simbolizaciones primarias y secundarias. *Revista de Psicoanálise da Associação Psicanalítica de Mendoza, 69*, 219-241.

Ruggiero, I. (2007). Autodestrutividade na adolescência: entre a repetição e a elaboração. *Revista de Psicanálise da Sociedade Psicanalítica de Porto Alegre, 14*(2).

Ungar, V. (2000). Transferência e modelo estético. *Psicanálise, 2*(1), 155-177.

Winnicott, D. W. (1975). La capacidad para estar a solas. In *Los procesos de maduración en el niño.* Laia. (Originally published in 1958)

Winnicott, D. W. (1975). O papel da mãe e da família no desenvolvimento emocional infantil. In *O brincar e a realidade.* Imago. (Originally published in 1967)

11. An intuition of the aesthetic paradigm in Freud? Reflections on the aesthetic paradigm of psychoanalysis and on developments in metapsychology

Freud (1919/2010), in his work "The Uncanny", writes that aesthetics is the area of knowledge dedicated to studying "the theory of the qualities of feeling" (p. 329). He points out, nevertheless, that psychoanalysts work in other areas of psychic life and do not deal with "subdued emotional activities which, inhibited in their aims" (p. 329), which are the material of aesthetics. However, he makes a reservation, pointing out that the psychoanalyst may eventually become interested in an area of aesthetics, as would be the case with the analysis and the study of the "uncanny". Again, Freud was concerned with characterizing psychoanalysis as an objective science, but, as we will see in more detail later, psychoanalysis, especially after Bion and Meltzer, has changed in this aspect. It is no longer just interested in the qualities of feeling but understood that feeling is one of the first ways of knowing the "truth" of experience, constituting what came to be called the aesthetic dimension of psychoanalysis (Levy, 2017) or the aesthetic model of psychoanalysis (Ungar, 2000).

Bion placed emotional experience, human emotionality, and its symbolization at the core of the expansion of the mind. As a consequence of this approach, despite the recognition that life and death drives and their derived unconscious fantasies remain in the background, attention in this psychoanalytic current has been focused on the emotions and sensations experienced in the encounter with the object and in the subject's relationship with their own body and with the world. However, although he developed the drive model throughout his metapsychology, we will see that at many moments Freud was concerned with the "qualities of feeling", proper to aesthetics, and not to psychoanalysis, according to himself. What is more, we will see that several of his brilliant works and insights stemmed from his aesthetic experiences.

Developments in metapsychology

Meltzer (1984/1987), in his book *Dream Life*, studies the developments in psychoanalytic metapsychology made by Klein and Bion. He states that in addition to the four classic metapsychological dimensions of psychoanalysis established by Freud – the genetic, the dynamic, the topographical, and the economic – Melanie Klein introduced the geographical dimension and Bion, the epistemological dimension. In other words, according to Meltzer, after the contributions of the two English authors, when analyzing a psychic event, in addition to the classic metapsychological dimensions already mentioned, we must understand the geography of the phenomenon, whether it is located in the subject's inner world or whether it has been projected onto the object. And we should also understand it from the point of view of knowledge (K-link), whether it is at the service of knowing the psychic reality of the subject or the object or whether it has the function of obstructing this knowledge.

Giuseppe Civitarese (2018), in his book *Sublime subjects*, especially in the first chapter, describes and substantiates another metapsychological dimension present in Bion's work, which would be the aesthetic dimension of the sublime. Other authors have previously described the aesthetic model of psychoanalysis inspired by Bion and Meltzer (Ungar, 2000) or the aesthetic dimension of psychoanalysis (Levy, 2017). In his book, Civitarese adds depth and consistency to the study of the aesthetic paradigm proposed by Bion by studying the roots of Bionian concepts in art, poetry, and philosophy. With this, it can be thought that today, when analyzing a psychic event, in addition to the metapsychological dimensions mentioned above, we must understand whether this phenomenon provides an aesthetic experience capable of elevating mental functioning, in other words, whether it is a sublime aesthetic experience.

Civitarese (2018) searches throughout Bion's work for evidence of the influence of the pre-Romantic and Romantic aesthetics of the sublime on his concepts. To do this, he studies the fundamental concepts of the English author's work, one by one, identifying their roots in the aesthetics that originated in the 18th century, and which profoundly marked poetry, literature, the plastic arts, and philosophy.

Why the *aesthetics of the sublime*? An aesthetic object is capable of promoting an aesthetic experience in others; that is to say, an experience of intense emotions, sensations, pleasure, rapture, but also of mystery, uncanniness, and sometimes – why not? – terror. The aesthetics of the sublime has its own style that differs from the usual canons of beauty, such as measure and harmony, and is capable of leading to an "elevation of the soul" and, in the case of psychoanalysis, mental growth (Civitarese, 2018).

There are always themes of mourning, of the danger of death to be overcome, of the fracture between nature and man, between the finite and the infinite, and between immensity and smallness. The Bionian and the post-Bionian conceptions regarding the constitution of subjectivity, of the human subject, involves precisely this theme: the feeling of helplessness, the dread of death due to the loss of the object, due to the absence of representation, and the overcoming of this experience through symbolization. The symbol created represents the absent object, while promoting an experience of psychic growth and relief from the preceding pain. The gap between mother and baby, between subject and object, between body and mind, is equivalent to the gap between nature and humanity and the ability to dream it, to represent it, is what constitutes human subjectivity.

From the subject's earliest object relations, he needs to free himself from the corporeal (originally from the mother's body and later from his own bodily sensations) and ascend to the symbolic, to the representational, in a truly heroic struggle, as depicted in 18th-century paintings. The subject must face the fear of helplessness, the loss of the object; from there will emerge the new human and symbolic "hero" (Civitarese, 2018). Thus, like the great heroes, the subject needs to face the "catastrophe" of the fear of object loss and helplessness in order to be constituted, and transform it into symbols that can be containing and soothing.

From this perspective, becoming a subject means being attuned to the other – the other being external objects or one's own body – and gradually forming representations of emotional experiences with this other in increasing degrees of abstraction. In this way, the bodily, the sensory, the affective-emotional, and the more abstract, logical, rational categories are integrated into a continuum that is proper to the human being. Ideally, a human being, without being dominated by splitting processes, should be capable of the most abstract rationality and the greatest sensitivity to the smallest details of the human and of nature, argues Civitarese (2018).

Understanding sublimation through the aesthetics of the sublime (the transformation of sensory experiences into symbolic products of high abstraction), art is no longer seen as an example of the capacity for sublimation restricted to a select few individuals capable of reaching higher levels in culture (Civitarese, 2018). It is now seen as a metaphor for what happens to all individuals in their processes of moving from "nature to culture", or from body to mind.

Freud and the aesthetic experience

Later, Meltzer (1988/1995) gives his masterly description of the aesthetic conflict. An ordinary beautiful baby looks intrigued, fascinated, seduced, and enchanted at his ordinary beautiful mother. Passion and sensuality exude from both sides of this relationship. He, the baby, the prince, is looked at with love, fear, irritation, sensuality, and mystery by his majestic mother. And she, the great fairy, is likewise looked at, admired, feared, desired, loved, hated, by the wonderful ordinary baby, enchanted by her beauty – in the sense that it floods him with sensations and bombards his sensoriality – but intrigued by the mystery of her inner self, which is unapprehensible to the senses. This is the aesthetic conflict.

Meltzer places the aesthetic conflict as the starting point of development, postulating that it remains so throughout life, as an essential element of mental growth. From this point of view, creative thought is constituted in the effort to give representation to the "other" and the enigmatic of its intangible interior. The presence of the object and its mystery puts the mind to work, to create symbolic forms that represent something of the emotional experience. In other words, this dual element, a presence that is intensely rich in sensory stimuli, which is why it is beautiful, breathtaking, and in mystery, due to the unreachable, unattainable nature of the object's interior, is essential to the development of speculative imagination, of creative thought.

This would be a poetic function of our unconscious (Meltzer *et al.*, 1986/1990; Civitarese, 2014), in that it creates images, whenever possible, that contain the emotion of the encounter with the other. Or, if these emotions are unbearable, they can be evacuated from the mind through action, defensive projective identification, or hallucinations. In other words, here, the emotion experienced in the encounter with the other is the starting point for the process of knowing the truth of that experience. In Meltzer's opinion, emotion gives meaning to the experience and its meaning is built in a long process of symbolic construction which, in the analytical situation, viscerally involves the analyst.

As we will see soon, Freud dealt with the fate of the aesthetic experience in various writings, or he himself made sublime contributions to psychoanalysis from an aesthetic experience.

Gabriela Goldstein (2019), in her book *The Aesthetic Experience*, looks for aesthetic experiences in various Freudian works that place them in a truly poetic dimension. For example, Freud's (1914/2012) analysis of his experience on the Acropolis is based on Oedipus and the guilt of living something not experienced by his own father. Goldstein, however, adds a new perspective for understanding this experience. She highlights the process of splitting and estrangement in Freud's aesthetic experience due to his contact with the sinister and the beautiful, understanding the Acropolis as an aesthetic object capable of awakening this experience. Goldstein supports and substantiates the hypothesis that, when faced with the "beauty" of the Acropolis, Freud "loses himself", gets carried away, and alienates himself, an experience he also had with Michelangelo's Moses.

> *in what can be an aesthetic experience and becomes so disturbed that we might think that something is preventing him from accepting being moved so intensely that he finds it strange to see himself as part of that experience. Thus, Freud perceives a certain personal condition that applies to the object of an aesthetic experience. He needs to find out why certain works subject his soul to "such violent*

> *impressions". He admits, however, that they are accessible as long as they are comprehensible by reason and reducible to concepts. (Goldstein, 2019, p. 35)*

Perhaps one of the works that brings Freud closest to the aesthetic paradigm described here is "On transience" (1916/2010). In it, Freud and his interlocutor poet share an experience and engage in a dialog that could easily be attributed to 18th-century poets. While on a walk with Freud, the poet expressed his sadness at the transience and impermanence of beauty, referring to the beautiful summer landscape that would soon be replaced by that of winter. Freud then remarked that:

> *No! It is impossible that all this loveliness of Nature and Art,* of the world of our sensations *and of the world outside, will really fade away into nothing. . . . Somehow or other this loveliness must be able to persist and to escape all the powers of destruction. (p. 248, my emphasis)*

Freud, like a poet, explicitly refers to the loss of the "beautiful" object, the aesthetic object, but intuits and proposes that it must subsist in some form. Freud states that the transience of beauty – we could say of the aesthetic experience – cannot imply its depreciation. In fact, he argues, it should imply an increase in its worth, but he attributes its value to its rarity in time. He then adds that "the value of all this beauty and perfection is determined only *by its significance for our emotional lives*" (p. 249, my emphasis), so it does not have to survive us, it does not depend on duration.

Finally, he concludes that it was *the revolt against the mourning of loss that prevented the poet from enjoying beauty*: as he was running away from the pain of mourning, his enjoyment of beauty was prevented by its transience. He goes on to say that once the mourning is over, "we shall build up again all that war has destroyed, and perhaps on firmer ground and more lastingly than before" (p. 252).

Now, does not all this come close to what we were talking about with regard to the aesthetics of the sublime, of romantic agony, described by Civitarese and which Bion and Meltzer brought to psychoanalysis in the form of concepts about primitive development, the primitive mother-baby relationship, and the analytical relationship? In other words, the aesthetic experience with the aesthetic object, wherever it occurs, is beautiful because of the intensity of emotions it arouses and the stimulating mystery that accompanies this object, and is fleeting because of its transience. It is the aesthetic experience that leads to psychic growth, to the expansion of the mind, because the sadness at its loss is overcome and eternalized by the symbolic reconstruction performed by the subject. It is the dangerous and painful passage from nature to the human, from the real to the symbolic, from emotion to symbol, albeit always intersubjective, in the relationship between two. And why is it painful? Because it implies a loss, a mourning, Freud explains. Bion would also claim that it is because in this crossing there is intense emotional turbulence, an oscillation Ps ↔ D, an uncertainty that needs to be tolerated.

Freud sensed all this. He sensed the importance of the mourning process in overcoming pain due to the transience of the experience aesthetic. What is more, as I said before, he used his aesthetic experiences to make brilliant imaginative conjectures about the mystery of his aesthetic object. One of the most striking examples is Freud's experience before the sculpture *Moses* by Michelangelo. The father of psychoanalysis spent hours in front of the imposing sculpture, moved and conjecturing, building the whole imaginary scene that would precede and succeed that instant engraved in stone.

Despite all this, Freud could not at that time conceptualize the aesthetic experience as a model for the analytical method, because his model of science did not allow it.

Recently, Gabriela Goldstein (2019), based on her analysis of Freud's experiences in situations such as the Acropolis and before

Michelangelo's *Moses,* and also on her knowledge of aesthetics, provides a true metapsychology of the aesthetic experience, as she describes its dynamics; what its object would be; and its topography, placing it in the transitional space described by Winnicott.

Final comments

This approach, which places emotion at the center – and as a link – of the subjective experience between two subjects and the unconscious with the poetic task of constructing images full of meaning that translate this emotionality, constitutes the aesthetic dimension of psychoanalysis. From this perspective, the emotional experience promoted by aesthetic experience is the starting point for knowledge. Emotional experience itself would be the first category of knowledge, followed, of course, by symbolic processing and other categories of thinking.

Perhaps this is another of the great paradoxes in Freud's brilliant work: on the one hand, he tries to place psychoanalysis within the scope of the objective natural sciences, using Newtonian, linear and causal physics as a model; but, on the other hand, he is concerned with studying the "subdued emotional activities, inhibited in their aims", with the "qualities of feeling", which would be the object of study of aesthetics, using his aesthetic experiences to get to know himself and his aesthetic objects.

References

Civitarese, G. (2014). *I sensi e l'inconscio.* Borla.

Civitarese, G. (2018). *Sublime subjects: aesthetic experience and intersubjectivity in psychoanalysis.* Routledge.

Freud, S. (2010). A transitoriedade. In *Obras completas* (Vol. 12). Companhia das Letras. (Originally published in 1916)

Freud, S. (2010). O inquietante. In *Obras completas* (Vol. 14). Companhia das Letras. (Originally published in 1919)

Freud, S. (2012). Moisés de Michelangelo. In *Obras completas* (Vol. 11). Companhia das Letras. (Originally published in 1914)

Goldstein, G. (2019). *A experiência estética: escritos sobre psicanálise e arte*. Triângulo Graf. Ed.

Levy, R. (2017). Intimacy: the drama and beauty of encountering the Other. *International Journal of Psychoanalysis*, *98*, 877-894.

Meltzer, D. (1987). La ampliación de la metapsicolopsicologia de Freud realizada por Klein y Bion. In *Vida onírica*. Tecnipublicaciones (Originally published in 1984)

Meltzer, D. (1995). *A apreensão do belo*. Imago. (Originally published in 1988)

Meltzer, D. et al. (1990). *Metapsicología ampliada: aplicaciones clínicas de las ideas de Bion*. Spatia. (Originally published in 1986)

Ungar, V. (2000). Transferência e modelo estético. *Psicanálise*, *2*(1), 155-177.

Part III
Adolescence

12. Adolescence[1]

Adolescents can be understood and studied from multiple angles: psychological, cultural, sociological, biological, and many others that could be mentioned. The focus of this chapter will be on the psychological standpoint, basically using the psychoanalytic framework.

Although adolescence is a universal process, it takes on peculiarities according to the prevailing culture. In this sense, at the end, we will examine some of the repercussions of today's culture, at the beginning of the 21st century, on youngsters, insofar as it alters their relationships with the environment.

The universal nature of adolescence can be illustrated by a text written in the 4th century BC by Aristotle (quoted in Blos, 1979/1981), in which he portrays the changeable, voluble, irritable, challenging character of the adult world, prone to noble acts. There are, therefore, some invariants that have been maintained over the centuries. Those invariants rest on the need for the new generation to challenge the adult world and its rules, in order to acquire its own identity, distinguished from its previous generation. This attitude is based on an inescapable feeling of self-sufficiency and greatness. If, on the one hand, this contestation generates a situation of conflict, on the other, it results in an indispensable cultural renewal.

1 This chapter was previously published in: C. L. Ezirik, & A. M. S. Bassols (2013). *O ciclo da vida humana: uma perspectiva psicodinâmica.* Artmed.

From the psychoanalytic point of view, the adolescent is a subject in process of transformation, immersed in a profound process of reviewing their internal world and their childhood legacies, with a view to adapting to the new body and the new drives resulting from puberty. To illustrate this, we will use an image created by a young adolescent in the midst of the pubertal process (Figure 12.1).

The volcano, in an obviously phallic shape, illustrates, on the one hand, the perplexity with the development of the genitals and their new secretions. On the other, it depicts how puberty is felt as an internal volcanic eruption of unknown, feared forces yet at the same time renewing. The curious thing about this drawing is what the almost 11-year-old patient said about what was happening at the base of the volcano: "The problem is that there were children playing ball near the volcano and they didn't realize how much danger they were in". It seems that our initial adolescent, with this comment, was expressing how much he felt that the eruption of puberty was casting him into adolescence and threatening his childhood. In other words, he was ceasing to be a child and sensed that he would lose, or leave behind, a series of characteristics and patterns of behavior and relationships typical of that phase. This shows the fractured, fissured nature of puberty.

The adolescent process

Once upon a time, a beautiful princess pricked her finger on a spindle and fell into a deep sleep… It was the evil witch's curse. It would take the princess' great love – the handsome prince – to come to her and kiss her in order for her to wake up. He had to overcome several obstacles: the evil witch and her various means of blocking his access to the princess. He fought against dragons and thorny hedges before he finally found the princess, kissed her and she woke up and they were married happily ever after.

This classic of children's literature masterfully illustrates the process and vicissitudes of development from puberty onwards, that is to say, from the first bodily transformations to heterosexual genital life. Confronted with the new body resulting from pubertal transformations – in the story, menarche is represented by the blood of the stung finger –, with the new drives and new postures required by development, the youngster turns to the inner world (deep sleep) to overcome the bans of the inner objects introjected throughout childhood development. This deep dive into the inner world will allow for a radical revision of the subject's relationship with inner objects, with childhood parents and their prohibitions. The young person, like the prince in the fairy tale, must engage in a real struggle against these archaic objects, face the hedges they have erected to prevent their access to genitality, and overcome them. The difference is that this struggle takes place in the inner world and is made possible by this turn inwards.

This "withdrawal" into the inner world can be seen in various ways: daydreams, moments of isolation in the adolescent's room, diaries, feelings of unreality. It is important to point out that this phenomenon is evidence of the increase in narcissism typical of the first moments of adolescence. The pubescent turns inward. They are concerned with what is going on inside them, whether in a bodily sense or in terms of their internalized object relations and the identifications made during the resolution of the Oedipus complex and consolidated during latency. Or even in terms of the prohibitions inherited from childhood regarding masturbation and manipulation of the body. It is only at a later stage that he will be able to turn to the other. In this sense, I believe it can be said that the evolution of love relationships in adolescence (Levy, 1995) takes place in the sense of narcissism toward the discovery of the other. In a way, this new "birth", or the birth of this new subject, mirrors the first steps of development: it evolves from narcissism to object love, from autoeroticism to genitality. The next chapter will study the symbolic rearrangement occurring in adolescence, in the sense that the system of representations of self, objects, and the world built up throughout childhood goes bankrupt. It can no longer cope with representing the new body and the new vision of objects and the world. It needs to be reordered, virtually rebuilt. Adolescence seen from this angle is understood as a major process of symbolization.

In this chapter, studying the standpoint of narcissism in adolescence, I will try to briefly address some of its vicissitudes in adolescence, given its relevance at this time of life. It might be possible to graphically illustrate the trajectories of narcissism (love of self) and object love (the capacity to love others) throughout adolescence as follows:

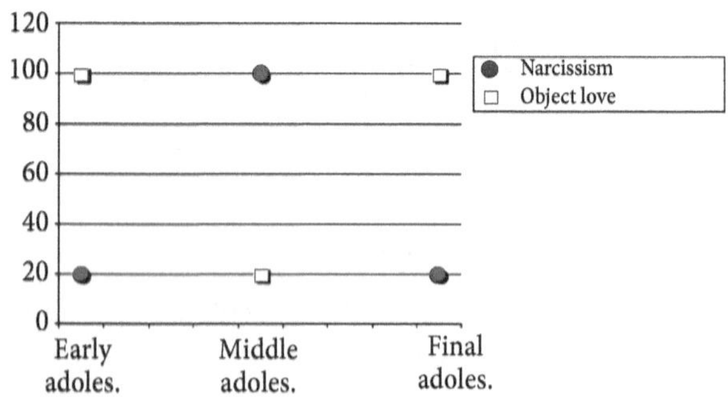

As the graph shows, both object love and narcissistic love are never at zero, because there is always some degree of love for oneself or others, except perhaps in very pathological states that are of no interest at the moment. On entering adolescence, or – if preferable – at the end of latency, the object love curve is at a high value because the affective investment and appreciation of parents at this point in life is high. Throughout latency, children idealize their parents, imagining not only that they are big and strong, but also that they know everything they need to know.

For Meltzer (1972), adolescence begins precisely when there is a fracture in the belief in the omniscience of the parents, which, added to the youth's increase in height, makes them see their parents from a different perspective, from the top down. With this evolutionary step, the young person is thrown into a mental state in which the confusional anxieties are prominent. We could summarize and imagine them as follows: *If my parents don't know everything, then who does? I must know. So, who am I? Am I big or small? Am I a man or a woman? Adult or child?* A significant part of adolescence, in Meltzer's view, will consist of trying to resolve these questions, as well as the defenses that are erected against the psychic pain that results from this state.

One of the defenses against the confusional and depressive feelings (loneliness and helplessness) resulting from the separation from parents becomes the idealization of oneself. The peak of this process occurs in middle adolescence, when love and idealization of oneself reach their maximum. However, it is expected that, towards the end of adolescence, narcissism may decline to give way again to object love, but now not so much to parents, but to exogamous objects, with a view to forming new family units.

The increase in narcissism after puberty can be understood from different angles: as the increase in preoccupation with oneself, as mentioned above; as the withdrawal of cathexis from infantile objects and their direction towards the ego, as Blos (1965, 1979/1981) comments; however, in any case, it is a fundamental element in enabling the adolescent to face the loneliness that arises from growing autonomy and to strengthen the fragile identity of this "new" subject. The narcissistic valorization of the self becomes an important way of coping with the depressive anxieties that arise from the loss of the infantile condition and the "parents of childhood" (Aberastury, 1978), with the confusional anxieties arising from the loss of the belief in the parents' omniscience (Meltzer & Harris, 1972) and with the paranoid anxieties mobilized by the struggle that takes place in the inner world. This intensification of narcissism, far from being pathological, is an essential psychic reordering that occurs for the sake of development and will leave its mark in various ways during the adolescent transition.

In contemporary culture, where there is an increase in narcissism and even narcissistic pathologies (Han, 2017; Levy, 2022), we can observe a prolongation of narcissistic investment in the self and a difficulty in establishing loving object links.

I will now try to comment, in a generic way, without considering the infinite possible individual variations, on the trajectory of each of the characters in this story: the boy, the girl, and their parents.

Adolescence in boys

As well as feeling fragile regarding his emerging masculinity, the young boy, beset by the onset of puberty, feels in his mind the female figure equated with the omnipotent, faithful mother of his childhood. In the fairy tale mentioned earlier, the mother is represented by the almighty, gigantic mother/witch. This makes women, in general, very feared and avoided in early adolescence.

As a result, male figures, the father, the homosexual "gang" with all its demonstrations of power and strength, become important elements of narcissistic reinforcement and consolidation of male identity. It should be made clear that when we talk about homosexual cliques, we are not referring to psychopathological states but only to the fact that libidinal investment and idealization are directed towards people of the same sex. Closeness to idealized male figures is intended to allow the feeling of being masculine to be strengthened through introjection. In the fairy tale, this is alluded to through the sword/penis that the prince is equipped with to fight against the phallic witch-mother. Love relationships at this time are of a homosexual, narcissistic nature, in an eminently sublimated way, although there may sometimes be homosexual acts of an experimental nature. This is one of the risks we see at this stage of development: that the young boy has problematic adults around him who, seeing themselves "loved" by the early adolescent, abuse them sexually.

The peer group is also becoming increasingly important in terms of the "socialization of guilt" insofar as the "transgressions" – and here there is a shift away from the transgressions made in the territory of masturbatory fantasies – cease to be the individual's alone and become collective, with shared responsibility. This will have the major effect of attenuating the superegoic rigidity inherited from childhood, which, together with the new identifications, will enable the subject to deal with the tasks of his new evolutionary moment and, subsequently, to encourage him to approach girls.

Once the young man has overcome childhood prohibitions on masturbation, body exploration, and sexual games, and as he feels more confident in his incipient masculine identity, he begins to approach the opposite sex. The first approaches, in later adolescence – the endless list of girls he has dated – also have a basically narcissistic objective of reinforcing self-esteem and the feeling of masculinity, as well as being experiments that will help in the task of getting to know his body. There is still no tenderness or consideration for the other as an object of love in these experiences. Perhaps this is the peak of narcissism, so that now we are faced with the omnipotent adolescent, arrogant and bearing the omniscience that in latency was attributed to the parents. This state of maximum narcissism, if we can call it that, will allow the youngster not only to deal with the fear, loneliness, and anxiety resulting from the de-idealization and estrangement from their childhood parents but also to carry out the experimentation that is essential for the maturing process. As mentioned earlier, in contemporary times this moment can last longer than in previous eras.

Feeling more powerful and able to tolerate female closeness, and at the same time needing this closeness in order to have a container on which to project his feminine aspects, the male adolescent is suddenly surprised by a new feeling of love, desire, and tenderness for a woman. The increasingly late departure from the homosexual clique and the heterosexual rapprochement is a defining moment in adolescent evolution and generates reactions of censorship towards the departed on the part of those who remain. These first heterosexual love relationships in adolescence, as well as showing the progressive decline of narcissism and the increase in love for the other, initiate a succession of attempts to elaborate the reactivation of Oedipal desires and fantasies, with the first choices being related quite directly to the subject's parental figures.

Adolescence in girls

The path followed by the girl in her adolescent psychosexual development is significantly different. The adolescent girl, mobilized by menarche and the new pelvic sensations coming from the functioning gonads, feels even more drawn to turn inward. For the first time in her development, she can form a clearer image of her female body and somehow "feel" her internal organs. Because the genitals are external, boys can manipulate them from the beginning of their development and thus form a mental representation of them. It is only from puberty onwards, as a result of these coenesthetic sensations, that the girl will be able to form mental representations of her internal genitalia. This will be further facilitated by the development of her capacity for abstract thought, which enables her to form a representation based on internal sensations (Plaut & Hutchinson, 1986). As a result of all this, she finally feels initiated into the "mystery" of the inside of the female body, which is a source of great pride and feelings of superiority over the boys, who are – and often feel – excluded from such a "secret". As in the mentioned tale, the young woman then turns more intensely to her inner world, becomes much more introspective, and devotes herself intensely to daydreaming.

However, while for boys, getting closer to their father is seen as a way of reinforcing their masculine identity, in the case of girls, although there is a closeness with their mother, it is much more feared due to fears of primitive fusion. This difference is based on the following. Typically, in normal development, the mother is the first object of libidinal relationship and the father is the second. At the beginning of childhood, following weaning and the process of separation and individuation (Mahler, 1979), the child separates from the mother and moves closer to the father, with this movement having a strong evolutionary significance. During puberty and early adolescence, getting closer to the mother takes on the meaning of returning to the first object, arousing an anguish of regressing to the most primitive relationship in life. The girl then turns, first and most decisively, to heterosexuality. The reinforcement of incipient femininity will therefore take place by accentuating feminine characteristics and seductively approaching male figures. We see young, coquettish pubescent girls, little "women", interested in older boys and men. Nowadays, with greater tolerance of sexual diversity, especially homosexual relationships, we will often see a change in this characteristic and we will find young teenagers still idealizing and getting close to women, without this turn towards heterosexuality, often with homosexual experimentation or even lasting homosexual affective links.

If, in the case of boys, we see the idealization of athletes as role models and find in their bedrooms, for example, posters of great basketball or soccer players, in the case of girls, we usually see posters of actors, hunks, who easily turn into platonic crushes. Also in the case of early adolescent girls, there is a risk that they will become involved in premature sexual relations or be victims of sexual abuse by adult men. These men take advantage of the ease with which girls fall in love with older men, as a result of displacements and sublimations of their oedipal fantasies. Even adult women in a homosexual object choice may approach early adolescents who are still defining their identity.

For young girls too, the first love relationships will have a more narcissistic character, an affirmation of their femininity and a working-through of primitive relations with both mother and father. The film *The Lover*, by Jean-Jacques Annaud (1991) – a veritable study of the psychopathology of female sexuality in adolescence – seems to illustrate this well. The main character, confronted with loneliness, sadness, and feelings of abandonment, first finds comforts in a homosexual relationship, with maternal overtones, with her fellow boarder. Nevertheless, not least because of the regressive nature of this relationship – the main character very decisively turns to heterosexuality with her lover, in a forbidden, borderline incestuous relationship. It could be said that Oedipal fantasies are acted out, rather than worked-through via displacement or sublimation, which often occurs in adolescents with more intense emotional difficulties. As mentioned earlier, we have often seen young adolescent girls remain in this first "homosexual" approach for a longer period or permanently.

In both sexes, there is an evolution from the first experiments (casual dating), in which one seeks narcissistic affirmation and bodily knowledge, to the beginning of proper, steady dates, dominated by a feeling of tenderness and possession over the other. It is interesting to see how the quality of these relationships evolves in another way. Initially, they are revivals very close to the adolescent's relationship with their original objects, marked by intense dependence and idealization, lived in the midst of great passion and accompanied, initially, by the feeling of having found – or re-found, one might say – the love of their lives. These relationships, still so close to the links with the original objects, can be either direct substitutions (the new object being endowed with the same characteristics as the original object) or their opposite (the new object contradicting all the expectations of the original object). This indicates that the internal struggle (or relation) with the original object is still dominant.

Once they have established heterosexual relationships, adolescents evolve in a cycle that oscillates between infatuation and mourning. They fall in love because the new object is perceived as having the attributes of maximum perfection that, in latency, were attributed to their parents. However, it is then de-idealized and a new mourning is experienced. This succession of infatuations and mourning allows the subject to progressively work through the greater mourning resulting from renouncing their childhood parents. At each step of this evolution, the new objects are progressively more distant from the original incestuous objects. It is expected that, by the end of adolescence, the loved one, although still related in some way to the parents in the unconscious fantasy, will be far removed from them and will also be loved for their own qualities and characteristics.

The group

Faced with the feeling of helplessness arising from disillusionment with their parents, the need and desire to acquire greater autonomy and self-identity, the loneliness arising from their new position, the perplexity and anxieties about their new body and the new strength of their drives, adolescents, in Meltzer's (Meltzer & Harris, 1972) view, will oscillate between four communities. On the one hand, these "environments" in which the youngster circulates function as psychic refuges and, on the other, they are a way of organizing confusion and avoiding the feelings of loneliness and abandonment that emerge once again. These are: the family, the adult world, adolescents, and isolation. Normality would be the possibility of oscillating between these four communities in a flexible way, while adolescent psychopathology would be the rigid fixation on one of these communities. The adolescent in the family follows the pattern of latency, accepting the model of their parents as their model of life, with minimal sexual experiences, reproducing the family scheme that their parents presented to them. The adolescent in the adult world would be the pseudomature incursions in which the youngster acts "as if" they were an adult, with the motivating force not being maturation and the definition of objectives, but the rapid and forced entry into adulthood to show their parents what an adult looks like. The adolescent community, initially with the homosexual pubescent group, then with the mixed group, and later with the couples' group, will be the appropriate container for the adolescent's depressive, paranoid, and confusional anxieties. Isolation would be the refuge frequently used by adolescents as a way of carrying out all the reflection and elaboration of adolescence. According to Meltzer (Meltzer & Harris, 1972), the most serious type of psychopathology would be when isolation becomes the predominant mode of functioning. These are situations in which the de-idealization of the parents was very intense and abrupt, without the conditions to transfer the idealization to another system (politics, the community of adolescents), leading the adolescent to take refuge in a narcissistic organization, in which he imagines himself self-sufficient, capable of building himself up as if he were his own father and mother. They develop a quiet megalomania and the feeling of having a mission to fulfill in the world.

The community of adolescents, the group, will play a key role in the adolescent's mental life. On the one hand, through a complex game of projective identifications, several genital or pre-genital fantasies will be "enacted". For example, the formation of couples, with all the triangularity and rivalry possible, or the acting-out of unusual anal sadism. On the other hand, the "socialization" of narcissism in adolescence through the group, or to put it another way, the projection onto the group of the omnipotence, omniscience, and grandeur of the idealized object, has the function of offering a new container for the youngster to face the anxieties of the period.

The group will also play a role in containing partial aspects of the self. By momentarily remaining outside the subject, these aspects give him the feeling of being free of them, allowing for transitory identifications that ensure the youngster certain tranquility. It is natural to find situations in adolescent groups where, for example, the fragile or devalued aspects of the members are projected onto a member who is harassed and mistreated. And the same happens with countless other undesirable feelings, such as feminine aspects in boys, and so on. In the same way, idealized characteristics that the adolescent, at a certain moment, feels they do not yet possess can be identified in some member of the group, the leader, who is felt to have all the attributes of strength, power, beauty, or intelligence. Of course, we know that this type of group functioning occurs in all human groups, but in adolescence, due to the characteristics mentioned, it takes on a greater intensity.

Psychopathology then sets in when the individual becomes fixated on narcissistic solutions, with the adolescent community, as a container, occupying a secondary or non-existent place: the subject takes refuge in isolation or in other psychic refuges in which omnipotence and idealization – often of one's own destruction – play a central role (drugs, sexual perversions, eating disorders, destructiveness in general). From then on, there is a series of nosographic scenarios whose backdrop are complex narcissistic organizations. A spurious "containment" of anxiety is created: refuge becomes a prison and omnipotence ceases to be a transitory way of dealing with feelings of powerlessness. It becomes a way of permanently denying reality, as already illustrated in other work (Levy, 1996, 2012).

In adolescents who are closer to normality, there is a more adaptive use of psychic refuges, serving as a protective mental space to which they can turn whenever anxiety overwhelms their capacity for tolerance. Individuals who have internalized objects that are very disturbing or have problems in managing their destructiveness, their whole personality becomes caught up in the workings of these pathological organizations.

The family

At this evolutionary moment, it is not only the youngster, the adolescent, who will undergo structural changes. The family will also have to change its internal structure and the patterns of relationships between its members, modifying its roles in order to accommodate the evolutionary demands of the moment. Families that are too rigid and lack the capacity to make this structural adaptation will tend to produce psychopathologies in adolescence or suffer serious internal fractures.

As mentioned earlier, the family is one of the "environments" or communities in which normal adolescents circulate throughout their evolutionary process. It will be essential for them to be able to count on this refuge, which they will turn to after their exploratory forays into the extrafamilial world. This is the time to return for a refueling (Mahler, 1979), to make sure that there has not been a real loss and break with his parents, that he still has them, albeit in a new form at this new moment in his life.

Parents need to have the flexibility to accept this return after having been despised and, at times, even belittled by their teenager. They must – and for this they will also need a period of adaptation – relate to their teenager by accepting and respecting the moments of estrangement and rapprochement. Families that do not have the flexibility to adapt to these new family configurations and ways of relating to their children will be doomed to tormenting conflicts at this point in their lives.

In addition, caught up in their mid-life crisis, parents are confronted with their young child, who has an exuberant body and health and has their whole life ahead of them. Adults, at this point in the life cycle, are faced with the situation of having already passed the half-way point in their lives and are inevitably re-evaluating their projects and achievements, often resulting in frustration as they realize that they have strayed or not achieved what they had hoped for. At other times, they experience a sense of fulfillment and accomplishment for what they have achieved so far. At the same time, they realize that their bodies are no longer those of their youth and that a period of inevitable aging is approaching. For all these reasons, they experience ambivalent feelings towards their children: they admire them while envying their beauty and youth and feeling jealous of their new relationships. Fortunately, most parents are mature enough to adequately deal with this conflict. However, in today's culture where narcissism, image, and the young body are increasingly idealized, we see more and more adults having to deny the passage of time and undergoing endless cosmetic procedures in the illusion of keeping their bodies young. Confusion is often created in the sense that parents try to present themselves as still young, frequently engaging in adolescent behaviors, which will hinder the youngster natural process of differentiation. Sometimes this confusion "pushes" the youth to take on increasingly bizarre behaviors and appearances in their eagerness to differentiate themselves (Levy, 2013, 2021).

Parents of teenagers face yet another challenge when it comes to allowing their children's sexuality to flourish. They need to let it take its own course of maturation, without pushing it towards early practices, which are often overstimulated by our culture's cult of sexuality (Levy, 2007) but neither should they impose obstacles, since it is natural and desired. If parents have not adequately resolved their own conflicts regarding the loss of youth or their sexuality – to cite just two examples – they may compete with their children or hold them back in their experiences, as we have mentioned. A common situation, by way of illustration, is the father who, troubled by aspects of his own sexuality, is disturbed by the emergence of sexuality in his teenage daughter. He is tormented when he sees other men looking at her with desire and, as a result, he tries to stifle the young woman's sexuality and tyrannize her to make sure that there is no trace of eroticization. A study was conducted in an outpatient clinic for adolescents (Cournut-Janin, 1988). It was based on a search motivated by family crises, with aggression and running away from home, caused by the use of the first lipstick by adolescent daughters.

There are characteristics of the adolescent process and family interactions that are unique to our time. In previous eras, the difference between the generations was deeply marked. Today, and increasingly, we are living in a unique moment, at least in our culture. Extensive research into Brazilian adolescence, conducted for MTV (Rocca, 1999), shows that the line between adulthood and adolescence is being redrawn. Today's mature adults are fully active and, more than that, immersed in a quest for rejuvenation. They are driven by the aphorism that "life begins at 40". An example of this is that in maternity wards, women in their 40s or older are having children beside young people in their 20s.

Alongside this challenge to biology, which has also been stimulated by advances in the medical field and greater awareness of the importance of preventing fatal diseases, there is another phenomenon in progress: this same research shows how, in the world of young people, current idols coexist with idols from their parents' generation (Beatles, Caetano Veloso, Gilberto Gil, and Rita Lee, for example). This new phenomenon has several facets. On the one hand, it brings parents and children closer together, creating common interests, values and languages, to the extent that this survey found that large segments of middle and upper-middle class young Brazilians feel a sense of well-being and security in their parents' home, and have no desire to leave it. On the other hand, this quasi-overlapping of interests and values creates greater difficulty in differentiating between the generations, which is necessary for the adolescent's process of separation and differentiation. This has forced young people to find new ways of differentiating themselves, for example by worshipping new idols and rhythms (reggae, rap, electronic music, funk music etc.). Often, middle-class or upper-middle-class young people look for models of identification in rappers or funk music singers from the periphery, also in an attempt to differentiate themselves from their parents and their cultural environment.

Parents of teenagers are therefore expected not to give up their adult status and to maintain their role as parents who educate their children, even though they may still have points of contact with their children when it comes to interests.

Virtual world

As has already been mentioned, since Ancient Greece there have been invariants that are part of all adolescent generations: for instance, the fact that they have new aesthetic and linguistic characteristics that are aimed precisely at differentiating them from the adult world in force. However, each generation of adolescents has some variable traits that characterize it.

The millennium generation of teenagers, who are totally globalized, have their own unique characteristics. This generation was born in the 1990s, 2000s and 2010s, having grown up and developed immersed in cyber language and culture. If we understand that the subject's subjectivity is a property that emerges from tensions between biology, family relations, and culture, we can say that these youngsters have also been shaped by the internet (Levy, 2011). Their minds have grown up in the online environment, with no rigid structures or notion of hierarchy. It is an environment where everything can be remixed and temporal and spatial boundaries have been abolished, as well as the boundaries between public and private, to the point where the personal content of their social media pages often takes on stratospheric proportions. Since adults were absent for a long time from the environments where these young people circulated solitarily, they had to create their own filters.

Used to connections rather than links, Bauman (2011) points out that these have become weaker, either because of the sudden change in family ties, which have become more volatile (Levy, 2006, 2013) or because, at the slightest frustration, youngsters can disconnect from online contact, without experiencing the depressive anxiety of ending a friendship relation in person. This aspect – less consistency in links in general – may be responsible for an increase in feelings of emptiness and depression today (Levy, 2022).

Life in civilization swings in the balance between two essential factors: freedom and security (Bauman, 2011). In *Civilization and its discontents*, Freud (1930/1969) found, among many other things, that in his time (modernity), in exchange for security, man gave up too much of his freedom (sexual, civil, mobility). If, on the one hand, millennials have lost out on security and stability in their relationships, on the other, they have gained a lot in freedom. This is a generation that lives globally, is versatile, not attached to rigid models, has spectacular creative potential and lives in an unprecedented range of opportunities.

The teenager at the analyst's office

The relationship with the adolescent in the psychotherapist's or psychoanalyst's office will vary greatly according to the stage of the adolescent process the young person is in. In early adolescence, the presence of parents in the first interviews is well tolerated by the adolescent because childhood is still close in time. In middle adolescence, the biggest challenge is for the therapist not to be mistaken for a parental figure and for the youngster to see them as an ally in the process of gaining independence and building their new identity. To this end, one of the certainties that the therapist must offer is the guarantee of absolute confidentiality – which, incidentally, should occur at all stages of life. When an interview with the parents is necessary, as well as inviting the adolescent to take part, the therapist should talk to the young person about the interview and assure him, if he does not take part in it, that the issues will be disclosed to him. In late adolescence, parents generally do not take part in the therapeutic process, as the young person is already approaching adulthood, except in special situations and serious pathologies involving risks.

In addition to all this, the adolescent therapist must be ready to understand the language of this time of life, the culture in which the young person lives, and be able to use a language in which, without "dressing up" as an adolescent, they can communicate in such a way as to be understood. As has already been said, social networks and the virtual world as a whole will be a constant presence in our offices; their relations with the web pass through our offices in various ways, and if we do not want to remain apart and distant from these youngsters, we must really embrace this phenomenon, understand it and relate to it, with its facilitations and its vicissitudes.

Final comments

As we have seen, the adolescent process is rich and complex. It involves parents, children, society, and culture, and while on the one hand it brings with it conflicts and tensions in many situations, on the other it is society's guarantee of a constant renewal of values. Youngsters, with their vigor, their courage, and their subversive spirit of the adult world, question customs and vices that adults, with their prudence, have often settled into.

Thus, the adolescent process has double importance: it is, on one side, a moment in the life cycle that allows the individual to mature, review, and re-elaborate situations from their childhood and prepare for adulthood, and, on the other, a renewing element in the cultural process.

References

Annaud, J.-J. (Director) & Brach, G. (Screenwriter). (1991). *L'Amant* [movie]. Pathé.

Aberastury, A. (1978). *Adolescência.* Artmed.

Bauman, Z. (2011). Interview recorded for the *Fronteiras do Pensamento* activity, Porto Alegre.

Blos, P. (1965). The second individuation process of adolescence. *Psychoan. Study of the Child, 22*(1), 162-186.

Blos, P. (1981). *La transición adolescente.* Amorrortu. (Originally published in 1979)

Cournut-Janin, M. (1988). Le premier rouge à lèvre ou La peur de la fèminité chez les parents de l'adolecente. *La Psychiatrie de l'Enfant, XXXI*(2), 301-311.

Freud, S. (1969). O mal-estar na civilização. In *Edição standard brasileira das obras psicológicas completas de Sigmund Freud* (Vol. XXI). Imago. (Originally published in 1930)

Han, B.-C. (2017). *Topologia da violência.* Vozes.

Levy, R. (1995). As relações amorosas na adolescência. *Revista de Psiquiatria do Rio Grande do Sul, 17*(1), 63-67.

Levy, R. (1996). Refúgios narcisistas na adolescência – Entre a busca de proteção e o risco de destruição: dilemas na contratransferência. *Revista Brasileira de Psicanálise, 30*(1), 223-240.

Levy, R. (2006). Adolescência: O reordenamento simbólico, o olhar e o equilíbrio narcísico. *Revista de Psicanálise da Sociedade Psicanalítica de Porto Alegre, 13*(2).

Levy, R. (2007). *A adolescência no Brasil, hoje.* Paper presented at Convegno Essere Adolescente Oggi, Milan.

Levy, R. (2011). *As redes sociais e a aliança com os adolescentes.* Paper presented at the XXXII Annual Conference of CEAPIA.

Levy, R. (2012). Dando "pensabilidade" ao impensável: criando "andaimes" ao pensar em adolescentes com transtornos severos. *Revista Brasileira de Psicanálise, 46*(3), 78-89.

Levy R. (2013). O tempo da incerteza – Elogio ao pudor: em defesa de um certo mistério necessário à simbolização. *Revista de Psicanálise da Sociedade Psicanalítica de Porto Alegre, 20*(2).

Levy R. (2021). Disrupções na cultura: violências visíveis e invisíveis. *Revista de Psicanálise da Sociedade Psicanalítica de Porto Alegre, 28*(1).

Levy, R. (2022, Mar.). *Uma ética para o século XXI.* Paper presented at the XXVIII Congress of the Brazilian Federation of Psychoanalysis.

Mahler, M. (1979). *O processo de separação e individuação.* Artmed.

Meltzer, D., & Harris, M. (1972). Seminários de Novara. Teoría psicoanalítica de la adolescencia. Psicopatología de la adolescencia. In *Quaderni di psicoterapia infantile.* Novara.

Plaut, E. A., & Hutchinson, F. L. (1986). El rol de la pubertad en el desarollo psicossexual femenino. *Libro anual de psicoanálisis* (p. 143).

Rocca, W. (1999). *Dossiê MTV – Estudo de valores e perfil do universo jovem no Brasil.* Carried out for MTV Brasil by Wilma Rocca & Associados.

13. Adolescence: symbolic reordering, the gaze, and narcissistic balance[1]

Today, as we are at a time of great change in our culture, in which modernity is strongly shaken by post-modernity, we have felt an intense need to understand its impact on the adolescent process. Precisely because they are in direct contact with the cultural frontier and are a subject undergoing rapid change, we see cultural modifications expressed in them in an obvious way. We see that the adolescent process is being modified, pushed forward, prolonged, and intensified. In short, it is as if we are watching adolescence being stretched, twisted, and turned right before our eyes.

In turn, even if we only study adolescence from an intrapsychic point of view, we can do so from various angles: that of the process of separation and individuation; that of the reactivation of pre-genital drives and the emergence of genital drives, with the consequent re-edition of the Oedipus complex; that of the vicissitudes of narcissism, as mentioned in the previous chapter (Levy, 1994, 1996).

At this point, I would like to study the adolescent process from the point of view of narcissism, focusing on a particular phenomenon: the symbolic reordering that takes place at this point in life, with the anxieties arising from this process, its impact on the subject's narcissistic structure and its points of contact with our culture. Going into

---

1 This chapter was originally published in a book on adolescence in Italy and, in Brazil, in: *Revista de Psicanálise da Sociedade Psicanalítica de Porto Alegre*, 13(2), 2006.

a little more detail, I want to postulate that there is a type of anxiety specific to this process of symbolic reordering, which is the anxiety of annihilation. As a complex phenomenon, adolescence and the whole process of subjectivation that it encompasses cannot be covered from a single point of view. There is no single theory or standpoint that can deal with an event of such complexity.

Symbolic reordering in the adolescent process

The human subject is a being that develops essentially in a symbolic world (Levy, 2000) and, for this reason, Cassirer (1944/1997) argues that man should not be called a rational animal, but a symbolic animal. According to Cassirer, the great divide between man and other animal species is the existence of a symbolic system, an intermediary between the stimulus-receiving system and the effector/motor system. Thought, as a symbolic system, mediates the immediate reaction, as Freud said in "Formulations on the Two Principles of Mental Functioning" (1911/1969).

The adolescent process is no different. It is constituted by the disconnection of previous systems of representation set up by the self (Cahn, 1999) throughout childhood and the creation of a new system of representations to deal with the new body, the self itself, objects and the world itself. Throughout this painful process of deconstructing and reconstructing a system of representations, we then witness the emergence of a new subjectivity in the subject's symbolic universe, with all the vicissitudes of such an endeavor.

Why am I not simply referring to the construction of a new identity in adolescence? Precisely because I want to focus attention on what happens metapsychologically, in the subject's phantasmatic world, and follow this major process of symbolization that is adolescence and a particular type of anxiety that emerges from it.

The new adolescent body emerging from puberty, with its new forms, new drives and new potentialities, imposes an unprecedented amount of work on the mind. It confronts the adolescent with a *disturbing stranger* (Cahn, 1999) that needs to be represented internally to recreate a feeling of familiarity with oneself. As Piera Castoriadis-Aulagnier (1975/2004) describes, symbolizing means assimilating a "foreign body" into a given system of representations. Of course, at this point, I am referring to the "foreign body" in a double sense: as a foreign element that needs to be assimilated and as a biological body that is foreign to the subject himself.

What makes this phenomenon even more disturbing is that the *disturbing stranger* is strange not only to the subject but also to others, so that the surprised gaze of others contributes even more to the feeling of strangeness so common at this time of life. According to Cahn (1999), it is this feeling of strangeness to oneself and to others that gives adolescence the thickness and specificity of its psychic transformations. And, since we are discussing the reordering of the system of representations of the self and others, the collapse of one system and the construction of another, in addition to the feelings of strangeness mentioned earlier, we will also be confronted with deep anguish of annihilation, often a feeling of imminent death – which is, as mentioned, the anxiety I intend to focus on in this work. The self, since it is a symbolic construction, feels threatened.

Throughout childhood, the subject had built up a system of representations of the self and of objects that guaranteed some stability in their self-image. With this radical process of symbolic reordering, in addition to the loss of childhood and the infantile body, there is the loss of representations of self and objects, an experience that causes a feeling of terror. Winnicott himself (1951/1975) already claimed that the greatest psychic suffering exists when one loses not the object, but its representation. At the end of this same work, Winnicott introduces the question of the negative in psychoanalysis, pointing out that when there is a loss of representation, sometimes the only possible reality of the object is its lack: the only presence of the object is its negative. These are individuals who will cling to the lack, the absence and, therefore, to suffering as the only real thing. How does this relate to the subject I am dealing with? There are adolescents who, faced with the loss of self-presentation and the feeling of not existing, will often cling to the negative as the only tangible reality: suffering, feeling pain, being destructive is a way of being.

More contemporaneously, Botella and Botella (2002) tell us how the traumatic situation is created by the inability of the subject to create representations of a certain experience that can link the affects it arouses. In this sense, we can anticipate that adolescence will become traumatic to the extent that the subject is unable to recreate a system of representations that can deal with this new experience and therefore fail in this unprecedented experience of subjectivation.

As a result of this symbolic reordering, I suggest that insufficiencies of mentalization (Marty, 1990, 1992) are inevitably created – to a greater or lesser degree – in adolescence, so that the body plays a central role in the attempt to control the anxieties of the period.

A particular mind-body link is established at this point in life because, on the one hand, the body places a demand for representation (Aisenstein, 2009) in which the mind must be the container of the symbolic representations of the new body, the new emotional experiences it triggers, and the new perception of the world. On the other hand, faced with the aforementioned insufficiencies of mentalization, the body will often have to "contain" unsymbolized emotions, preventing them from being thrown into the infinity of external reality (Lutenberg, 2005), and then returning in the form of hallucinations, typical of psychosis. This establishes a particular container/contained relationship in adolescence. The body presents itself as an intermediary space between the mind and the infinite universe of external reality when the mind is still incontinent to symbolize the infinitude of new experiences in adolescence.

The attempt to acquire a narcissistic balance

In his various works, Meltzer (1973/1979, 1992) developed the study of mental geography, that is, the study of mental spaces, the transit between them, their compartments, their characteristics, including their importance in adolescence. He sought to study the various types of projective identification into objects and their communicative, structuring, and defensive purposes.

In his book *The claustrum* (1992), Meltzer describes the consequences of these fantasies for the psyche. He differentiates between projective identification, which has more adaptive and communicative purposes, and intrusive identification, with fewer possibilities of reversibility, in which the individual appropriates the object, transforming it, in his fantasy, into a cloister that imprisons, rather than a container. These are situations in which the self is dominated in its functioning by this intrusion, determining that the individual's entire sense of identity is compromised. Referring to adolescents, he comments that

> *the vision of the cloister illuminates this change in the sense of identity, making it possible to recognize that they are different not only from what they were before, not only in their mental qualities, but also as regards the world they are inhabiting. (p. 147)*

In another paper, "Narcissistic refuges in adolescence: between the search for protection and the risk of destruction – dilemmas in countertransference" (Levy, 1996), I described in detail what these mental spaces with structuring and defensive functions are and how they are constituted in adolescence. I tried to describe the destructive aspects involved in these mental organizations and their repercussions on the psychoanalytic technique, especially on countertransference.

In their quest to defend themselves from their depressive, paranoid, confusional, and annihilation anxieties and, especially, from this feeling of depersonalization resulting from the symbolic "dismantling" in the adolescent process – which I am trying to study nowadays – youngsters will move psychically not only between various communities (the family, the adult world, the group, and isolation; Meltzer & Harris, 1972), but also between various objects. Through projective identifications that are more or less intrusive, parts of the self will "circulate" through a complex geography, creating more or less transitory identifications with more or less damaging consequences for the self. That is, as they lose their representation of themselves, adolescents seek to "appropriate" some self, some identity.

I want to emphasize that these defensive maneuvers aim to protect against the anxieties already mentioned, but, for the focus I want to give here, they also aim to create a feeling of narcissistic stability. The subject needs to recognize themselves as existing, first and foremost. By being something, being someone.

The importance of the gaze

Claiming to be influenced by Lacan, Winnicott (1967/1975) asserts the importance of the gaze of the other, initially the mother, in the constitution of the subject. He states that the precursor of the mirror is the mother's face. Very skillfully he comments that when the baby looks at the mother's face, it sees itself. The mother who manages to "look" at the baby becomes like what she sees there. The baby's sensation gains meaning on the mother's face. It is in this interplay, of showing oneself and being seen, that the subject's self-image is built, which will become the "truth" about oneself. There is an enrichment in this exchange, because what is felt gains meaning "in the world of things seen". Winnicott adds that babies whose mothers cannot look at them, will look at their mothers and will not see themselves. In normal situations, when the baby looks at the mother, it seeks and finds the meaning that should be there.

Winnicott coined a phrase very similar to Heidegger's descriptions of the constitution of the truth of being. He says: "When I look, I am seen; so I exist". In other words, it is in the dynamics of seeing and being seen that the feeling of existing occurs. In intimate human relationships, we see ourselves, we find our "truth" in the faces of others. We create our emotional state in others and this is reflected in the image we are shown.

Another work, called *The first lipstick* (Cournut-Janin, 1988), comments on episodes of violence detected in a French outpatient clinic. The violence was perpetrated against pubescent girls by their own families when the girls began to put on make-up and present themselves in a more feminine way. This was due to the anxieties they aroused in their parents. One would expect these anxieties to be linked to incestuous libidinal fantasies aroused in their parents, and perhaps they were. However, what is interesting is the original approach taken in this study: they conclude that what caused the greatest anxiety was the way in which the girl came to be seen by other men. By presenting herself as feminine and attractive, she aroused the desire and gaze of men and this gaze had a double consequence: on the one hand, it was fundamental for reinforcing the girl's feminine identity – through the development of representations of herself as a woman – and on the other hand, the gaze of men aroused homosexual anxieties in the girls' fathers.

A quick illustration

Ciro sought treatment at the age of 15, because he had strong feelings of depersonalization and unreality, which triggered anxiety attacks, sometimes panic, due to the horror he had of losing his identity and becoming psychically disoriented. He had what he called a feeling of "being and not being". You could say that even his material existence, his body occupying a space in the world, was questioned by him.

He feared that, by moving around the city alone, he might lose his self-awareness, become disoriented, not know whether he was asleep or awake, dreaming or in wakefulness, and thus commit some careless or reckless act that would lead to his death. This gave rise to an incapacitating phobia that prevented him from going to school, going out with friends, and sleeping alone peacefully at night. His clinging to his mother was intense, as he believed that only she could prevent the worst from happening. He went to great lengths to keep her close to him 24 hours a day. What was important to Ciro was not what his mother said, but simply having her by his side, having her gaze.

What interests us for this topic is Ciro's need to be seen. If he did not feel that he was being looked at, he feared that he no longer existed, in other words, that even his own body was not visible. To be looked at, then, every day he would change something about his appearance, magically making "his body exist": the color of his hair one day; an earring another day; a piercing; shaving his hair; in short, he made changes to his appearance that caused surprise in others around him. Being looked at with surprise reassured him, because it gave him the feeling of existing, of being real. As he got better and reassured himself, this certification of his existence and identity took on new forms.

He began to feel a curiosity to discover what the other person's gaze was capable of seeing. To put it another way: as Winnicott describes, he wanted to put himself in the position of the object and look at himself from the position of the object. The self exists as a subject, which is the very feeling of existing, but it can take itself as an object, which consists of the possibility of occupying the position of the object and looking at oneself (Ogden, 1996). Of course, in Ciro, this interchange of positions with the object took on a very intrusive form, as Meltzer describes. So Ciro, who had been dedicating himself to photography, devised a plan. He knew a beggar who frequented his neighborhood, with whom he maintained fanciful contacts. First, Ciro asked to take some photos of him, especially of his face, getting progressively closer until only his eyes were in the frame. Then he gave the beggar the camera and asked him to take pictures because he wanted to "see what Marcos saw".

Another activity he did with his camera was an interesting job in a poor community in Porto Alegre. He told me: "I realized that these poor people don't have family photos at home". He started visiting the community at weekends and taking family photos. He was happy to see them waiting for him at their homes, in their best clothes, to take the family photo. Ciro thus helped them to develop a family identity through a visual, photographic representation of the family. He gave them an image of themselves. Through his gaze, recorded by the camera, he gave them a family identity. They could now see themselves. Obviously, Ciro was sensitive to the needs of these families and to the flaws in their representations because he had experienced them himself. And he himself used the gaze in its multiple unfoldings to try to create representations of the self that would reassure him.

Today's culture and the question of image

Returning to the beginning, the adolescent process and adolescent psychopathology, in their multiplicity of boundaries, are open and in permanent contact with culture. Postmodern culture has been characterized by the fluidity of human relationships and by a new type of discontent characterized precisely by the inconsistency and fragility of links (Bauman, 1997, 2001). In addition, in today's culture, we are witnessing a crisis and a questioning of the functions of authority, especially in our country, of values and ideologies (Cahn, 1999), as well as a blurring of the limits that creates ethical and moral disorientation. Obviously, previous cultural moments were never lost paradises. There was an established order, a *status quo,* against which young people rebelled with an ideology that gave them a clearly defined identity.

Raymond Cahn (1999) describes clearly some of the poles of conflict in today's adolescence: increasingly total freedom in customs, but increasingly severe demands in terms of skills; the stimulus to consume increasingly tempting products, but increasing difficulty in obtaining them; the liberation of sexuality in behavior, but increasing distance from life with a couple and parenthood. These are poles of conflict that generate anguish that is often unsolvable, often leading to pathologies of behavior. Added to these conflicts is a family situation in which parents have difficulties recognizing and setting limits between the sexes, between generations, between "good" and "evil" and between true and false. In addition, these contemporary parents often share with their teenagers the same feeling of uncertainty about the future, of material precariousness and helplessness, and of questioning institutions.

What happens is that adolescents, faced with the anguish resulting from the loss of their representations of themselves, on the one hand, retreat into the inner world in an effort to reconstruct them. On the other hand, they turn to outer objects to use them as mirrors to help them reconstruct their own image, so that they reflect something that guides them, be it a beautiful image or a repulsive one, but an image nonetheless. However, in the picture we are describing, the adolescent looks at the object and it reflects a confused image, either of himself as an adult, or of the young person, because he does not know whether what he is seeing is right or wrong, good or bad; or, worse still, the object does not reflect any image at all, because it cannot "see" his child, which throws the child into a void of non-existence.

This failure in symbolic reordering – which would otherwise make it possible to construct a self-image that guarantees narcissistic stability – leads to an unfinished process of subjectivation. This, in turn, leads to narcissistic pathologies that affect conduct and the body

(delinquency, anorexia, bulimia, drug addiction etc.). Narcissistic defenses seek to resolve the insufficiency of psychic elaboration (Cahn, 1999).

An illustration of what we are describing: in May 2006, Claude Askolovitch published an article in a French magazine, *Le Nouvel Observateur*, with the following headline: "The truth about youth violence – when blows replace words". The title speaks for itself, but the content of the article refers precisely to the substitution of conduct for the symbolic in the demonstrations of young French teenagers. More than that, it describes the flaws in this process of subjectivation, its explicitness in conduct, and the extent to which youngsters have needed reinforcements to construct an image of themselves.

The article recounts incidents of violence committed by youngsters throughout France (Nice, Orleans, Orly, Paris etc.) which have some common elements. They are all kinds of violence (such as sexual violence, beatings) in which there is no real awareness of what has been done. For example, 13- and 14-year-olds in Nice who sexually assaulted a classmate, forcing her to perform various sexual acts, but who did not see any major problems *because they never beat her...* Another common element – the most striking for the purposes of what I am describing – is that most of these violent acts were recorded in photos or videos taken on cell phones. This practice has now been called "happy slapping". In other words, the aggressors are the main characters, the protagonists of films they make, as if they needed to have an image record of themselves carrying out violent acts.

We are, as mentioned earlier, in the narcissistic effort to construct an image of oneself through the use of the real external image and violence as positive proof of one's existence. It seems that destructiveness is the only part of the self that they feel they possess. Let's see what Michel Redon, deputy prosecutor at the Nice court, says:

> *These boys give the impression that the image is the only way for them to exist in the face of their own nothingness. The victim becomes an extra in their movie, she is unreal. The essential thing for them is that they can, thanks to the proof of the image, demonstrate that they are men.*

There is yet another element of our time that goes hand in hand with all this, that I would like to address. It is the presence of the internet in the lives of teenagers, especially all the social media existing today, where young people post photos of themselves, their families, or friends, to be seen by others on the web. There are millions and millions of youngsters connected to these media, exposing themselves, their friends, and their families. What could this be if not something very similar to what Ciro did with the families of the poor community in Porto Alegre? It seems that this phenomenon has become a way of showing oneself and being seen – with the right to testimonials, even. From one point of view, we know that it is a way of alleviating the feeling of loneliness that is so common in adolescence and in our culture in general. In many ways, our culture goes through phenomena (loneliness, loss of references, diffusion of identity, return to the body, and acting out etc.) very similar to those of adolescence and therefore does not offer youngsters any containment.

What has attracted attention is that many of these social media sites show young teenagers in their underwear, or half-naked, in poses reminiscent of celebrities or prostitutes. Naive photos of youngsters exposing themselves are confused with prostitutes offering themselves. Even pubescents are exposing themselves in their underwear to classmates via webcams. I think that in the culture of narcissism, in which the image is enthroned, in which superficial values are privileged over deep ones, and in which aesthetics is privileged over ethics, the cult of the image is offered in an attempt to strengthen the feeling of existing as a subject, often by exposing one's body and attracting gazes precisely because of this. Winnicott's *I am seen, so I exist* occupies this virtual space, since relations with real objects are so fluid, as we have already mentioned. "Celebrities" are born and die with the speed of the internet. They are built instantly from almost nothing; all they have to do is appear in a Parliamentary Commission of Inquiry (CPI), a soap opera, or simply a reality TV show. And so the Winnicottian aphorism becomes *I am a celebrity simulacrum, so I exist.*

Final comments

The adolescent, through the adolescent process, seeks, among other things, a normal symbolic reordering, in other words, the reconstruction of the representations of the self and of objects. Such reconstruction is necessary for the subject's new subjective configuration, in order to guarantee narcissistic stability at the end of adolescence. Here we are on the terrain of normal narcissism: the subject being able to look at himself and say: *I exist and this is me*. However, since we are talking about borders, when this process of subjectivation fails, the subject will resort to narcissistic solutions, already in the realm of psychopathology, as the only way of being. With these solutions, youngsters seek to reassure themselves that they exist in reality. These narcissistic refuges, which should be transitory, often become consolidated structures.

This symbolic reconstruction of the self undertaken by the subject must, by the end of the adolescent process, have been able to create images of the subject and his objects that guarantee him, in addition to a sense of tranquility about his existence, a feeling of clarity and stability about himself. Youngsters must have created representations of their objects that serve as a reference for them – inspirational objects, in Meltzer's (1973/1979) words – and have answered the questions: "*Since I exist, who am I? Whose body is this? Who are my objects and what are they for?*" in order for personality structuring to take place properly. When the self-images are too dissociated, the anguish too intense, or when the object images are too split, charged with hatred or other disturbing emotions, this process will be compromised. Or, to put it another way, if the subject turns to his real objects and does not find in them an attitude that favors this symbolic reordering, not finding their gaze, or finding a gaze that increases the confusion, the risk of narcissistic exits, in the context of pathology, is very high. The body may become over-invested, either through libido or destructiveness, in the search for narcissistic affirmation; or the object may be rejected, because its recognition may imply a sense of annihilation of the self.

I hope that throughout this work I have been able to explain clearly enough the importance of the processes of symbolic reconstruction in the adolescent process, their intersections with the importance of the gaze, the role of the body, and the way in which this occurs in our culture.

References

Aisenstein, M. (2009). *Les exigences de la représentation*. Paper presented at the XXX Congrés des Psychanalystes de Langue Française.

Askolovitch, C. (2006). La verité sur la violence des jeunes. *Le Nouvel Observateur, 2168*.

Bauman, Z. (1997). *O mal-estar na pós-modernidade*. Jorge Zahar.

Bauman, Z. (2001). *Modernidade líquida*. Jorge Zahar.

Botella, C., & Botella, S. (2002). *Irrepresentável: mais além da representação*. Criação Humana.

Cahn, R. (1999). *O adolescente na psicanálise: a aventura da subjetivação*. Companhia de Freud.

Cassirer, E. (1997). *Ensaio sobre o homem: introdução a uma filosofia da cultura humana*. Martins Fontes. (Originally published in 1944)

Castoriadis-Aulagnier, P. (2004). *La violencia de la interpretación: del pictograma al enunciado.* Amorrortu. (Originally published in 1975)

Cournut-Janin, M. (1988). Le premier rouge à lèvre ou La peur de la fèminité chez les parents de l'adolecente. *La Psychiatrie de l'Enfant, XXXI*(2), 301-311.

Freud, S. (1969). Formulações sobre os dois princípios do funcionamento mental. In *Edição standard brasileira das obras psicológicas completas de Sigmund Freud* (Vol. XII). Imago. (Originally published in 1911)

Levy, R. (1994). *As relações amorosas na adolescência.* Paper presented at the XVII Jornada Sul-Riograndense de Psiquiatria Dinâmica, Gramado.

Levy, R. (1996). Refúgios narcisistas na adolescência – Entre a busca de proteção e o risco de destruição: dilemas na contratransferência. *Revista de Brasileira Psicanálise, 30*(1), 223-240.

Levy, R. (2000). *Do símbolo à simbolização: uma revisão da evolução teórica e suas repercussões sobre a técnica psicanalítica.* Dissertation for full membership of the Psychoanalytic Society of Porto Alegre.

Lutenberg, J. M. (2005). A criatividade negativa e as doenças psicossomáticas. *Revista de Psicanálise da Sociedade Psicanalítica de Porto Alegre, XII*(2), 329-351.

Marty, P. (1990). *La psicosomática del adulto.* Amorrortu.

Marty, P. (1992). Mentalizacion y psicosomática. *Revista de Psicoanálisis,* (3), 7-21.

Meltzer, D. (1979). *Os estados sexuais da mente.* Imago. (Originally published in 1973)

Meltzer, D. (1992). *The claustrum: an investigation of clautrophobic phenomena.* Clunie Press.

Meltzer, D., & Harris, M. (1972). Seminários de Novara. Teoría psicoanalítica de la adolescencia. Psicopatología de la adolescencia. In *Quaderni di psicoterapia infantile.* Novara.

Ogden, T. (1996). *Os sujeitos da psicanálise*. Casa do Psicólogo.

Winnicott, D. W. (1975). Objetos transicionais e fenômenos transicionais. In *O brincar e a realidade*. Imago. (Originally published in 1951)

Winnicott, D. W. (1975). O papel da mãe e da família no desenvolvimento emocional infantil. In *O brincar e a realidade*. Imago. (Originally published in 1967)

www.ingramcontent.com/pod-product-compliance
Lightning Source LLC
Chambersburg PA
CBHW031337230926
51848CB00002B/278
9788521230922